The Lean Company:
Making the Right Choices

The Lean Company:
Making the Right Choices

James A. Jordan, Jr.
Frederick J. Michel

Society of Manufacturing Engineers

Library of Congress Catalog Card Number: 2001-131047
International Standard Book Number: 0-87263-523-6

Additional copies may be obtained by contacting:
Society of Manufacturing Engineers
Customer Service
One SME Drive, P.O. Box 930
Dearborn, Michigan 48121
1-800-733-4763
www.sme.org

SME staff who participated in producing this book:
Cheryl Zupan, Staff Editor
Rosemary Csizmadia, Production Supervisor
Kathye Quirk, Graphic Designer/Cover Design
Frances Kania, Administrative Coordinator
Jon Newberg, Production Editor
Walter T. Kelly, Consulting Editor

Printed in the United States of America

Dedication

We dedicate this book to the millions of men and women who every day make the right choices that are shaping lean companies.

More personally, we dedicate the book to our wives, Joan Jordan and Lucille Michel, and our families who have given us their love and support as we have made our choices.

James A. Jordan, Jr. and Frederick J. Michel

Table of Contents

Preface

American manufacturing was on the ropes. It was just twenty years ago. American products were not competitive. The big companies that fueled America's post-World War II economy were losing market share. Quality was poor. Productivity was low. U.S. manufacturing companies had high overheads. "Above the floor" costs were going through the ceiling, rising much faster than the direct costs on the manufacturing floor. Large companies—most notably Chrysler—teetered on the brink of extinction, requiring extraordinary government intervention. Storm clouds were gathering over American icons like General Motors and IBM. Americans began to doubt the ability of the manufacturing industry to continue as a primary driver for the economic well being of the United States. Experts predicted that U.S. industry would lose more and more market share. Employment in the industry was expected to shrink to a level comparable to that in farming.

Three forces were converging to transform U.S. manufacturing enterprises. First, shareholders revolted, demanding more value, usually defined as greater short-term returns, for their investments. The economic difficulties of the early 1980s—stagnation, inflation, the highest interest rates of the late 20th Century—motivated shareholder activism. Shareholders demanded a better return on their investment, leading to a rash of leveraged buyouts and other mergers and divestitures intended to unlock shareholder value. This environment also led to shareholder-driven activism on corporate boards and a churn of corporate leadership.

Second, was the remarkable growth of information technology. Beginning in the 1970s, large companies started building proprietary global networks. These networks gave senior managers quicker access to information about a company's operations, information that used to be massaged by several layers of middle managers. Easy access to information made possible many of the restructuring and business process reengineering efforts. These efforts increased the productivity of managers by increasing their span of control. This led to more timely decisions.

The third force was international competition, most notably the Japanese. In the 1970s, '80s, and into the '90s, Japanese manufacturing gained mythical proportions and seemed to be unbeatable. Japanese manufacturing was feared and envied. Competitors that had started as low-cost producers of unexciting but functional products transformed themselves into excellent industry leaders. Consumers preferred the value built into Japanese products, and these innovative products commanded a premium. They viewed Sony as the best electronics company. Toyota, Nissan, and Honda gained the reputation of delivering far higher quality and better value products than U.S. car manufacturers did.

As U.S. manufacturing grew increasingly bleak, companies that prided themselves on leading their industries and being self-sufficient began looking beyond themselves for answers to their corporate angst. Companies started to focus on increasing shareholder value and on using information technology to restructure. A few also examined the Japanese successes, looking for lessons that could be translated into American factories.

In 1990, Womack, Jones, and Roos published *The Machine that Changed the World: The Story of Lean Production*. Six years earlier, the three authors, the leaders of the International Motor Vehicle Program (IMVP) at the Massachusetts Institute of Technology (MIT), had undertaken a study of the Japanese automobile industry. The resulting book lived up to the publisher's hype that it would show "how Japan's secret weapon in the global auto wars would revolutionize Western industry."

The Machine that Changed the World focused attention on Japanese production methods, and particularly on the Toyota Production System (TPS). The TPS emphasized the continuous refinement of manufacturing processes to reduce or eliminate costs. Lean manufacturing was born out of lean production. At first, the emphasis was on lessons for the factory floor, on the little "m" of manufacturing.

Quickly, however, people saw that the ideas of lean production were applicable to the entire manufacturing enterprise. Eventually, the ideas were seen to be independent of manufacturing and applicable to very nearly any organization delivering a product or service. This caused people to start talking about the big "M."

One of the places where the ideas of lean enterprise took shape was the Lean Aircraft Initiative (LAI), also at MIT, begun in 1993. The LAI was funded by the U.S. Air Force and supported by many contractors from the aircraft industry. Late in the 1990s, the LAI was renamed the Lean Aerospace Initiative.

The goal of the Lean Aircraft Initiative was to apply the lean concepts from *The Machine that Changed the World* to the aerospace industry, an industry that, in the wake of the end of the Cold War, faced unprecedented affordability challenges. The LAI was one of the first places where lean concepts were shown to be applicable to much more than production. LAI began to consider what it meant to talk about a lean enterprise. It described a prototypical lean company in the Lean Enterprise Model (LEM), a behavioral model based on two meta-principles, six principles, and twelve overarching practices.

Two other important activities took place in the 1990s that have helped the understanding of manufacturing's future. The Agile Manufacturing Initiative (AMI) was born out of the realization that 21st Century factories began to have the need to shift production inexpensively from one product to another. This need was driven by the accelerating pace of change in consumer tastes, technology, and economic conditions—and by merging parts of separate military and civilian manufacturing industries into multi-use capabilities. The second activity was the Next Generation Manufacturing (NGM) Project. NGM was a study of the future of U.S. manufacturing in the early 21st Century, with nearly 500 contributors, most experts from the manufacturing industry.

Together, these efforts developed a consistent and comprehensive description of a company, both lean and agile, that can survive in the coming global competition. However, companies still had problems. The experts in manufacturing processes and systems and the experts in enterprise integration described what companies should look like and how they should function. They alluded to the changes companies needed to make and even, in the case of the NGM Project, provided a framework for the actions companies needed to take.

None of these efforts, however, provided linkages needed between investments to achieve lean and agile characteristics and measurements acceptable to the financial community. The authors have developed a way to make those linkages, taking advantage of one of the most important recent developments of the accounting world—the Balanced Scorecard^{SM}, developed by Robert S. Kaplan and David P. Norton.

This book applies the authors' method to the problem of prioritizing investments in the many actions a company needs to take to become more lean. It starts with a discussion of the lean company, as described by the Lean Enterprise Model. Then it uses the results of the NGM Project as a way to categorize the many choices of action that companies have, describing linkages to corporate strategic goals and metrics that permit companies to assign value to specific actions. Finally, it considers the costs and risks of those actions in a decision model.

James A. Jordan, Jr.
Frederick J. Michel

BIBLIOGRAPHY

Jordan, James A. Jr., and Michel, Frederick J. 2000. *Next Generation Manufacturing: Methods and Techniques*. New York: John Wiley & Sons, Inc.

Kaplan, Robert S., and Norton, David P. 1996. *The Balanced Scorecard: Translating Strategy into Action*. Boston, MA: Harvard Business School Press.

NGM Project. 1997. *Next Generation Manufacturing: Framework for Action*. Bethlehem, PA: Agility Forum. http://www.dp.doe.gov/dp_web/public_f.htm

Womack, James P., Jones, Daniel T., and Roos, Daniel. 1990. *The Machine that Changed the World: The Story of Lean Production*. New York: Rawson Associates.

Acknowledgements

This book tells of the work of many creative and dedicated people. It is the result of the insights gained by observing their efforts. At times, we have even had the opportunity and the good fortune to be associated with some of their work.

We are especially appreciative of Cecil Schneider of Lockheed Martin, past President of SME, for his encouragement and insights into Lockheed Martin's efforts to become a lean company. Herm Reininga of Rockwell Collins and Bill Kessler of Lockheed Martin have given us access to the lean transformations in progress at those companies. We also appreciate the support and encouragement we have received from Jim Mattice of Universal Technology Corporation.

We thank Peter Liebhold of the Smithsonian Institution for directing us to important source material and Guenter Spur, Ph.D., h.c. (*honoris causa*), multiple, of the Technical University of Berlin for giving us information on the history of manufacturing technology.

We want to thank the Society of Manufacturing Engineers' Reference Publications Department and express our appreciation especially to Bob King, Cheryl Zupan, and the department's production staff. SME's Karen Wilhelm has also been most helpful in providing some useful insights.

Without the use of the Internet and the telephone, the writing and publishing would have taken many more months in view of the geographic separation of all participants. (Jim Jordan works in Cupertino, California; Fred Michel works in Alexandria, Virginia; and the SME book development staff is located in Dearborn, Michigan.) This has been a successful test for the modern information technologies that are changing the ways manufacturing companies operate.

Acronyms

ABB	Asea Brown Boveri
AMI	Agile Manufacturing Initiative
ASP	Application Service Provider
BMPCOE	Best Manufacturing Practices Center of Excellence (U.S. Navy)
BMW	Bayrische Motorenwerke
BPR	Business Process Reengineering
CAM	Computer-aided Manufacturing
CAM-I	Consortium for Advanced Manufacturing-International
CASA/SME	Computer and Automated Systems Association of the Society of Manufacturing Engineers
CEO	Chief Executive Officer
CFO	Chief Financial Officer
CIM	Computer-integrated Manufacturing
CNC	Computer Numerical Control
COO	Chief Operating Officer
ERP	Enterprise Resource Planning
FedEx	Federal Express
FMS	Flexible Manufacturing System
FTE	Full-time Equivalent Employee
GM	General Motors Corporation
HPWS	High-performance Work System
IBM	International Business Machine Corporation
IMVP	International Motor Vehicle Project
IMTR	Integrated Manufacturing Technologies Roadmap
IPPD	Integrated Product and Process Development
IPT	Integrated Product Team
I/S	Information System
IT	Information Technology
JIT	Just-in-Time

JSF	Joint Strike Fighter
K-12	Grades 1 through 12, U.S. School System
LAI	Lean Aircraft Initiative
LEM	Lean Enterprise Model
LFM	Leaders for Manufacturing
M&S	Modeling and Simulation
MADM	Multi-attribute Decision Making
MEP	Manufacturing Extension Partnerships
MES	Manufacturing Enterprise System
MIT	Massachusetts Institute of Technology
NCMS	National Center for Manufacturing Sciences
NGM	Next Generation Manufacturing
NIST	National Institute of Standards and Technology
NUMMI	New United Motors Manufacturing, Inc.
PC	Personal Computer
PERT	Project Execution Report, Time
PS/2	IBM Model Personal Computer
QFD	Quality Function Deployment
R&D	Research and Development
RIT	Rapid Improvement Team
ROI	Return-on-investment
RPI	Radical Process Improvement
RPPR	Rapid Product and Process Realization
SAVE	Simulation Assessment and Validation Environment
SME	Society of Manufacturing Engineers
SPC	Statistical Process Control
SUV	Sports Utility Vehicle
TMMK	Toyota Motors Manufacturing Kentucky
TPS	Toyota Production System
TQM	Total Quality Management
UAW	United Auto Workers
UPS	United Parcel Service
VP-HR	Vice President–Human Resources
WIP	Work-in-process
"5S"	Sort, Straighten, Sanitize, Sweep, and Sustain

Chapter One

The Lean Company

The business of manufacturing is undergoing more ups and downs, more cycles of change, than ever before. It is difficult to steer a course that yields profits year after year. Companies must be so lean that they waste nothing, but be agile enough to change course as customers change their demands. This book lays out a framework for a lean company, a company that can succeed in the dynamic environment of 21st Century competition.

People engaged in management and leadership positions will find the central themes of the book and its specific suggestions and recommendations useful as a road map for improving the competitiveness of their companies. The concepts discussed in the book can help them to develop an environment within their companies that will help them capture significant market share.

> Winning the 21st Century competition

Students in engineering and management can use the book to prepare themselves for leadership positions. The book provides them with an insight into the thought processes they need to adopt to achieve success upon entering their careers. Acceptance of the concept of leanness and its practices are recognized worldwide as the one approach for achieving success in competing in today's global economy.

SHOULD JENNY DO IT?

To introduce the lean company, consider the following vignette in the life of a mid-sized company:

> In late March, Dominic, the company's marketing rep for the Northeast, stopped by headquarters to see Jenny, the product development manager. The winter had been particularly brutal. The continually snowy conditions meant Dominic's customers were constantly complaining that the company's snow blowers did not throw the snow far enough. The blowers piled snow along the driveway, instead of throwing it back where it would not cause problems when it melted. Customers also complained that the snow blowers were too heavy.
>
> After some small talk, Dominic came to the point, "Can't you guys come up with a more powerful, lighter, snow blower for next season? It has to outshine the new ones the other guys are offering. Of course, it has to be cheaper, too." He paused, "It can't be that hard. There always seem to be more powerful motors around, and aluminum is lighter than steel."
>
> Jenny and the rest of the new product development team knew better. Usually it took the company at least 15 months to get a new product from concept to market. She could not escape from the fact that larger motors usually cost more than smaller ones. Aluminum is lighter, but the company did not have much experience with it and would need to make a learning investment. The company had worked hard to optimize the production line for its current model. It would be tough to keep costs low while changing to different motors and materials. Jenny knew she would have to argue for the up-front money that it would take to design the new blower and to modify the production line. Moreover, that meant she had to put together a business case. Still, Dominic made a compelling argument.

More and more manufacturing people are finding themselves in Jenny's shoes. The customers want what they want—now. If they do not get it, they will go somewhere else. If a company tries to give customers features they do not want, instead of ones they do, they will walk. They want low prices—it is up to the company to figure out how to keep its costs low enough to make a profit.

Every day, companies face tough decisions. There are many opportunities from which to choose. The issue is making the right choices and doing the right things now so the company—and its people's jobs—will be there tomorrow.

One answer is to do everything lean—responding accurately to the customer's changing needs in ways that minimize every kind of waste. Lean is not just a buzzword. Lean is a way of life. Lean applies to the production system. Lean applies to design and development. Lean applies to business systems. Lean applies to the whole company.

Lean is the way Jenny will get those snow blowers to Dominic's customers fast enough, cheap enough, and with the features that will satisfy them.

However, just being lean is not enough. Lean is a means to an end. For any company, the end that counts is making and sustaining profits over time. A company that survives will have a vision of growth, expressed as a set of measurable strategic goals. It will have leaders at all levels. It will take informed risks. In addition, it will use lean principles and practices throughout the company to achieve its goals.

Lean: a means to an end

This book describes the way a company can use lean practices and principles to make investment decisions. How an employee does his or her job is an investment decision. Every day a manager decides how to spend his or her time and how to use the resources the company makes available. Every day, a manager's employees make similar decisions, even if they are junior trainees on the line or in the back office. The company makes larger decisions, but they are all focused on the use of time and resources. A company can thrive if those decisions are lean. Companies that are not lean-thinking run the risk of being passed by in the market or eaten alive by the competition.

Lean is not a fad. It is not a quick answer to today's production glitches. Mostly, lean is a disciplined way to think about good manufacturing and business practices. As lean concepts have developed in the past decade, they have created the image of an integrated company where there are few wasted efforts or resources as the company responds to dynamic market forces.

There is little new to lean. Over the years, many companies, especially successful small companies, have used some of the practices now called lean. What is new about the lean company is that it has made an integrated whole out of these best practices, so that each feeds on the next. The company has brought these practices together in a way that paints a picture of the culture and operation of a company that has become successful, and will continue to succeed.

This book is about building a lean company. It does not teach the reader specific techniques for improving the production line or for improving customer relationships. It is about a discipline for making the choices the reader needs to face in laying out a production line. It is about the choices the reader needs to face in serving customers. It is about building a company where everyone is challenged to make the best decisions he or she can make for achieving the company goals.

PLAN OF THE BOOK

Lean cannot be thought of in a vacuum. Although lean principles and practices are universal descriptors of a successful business, their application has to fit in context. The descriptors are meaningless unless a company knows its goals. They are meaningless unless the company has an understanding of the dynamics of the marketplace, the competition, and the technological environment. In addition, they are meaningless unless the company can relate the application of lean principles and practices to achieving the company goals.

The themes in this book converge in an example of decision-making to achieve a lean company. The themes are:

- Lean companies require a vision of growth and a set of strategic goals into which employees must fit the visions of their own work.

- It takes leadership and communication to convey the company's vision and goals, and it takes a set of disciplined principles and practices to bring to realization the vision and achieve the goals.
- The hallmarks of a modern company are change and risk taking. Companies need to measure their progress to ensure that the changes that are made, and the risks that are taken, can and do move the company toward its goals.
- What one group of employees does will affect other activities in the company, just as those other activities will affect what they do. Time, energy, and resources will be wasted if the activities conflict. Alternatively, the activities can build on one another to achieve more than they would if acted on separately.
- There is a set of lean practices and principles that, if lived by, will help ensure that everything done in the company drives it toward its goals.

Figure 1-1 shows a roadmap of the book.

The modern understanding of lean in the United States started with the study of post-World War II experiences of Japanese manufacturers, especially with Toyota's production systems. It has matured into a description of entire companies. It has changed from a collection of very good best practices to a systematic transformation of the way companies think and corporate cultures behave. It has grown from an almost exclusive focus on the factory floor to a view of a successful integrated enterprise that includes customers and suppliers as well as the company itself. Chapters 2, 3, and 4 tell the history of lean manufacturing. They describe the dilemmas and challenges that confront companies today, providing the context for lean. Finally, the chapters present a set of lean principles and practices that describe the behavior of an efficient, responsive company. Chapters 3 and 4 tell *how*—using lean principles and practices. The authors have borrowed extensively in their discussion of lean principles and practices from the Lean Enterprise Model developed by the MIT Lean Aircraft Initiative. The MIT model is a systematic and comprehensive presentation of essential characteristics of lean behavior.

In Chapter 5, the discussion shifts to corporate visions and goals. Each lean company requires an organizing principle that is its

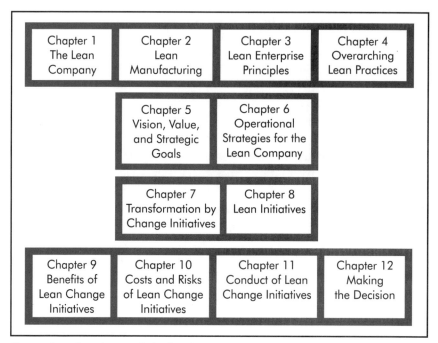

Figure 1-1. Roadmap of the book.

reason for existence and the rationale for all the activities that go on inside the company. The work of Kaplan and Norton on the so-called Balanced Scorecard℠ provides a way for a company to set measurable goals for a balance of financial and non-financial performance areas.

Chapter 6 is somewhat more technical and describes the operational strategies modern companies must employ as they compete in a changing world. These are taken from the recent description of the successful 21st Century manufacturing company developed by the national Next Generation Manufacturing Project. These strategies are the *what* of the choices that must be made. They are the content of the change initiatives undertaken as a company responds to its customers.

Lean does not necessarily come easily. When used it changes both what a company does and how it does it. Most people have difficulty with changes—especially changes they do not understand. Chapter 7 takes a broad look at change, the ways employees respond to change, and some of the techniques managers can use to minimize its adverse effects. Chapter 8 looks specifically at the transformation of a typical, so-called traditional, company into a lean one. Of course, this is a major change effort.

Chapters 9 through 12 provide an example of the application of lean principles and practices to the decision-making process a lean company should use in making investment choices. The example is the application to the choices that a company might make in changing significant operations. Chapter 9 provides a way to describe the change initiative's benefits in terms of company goals. Chapter 10 provides checklists for the costs and risks of the initiatives. Chapter 11 describes a discipline for conducting change initiatives in a lean way. Chapter 12 presents all the material that affects the actual decision-making process.

There is no magic switch Jenny can throw to give Dominic the answer as to whether he can start selling the new high-powered aluminum snow blower next week. However, if her company applies lean principles and practices in disciplined decision-making, she will make the right decision. She will make it quickly and systematically. In addition, it will be the best decision she can make—at least until conditions change and Dominic or one of his colleagues challenges her again.

Chapter Two

Lean Manufacturing

As the 1980s dawned, so too did the realization that Japanese manufacturing had become world-class, frequently winning the competition with U.S. and European manufacturing. This discovery was a long time coming. The growth and prosperity of U.S. manufacturers produced complacency, obscuring a development that should have been recognized in many industries as early as the 1950s, when Japanese manufacturing started rising from the ashes of World War II. In the 1960s and into the 1970s, social changes in the United States and the country's geopolitical agenda hid the changes occurring in Japanese manufacturing.

The Japanese import that revolutionized manufacturing

As a case in point, look at the automobile industry, which has been America's most important industry throughout the 20th Century. The industry's awakening to Japanese competition and its slow metamorphosis since the 1970s continues to be instructive.

Following World War II, the U.S. economy fueled a great demand for all consumer goods, especially cars. American manufacturers churned out successive models that stressed power, styling, and comfort—models that showed little concern for fuel efficiency in an era of plentiful, cheap gasoline. The quality of cars was hit or miss, certainly not a major discriminator among competitors.

Japanese manufacturers competed with Volkswagen, Fiat, Renault, and other European manufacturers, for the small, low-end market for cheap little cars. Then the Arab oil embargo in

1973 forced American consumers to consider seriously the fuel economy of foreign alternatives to domestic companies' offerings. The market share of Japanese manufacturers started to grow, based on lower prices and better fuel economy than the Big Three could offer. Japanese designs were more responsive to the changing market than the big gas-guzzlers Detroit was turning out.

Then customers found Japanese cars to be more reliable and of higher quality than Detroit's offerings. Japanese manufacturers began to introduce new models with even higher quality and more luxury, but still with superior fuel efficiency. Detroit's hastily produced compact cars suffered in comparison. By the end of the 1970s, it was clear in the United States that business as usual was a recipe for going out of business.

What made the Japanese such formidable competitors? "Made in Japan" had been a catchphrase for signifying cheap, shoddy imitations of U.S. or European designs. The Japanese were thought to use American research and development (R&D) without making R&D investments themselves. Many viewed the Japanese as a backward economy with labor that was paid very little, but that worked very hard. How did these stereotypes fit the realities of economically priced cars whose fit and finish were better than American luxury brands, and that incorporated advanced engines and other technologies?

Protectionist measures were proposed, intended to shield American manufacturers from Japanese competitive practices assumed to be unfair. These measures did not stop the free market demand for Japanese products. There was a need to separate myth from fact and to understand the Japanese success, in order to construct a strategy that might blunt further market penetration from the competition.

American manufacturers searched for answers

American manufacturers searched for answers and borrowed ideas with more or less success from Japanese and European competitors. Chrysler's K-car, pursuing a development strategy that had roots in Renault, proved successful as a platform for many variants that required little investment. However, General Motor's flirtation with robotics proved costly and cumbersome. Each of these moves toward adoption of best practices had potential to improve the companies' performances. None represented an integrated systems approach.

In 1985, MIT's International Motor Vehicle Project (IMVP) undertook a thorough study of practices in the worldwide automobile industry. By the completion of the study, as documented in *The Machine that Changed the World*, a systematic picture emerged. The IMVP researchers found the purest example of a set of integrated best practices in the Toyota Production System (TPS). They found a simple underlying principle behind the TPS—they called it lean.

HISTORY OF LEAN MANUFACTURING

Lean manufacturing is part of a progression that started with the industrial revolution in England. Guenter Spur, Ph.D. in *The Transformation of the Industrial World Brought about by Machine Tools*, attributes Puritanism, with its emphasis on the work ethic and more effective utilization of one's time, as creating a culture that was highly conducive to the development of modern manufacturing (Spur 1991).

The progression started with Abraham Dooby's invention of steel-making processes. The steam engine, patented by James Watt in 1769, provided a source of mechanical power that was much more versatile and portable than the water wheel. People started to think of finding ways to make things with the help of machinery. The steam engine permitted the simultaneous operation of several machines, providing the methodology for the quantity fabrication of parts, the replication of dimensional accuracy, and the improvement in productivity.

Even though turning had been an age-old skill, the lathe, invented by Henry Maudslay in about 1794, was significant for the fabrication of metal parts. Joseph Witworth (1803–1877) improved the accuracy of machine tools with the introduction of standards for the manufacture of leadscrews.

France, Germany, and Switzerland lagged somewhat behind England, but finally started to catch up during the first half of the 19th Century. The history of modern manufacturing in the United States had its origin in the federal armories of the early 19th Century (Hounshell 1984). The Springfield Armory in Massachusetts, especially under Colonel Roswell Lee, played a lead role in the development, first with the introduction of the interchangeability of parts and later the development of gaging for checking them. Although Eli Whitney has been quoted as the inventor of interchangeability, he is now seen as a promoter, rather than as a pioneer. The efforts of Springfield to coordinate its operations with those at the Harper's Ferry Armory played a major role in furthering the development of the process. The perfection of the lathe for the manufacture of rifle barrels and gun stocks was the next significant development, creating the foundation and allowing expansion of modern manufacturing in the United States. British visitors to the United States in the 1850s found the concept sufficiently different that they referred to it as the "American System." The demand for screws had become overwhelming and it encouraged William Sellers to develop the automatic screw machine.

Soon, the new technology spread to the production of consumer goods. After the invention of the sewing machine followed the production of typewriters, bicycles, and eventually, the automobile. None of these developments would have been possible without the parallel development of the machine tool industry. It grew out of the small arms industry, especially Colt's Patent Firearms Manufacturing Co. in Hartford, Conn. and Robbins & Lawrence Co. in Windsor, Vt. The makers of machine tools worked with manufacturers in various industries as they encountered production problems in various metalworking operations. The concept of interchangeability subsequently applied to other materials such as wood. The clock-making industry in New England became a major benefactor, bringing to mind names like Eli Terry.

The next major advance occurred when Henry Ford perfected the mass-production paradigm using the assembly line to manufacture a large volume of affordable cars. By the 1930s, the mass production paradigm was fabulously successful in creating products affordable to people from most economic walks of life.

The mass-production paradigm worked

The mass-production paradigm worked because it could take advantage of economies of scale. Demand for affordable vehicles grew larger and larger. Enormous factories with large work forces built nearly identical cars year after year. The workers did not have to know much. So many cars moved down the assembly line that workers kept busy doing a few simple operations repeatedly. In fact, many workers were immigrants who knew only enough English to be able to do their few simple tasks. Industrial engineers laid out the assembly process and taught line workers the few operations each needed to know.

Capital expenditure for fixed equipment and tooling at Ford's Rouge complex was amortized over decades. Production volumes were so large that manufacturers could use specialized machines with hard tooling for a single manufacturing operation.

The Rouge plant before World War II was almost totally integrated. Ford produced all the parts it needed in its own facilities. Ford had built 15 million Model-T cars by 1928 when it introduced the Model A. Other manufacturers were not so fully integrated. They depended on competing suppliers to make parts to exacting specifications established by the manufacturers. The bidding process was adversarial and focused on getting the lowest prices for large lots of parts.

Competition brought prices down. Markets grew and as they grew, mass production was adopted all over the world.

Then came World War II, which devastated very nearly all the world's industrial capacity and capabilities outside the Western Hemisphere. In the Western Hemisphere, the mass-production paradigm could, and did, live on relatively undisturbed—redirected in legendary plants like Willow Run to the mass production of planes, tanks, and even ships. In 1946, automobile companies turned out millions of cars to meet pent-up post-war demand. Europeans revived the mass-production paradigm with some remarkable successes, such as Volkswagen and its Beetle®.

Japan's industrial capabilities literally had been flattened by the summer of 1945. In the early post-war years, the Japanese had to start from scratch. They did not have a legacy of leftover war production factories and assembly lines to convert to peaceful production. They had miniscule markets. They were at the bottom of the economic spiral, with markets too small to generate the capital they would need to build the huge factories the mass-production paradigm demanded.

Creating a New Paradigm: the Toyota Production System

How could the Japanese serve small markets that were beginning to emerge out of the rubble? How could they compete against the foreign automakers with the advantage of economy of scale? The Japanese had to create something out of nothing and do it in a way that would allow them to compete against foreign manufacturers who did have markets sized for mass production success.

The Japanese government, with support from the U.S. occupation forces, provided protective cover for struggling Japanese industries while the domestic manufacturers tried to find a way. Toyota's first answer was to send Eiji Toyoda, a son of the company's founding family, to Ford's Rouge plant in Dearborn to learn the best practices of Ford. At the time, the Rouge was the most efficient manufacturing facility in the world, and among the largest.

However, the Rouge plant was the culmination of the mass-production paradigm. Just importing all the best practices of the Rouge plant would not work in Japan. Some might, and others could provide the cost and quality standards against which Toyota would have to compete. However, Toyota and Japan needed a different manufacturing paradigm.

Toyoda, an engineer by training, teamed with Taiichi Ohno in challenging the assumptions and processes of the mass-production paradigm.

Since the market for any model of vehicle was small and there was little capital for machines, each machine had to perform many jobs (Womack and Jones 1996). The Rouge had many specialized machines on its production lines. Changing tooling to allow a machine to perform a different job could take months. Toyota developed tooling systems that allowed machines to change tasks in a few hours. Thus, Toyota could use one tool for producing small lots economically.

Toyota could not afford a large work force. Production runs were too small for a worker to be employed full time on one simple task. Social pressures in a country desperate for economic stability forced the company into lifetime employment practices. Toyoda and Ohno realized that they had to get the most out of each worker, and that would happen only if the workers knew how to do many different tasks effectively.

Small-lot production meant there was always a lot of change going on. A hierarchical system of management and supervision could not keep up with the redefinition of tasks and the education required with each change. It proved better to turn over the responsibility for production to teams of workers, each with the skills to do many tasks, and to allow them to organize and perform the work. Industrial engineers gave the teams guidance and technical instruction. A coordinator, and a team leader who was a worker too, replaced the traditional foreman.

Toyota gave teams increasing responsibility: for housekeeping, tool repair, and especially for quality. The focus on quality led to *kaizen*, a formalization of the concept of continuous improvement. While kaizen describes a behavior expected of all employees every day, it is often punctuated by kaizen events or workshops that could last several days. In kaizen workshops, teams collaborate with industrial engineers. They suggest and implement improvements in the production system, so that the next production run yields higher quality, or can be done faster or cheaper than the last one.

Focus on quality went further, with an obsession for early detection and correction of in-process quality defects. Every worker was given the responsibility to stop the production line if he saw a defect he could not correct. Toyota trained workers to track down and correct sources of defects. After a while, there were few defects. The remaining ones were caught before they were propagated down the line into products, thus preventing costly rework. All vehicles that came off the line went immediately into the distribution pipeline.

Toyoda and Ohno took a challenging look at the way suppliers were treated in the mass-production paradigm. Toyota adopted an extension of the teaming concept that had made its assembly lines productive. It teamed with suppliers too, giving them knowledge, responsibility, and long-term stability. Toyota people would even help suppliers learn and improve the processes they used. In return, Toyota asked that suppliers adopt continual improvement processes, so that parts supplied to Toyota would be ever cheaper and of ever higher quality. Toyota encouraged suggestions for improvements from suppliers. It also encouraged suppliers to work together to share advanced processes and technologies.

Another important practice instituted by Toyoda and Ohno was kanban. The two men conceived a system in which product flowed, almost organically, down the production line, with just the right parts available at just the right time so flow was seamless. *Kanban* meant that parts would be produced only when they were needed, and delivered only when they would be used. A container or tag was returned to the parts supplier only when the previous batch of parts had been used up. The supplier then sent Toyota the exact number of additional parts needed. This is a pull system. The empty container pulled a new batch of parts from the supplier.

An especially important aspect of the supplier relationship was Toyota's insistence that suppliers provide parts *Just-in-Time* (JIT) for use on the assembly line. JIT meant Toyota did not need to devote space for parts inventory; nor did it carry the expense of a parts inventory.

After more than 20 years of refinement, Toyota's production system was ready in the 1970s when American consumers began asking for more fuel-efficient cars and American regulators sought both better fuel economy and lower-pollutant emissions. Toyota's production system was ready to provide the world's consumers with attractive, well-made vehicles that met their expectations and needs. By the 1980s, Toyota and other Japanese manufacturers that had learned and even improved on Toyota's best practices became formidable competitors.

At this point, IMVP did the study that looked deeply at the characteristics of Toyota's production system and reduced it to a new manufacturing paradigm they called lean.

The Lean Manufacturing Paradigm

The lean manufacturing paradigm is simple. Take a process. Focus on the intent of the process. Eliminate all parts of the process that do not contribute to meeting the intent, all those that do not contribute to value. Then look at each remaining part and work continually to lower its cost, make it timelier, and improve the quality of results.

This focus on eliminating all wasteful effort, the fat that did not contribute to achieving the desired outcome, resulted in

Toyota's lean production system. Lean and mean. Every bit of energy, every minute, every Yen, went into building cars and trucks that would give customers the outcome they wanted—reliable vehicles that would meet their needs for years.

> **Processes should be able to respond to change**

In recent years, there has been a second part added to the lean paradigm. The world is so full of change that no process is static. Processes should be able to respond to change, but they should do so with minimum cost of money, effort, and time.

Since the 1980s

Since the 1980s, the simple idea of lean has taken hold. It has been recognized as applicable to any process that delivers a product or service. Lean is not limited to automotive production lines. Lean concepts can be applied in fast-food shops and automotive repair shops, mortgage finance, and insurance companies. In fact, the concepts can be applied to almost any human endeavor.

In the early 1990s, two participants in the study that identified the lean manufacturing paradigm, James Womack and Daniel Jones, tried to help companies implement lean production systems. They realized lean was not a quick fix or a one-time thing for a company. Instead, lean was a different way of thinking, a different way of approaching the culture, organization, and operations of a company. Their formalized set of precepts called Lean Thinking[SM] has extended the ideas of lean beyond production lines to entire enterprises (Womack and Jones 1996).

One of the analytical techniques Womack and Jones described in their book was mapping so-called value streams. They pictured systems as streams of value. Raw materials and knowledge or information entered the system upstream. Products or services of value to customers flowed from the system downstream. In between were individual processes that added value to the product or service as it flowed through them. The model was simple, but powerful, allowing companies to examine the processes they used against the value they contribute. If processes did not contribute value, they could be eliminated. If they did, but at high cost, the process could be scrutinized for excessive cost elements. The Lean

Enterprise Institute provides proprietary tools, termed Value Stream Mapping^{SM} to aid in this type of analysis.

TPS, in its purest form, is a system that produces one product, a car model—maybe a family of models, built on a single platform. The focus of TPS is on making this production system as lean as possible. Toyota found it outgrew the thinking behind its flagship production system concept. The problem was that, as Toyota grew, it built separate production systems around several models or platforms. By the mid-1990s, Toyota had discovered that optimizing each of the production systems did not necessarily lead to a lean company. It found it could identify duplications of effort. It also found unique designs that might have been shared across systems. The company found it needed to think beyond the system for a single project and consider systems for multiple products. Toyota needed to integrate better designs, best practices, knowledge, and skills into an integrated super-system. Integration applied as well to the people of its several systems. The integrated super-system would still have lean production characteristics, but would be capable of extending lean concepts into all efforts to achieve corporate goals (Cusumano and Nobeoka 1998).

The Machine that Changed the World, started many thinking. If lean could make the Japanese automobile industry so fiercely competitive in cost, time, and quality, then lean could be a significant approach for any industry. By the early 1990s, the aircraft industry in the United States was under great pressure. On the military side, there was pressure to cut costs to make aircrafts affordable within post-Cold War defense budgets. On the commercial side, competition from outside the U.S. had increased—competition that punished any inefficiency or extra cost.

The Lean Aircraft Initiative

In 1993, the aircraft industry, the U.S. Air Force, and MIT formed a group, the Lean Aircraft Initiative (LAI), to examine ways to drive lean concepts into the industry. Aircraft manufacturing requires the assembly of a relatively small number of large, very complicated products. It lends itself to thinking about networked systems that encompass the manufacturers and their suppliers. Although LAI could, and did, examine techniques for making unit processes leaner, it also saw the value of applying lean to the whole enterprise.

One result of LAI's work was the Lean Enterprise Model (LEM), a description of the attributes of lean companies used extensively in this book.

Two other important activities took place in the 1990s that helped explain future manufacturing. Their results are used in this description of lean companies.

The Agile Manufacturing Initiative

In the 1990s, the Agile Manufacturing Initiative, which includes the results from the Agility Forum and several joint industry/academic applied research institutes and projects, was born from a realization that factories needed to have the capability to shift production inexpensively from one product to another. The accelerating pace of change in consumer tastes, technology, and economic conditions drove this need. So did the need to reduce the ever-increasing cost of military hardware by manufacturing its parts on the same production lines as parts used in civilian products. The Agility Forum at Lehigh University was an industry/academia/government-sponsored think tank that examined characteristics of agile production facilities. As with LAI and its application of lean to an entire enterprise, the Agility Forum quickly realized that agility—the ability to respond to unpredicted change—was a company-wide concept (Preiss et al. 1996, Goldman et al. 1997). The work of the Agility Forum was done in parallel with the development of the LEM with its emphasis on waste-free responses to changing circumstances.

The Next Generation Manufacturing Project

In 1997, the Next Generation Manufacturing Project (NGM) studied the future of U.S. manufacturing in the early 21st Century. NGM involved nearly 500 contributors, mostly experts from manufacturing (NGM Project 1997, Jordan and Michel 2000). NGM drew on:

- knowledge of lean that flowed from industrial experience;
- studies of the International Motor Vehicle Program (IMVP);
- work of the LAI;

- knowledge of agility that flowed from the Agility Forum and associated industry projects;
- wisdom of management of 21st Century manufacturing that came from MIT's Leaders for Manufacturing (LFM) program;
- pictures of the future of manufacturing technology coming from Oak Ridge Center for Manufacturing Technology;
- and the collective wisdom of about 500 practitioners of advanced manufacturing technology, processes, and systems.

The authors have used results of the NGM Project extensively in this book, especially in Chapter 6.

EXAMPLES OF LEAN MANUFACTURING

Many companies in many industries now embrace lean manufacturing and the extension of lean concepts across the enterprise (Liker 1998). Some of the most thoroughly considered experiences of companies that are undergoing transformation to lean, teach that transformation is a long, continuing process. Becoming lean is aptly titled, since few companies, once engaged in the transformation, believe that they will reach an endpoint.

Transformation requires vision and commitment at all levels, but especially at the executive team. Without a well-articulated and sustained vision, without visible and continuing commitment of time and resources by the company's executives to live lean, lasting transformation cannot happen.

Lessons from Toyota: the NUMMI Production System

John Shook, now co-director of the University of Michigan's Japan Technology Management Program and a partner in the Lean Enterprise Institute, was an important figure in importing Toyota's production system into the United States. After joining Toyota in Japan in 1983, he helped train cadres at the New United Motors Manufacturing, Inc. (NUMMI) plant in Fremont, Calif. and then at the Toyota Motors Manufacturing Kentucky (TMMK) plant in Georgetown, Ky. In his book, he describes some of the essential features of TPS and his experiences in transferring it to NUMMI and TMMK (Shook 1998).

NUMMI was the first full-scale demonstration of TPS in the United States. Since 1984, it has served as the laboratory in the U.S. for lean. NUMMI's goal is to build products with quality as high as anywhere in the world with costs that are the most competitive of any manufacturer. The function of NUMMI's production system is to meet those goals, efficiently and effectively, using three concepts:

1. Just-in-Time (JIT) production—the idea of JIT is not to produce products speculatively, but to build to order or to replace products that have been sold from dealers' inventories. The production process is a steady flow of materials and parts that are assembled into finished products. The ideal is to have no delays from start to finish. Finish is defined as receipt of the product by the customer. Synchronization has become an important term in NUMMI's and GM's lexicon. Synchronization in JIT production ensures that the right parts arrive at the right place on the production line—at exactly the right time, and in exactly the right quantity to maintain product flow down the line.

2. Jidoka—the quality principle. One of the basic concepts at NUMMI is to build quality into the production process itself. This concept, known in Japanese as *jidoka*, means preventing defective parts from going from one workstation to the next. NUMMI builds jidoka into machines and the production line so the line stops automatically when a machine breaks down, when defective parts are produced, or when other abnormal conditions occur. Jidoka also provides instructions for actions when team members encounter problems at their workstations. They are responsible for correcting the problem. If they cannot, they can stop the line.

3. Full utilization of team members' abilities. NUMMI's people work in teams. An important factor in the NUMMI production system is treating team members with trust and respect. NUMMI holds teams and team members accountable for their work. Everyone has responsibility to help solve problems and make decisions that affect them or their group. As much as possible, NUMMI has automated operations that are dangerous, require hard physical labor, or are monotonous and

repetitive. Team members routinely rotate jobs within their team to increase their value and the quality of their contributions.

The NUMMI production system uses many different techniques and methods to produce high-quality vehicles:

- Kanban—the *kanban* process of producing only what is needed to fill customer orders imported from Toyota prevents overproduction of parts and vehicles.
- Heijunka or production leveling—NUMMI keeps production costs down by efficiently building no more vehicles and parts than can be sold. One way to accomplish this is through heijunka. *Heijunka* is the overall balancing of the schedule to produce the variety and volume of vehicles produced in a given time period. The result of heijunka is a consistent production volume, driven by customer demand. Timelines can be developed for each product and for each product variation. The timelines of all the products produced in the chosen time period blend into a steady flow of work and a consistent schedule.
- Takt time—Takt time is the basic tool for building the time line (Shook 1998). *Takt time* is the time allotted to each job step of a process required for a given product. If you know takt times for all the job steps, you know how long the process will take for the entire product. If you know how long the processes will take, you know how long it will take to produce that product. You can then initiate production of the products needed to meet actual customer demand in a way that results in a steady flow of work to each workstation along the production line.
- Standardized work—NUMMI organizes each job so it is always done in the most efficient way possible, ensuring quality no matter which team member does the job. In standardized work, NUMMI establishes the takt time for each job, the order in which job steps are performed, and the parts that must be on hand.
- Kaizen—NUMMI teaches its team members to *kaizen* their jobs to achieve higher efficiency, better quality, and lower costs. Members actively search for continuous improvements by

finding waste in machinery, material, labor, and production methods.

- Poka-yoke—*Poka-yoke* monitoring devices are for in-process verification to support jidoka. They identify machine malfunctions in an effort to ensure failure-free production. Poka-yoke is also used to identify missing parts and improper assembly, and then automatically stop the conveyors or machines until the fault is corrected.
- Visual control and andon boards—NUMMI defines visual control as providing indicators that can show at a glance whether or not production activities are proceeding normally. *Visual controls* monitor the flow of work done by team members or machinery at each workstation. One of the visual tools used for this is the andon board. If a problem occurs at a workstation, the *andon* board lights up and an audible signal sounds to alert the group leader or team leader that there is a problem somewhere in his or her area. The andon board is triggered when a poka-yoke device identifies a machine malfunction—or when a team member pulls the andon cord or pushes a button at the workstation. The group leader or team leader then assesses the situation and takes appropriate steps to correct the problem. NUMMI uses other forms of visual controls to communicate different kinds of information. Examples include charts that display the status of quality, efficiency, attendance, safety, and training.
- Teaming—the work force in the NUMMI plant is divided into teams consisting of six to eight members. Each team is responsible for meeting NUMMI's objectives in areas such as quality, production, and safety. Teams are lead by an hourly employee. There are only two job classifications: one for production workers, and the other for skilled trades, such as tool and die handlers or general maintenance workers.

NUMMI was an immediate success. It was born in the shell of the Fremont plant that General Motors had closed in 1981. When GM closed it, the plant was assessed as having the worst quality statistics of any GM assembly plant, with absenteeism rates of more than 20%. NUMMI established a partnership with the United Auto Workers (UAW) and hired many of the UAW members who had worked for GM. Early quality audits were among GM's best and absenteeism was less than 2%. John Shook attributes the success to the sense of belonging and membership that the NUMMI work force developed. Membership led to accepting responsibility freely for achieving NUMMI's ultimate success.

Lean Electronics at Rockwell Collins

Lean was first demonstrated in the automobile industry, but in the past decade, companies in all industries have started the transformation. Rockwell Collins is one company where lean has met with significant success. Rockwell Collins is the business unit of Rockwell International responsible for aircraft electronic systems. Its customers are from all aviation sectors—general, commercial, and defense. Rockwell Collins is implementing lean concepts under the lean electronics banner.

Lean electronics is a dynamic process improvement philosophy that is a fundamental component of the company's culture. Its precepts are to:

- eliminate waste throughout the value stream;
- develop an agile enterprise infrastructure;
- create high levels of employee involvement;
- develop a mindset of perfection;
- establish predictable processes;
- and optimize use of human and capital assets to yield the lowest life-cycle cost.

Rockwell Collins identified three major categories of waste conditions: variability, congestion, and confusion. Figure 2-1 identifies enablers for the transformation to lean conditions including:

- Standard work and process control, using poka-yoke and visual controls lead to lean conditions of predictability and repeatability.
- Just-in-Time and process flow lead to synchronization and flow with minimal queuing and wait-time for work-in-progress.
- Design for manufacturability and transparency lead to simplicity and order.

Wasteful conditions	Lean principles	Lean conditions	Value	
			Work force	Customers
Variability	Standard work	Predictability	Stability	Quality
	Process control	Repeatability	Consistency	
Congestion	Just in Time	Synchronization	Flexibility	Availability
	Process focus	Flow	Responsive	
Confusion	Design for manufacturing	Simplicity	Waste elimination	Affordability
	Transparency	Order	Resource efficiency	

Figure 2-1. Enablers for the transformation to lean conditions.

The Decorah Experience

The 350-person Decorah, Iowa, facility is Rockwell Collins' model for the company's enterprise-wide plan to eliminate waste. In the first year after Decorah committed to lean:

- Product-line cycle time has been reduced by 50%.
- Work-in-process (WIP) has been reduced by 46%, having a dollar value estimated at $3.7 million.
- Defects have been reduced by 32.5%.
- 52 operators have been assigned to new work.
- Over 6,000 ft^2 of floor space has been freed to bring in additional products.

Plant Manager Kevin Myers credits Decorah's employees using lean principles and practices for the improvements. Rockwell Collins had already committed itself to High-Performance Work Systems (HPWS), a high-involvement/high-commitment approach to work. Employees are organized into semi-autonomous teams empowered to make decisions and act with minimal external approval. At Decorah, an employee team redesigned the layout of the plant. Employees immersed themselves in 5S (sort, straighten, sanitize, sweep, and sustain) events to make the workplace simpler, more orderly, and more transparent. The employees participated in more than 40 Radical Process Improvement (RPI) exercises to clean work areas and redesign product flow. RPI is Rockwell Collins' adaptation of Toyota's kaizen event.

Today, the plant is rearranged around product families, and assembly operators build complete radios in a continuous flow to meet a specific customer demand. Customers may be commercial or defense aircraft manufacturers, airlines, or aircraft operators. The assembly operators do not crank out circuit boards that are just placed in piles of inventory to await a need. In the past, specific functional areas, such as test, postcoat, and assembly were all grouped in clusters. Now, Decorah has incorporated the functions with the production line. Once product build starts, product flows down the line until it is shipped out the door.

Many of the steps taken at Decorah were just good housekeeping. With JIT, the company removed large, moving racks used to store inventoried parts. It reclaimed space that had been used as a repository for the scrap it salvaged and the equipment it no longer needed. After the housekeeping was done, Decorah employees started from scratch to set up the facility as a whole. They do not claim perfection; but they have achieved a good starting point for continuous improvement.

Before its processes were examined in RPI exercises, Decorah would ship products for intermediate processing to Rockwell Collins plants in Cedar Rapids and Manchester, Iowa. The parts might make four round trips and travel 900 miles. After RPI, the parts made a single, 200-mile, round trip to Cedar Rapids.

Becoming lean is itself a process

Becoming lean is itself a process that should be subjected to continuous improvement. Some of the things Decorah has tried were not successful, except as lessons learned. However, Rockwell Collins sees that as an inevitable part of the transformation to lean. The point is to plan the change, implement it, evaluate it, and quickly discard it if it is not successful. Move on and try something else.

Decorah is a real success story for everyone. The productivity gains meant fewer employees were needed to build the existing backlog. However, the plant's costs, quality, and work force productivity gave it competitive advantages that led to new work.

In turn, the new work provided the plant and its employees with greater stability and less dependence on any single product line.

Herm Reininga, Rockwell Collins Vice President of Operations, says of the employee response to lean: "Employees express excitement as they describe changes to their workplace and we have determined the keys to that excitement." These are:

- Employees have been an integral part of developing changes.
- It is all right to fail on a change.
- It is not bad to run another RPI and find a better way.

"During the last year we have moved product from and to each of Collins' 10 plants (all building civilian and military units on the same line). In some cases, we have performed the lean process before it moved. In all cases, we performed the process during the move. The results have all projects requiring fewer people at the receiving location. This is not perceived negatively by management or the sending location, but only as part of the lean process. Herein lies the real key to success for people to embrace long-term improvements," Reininga says.

Among the lessons Rockwell Collins has learned from its Decorah plant and its other transformation efforts are:

- All leaders must embrace lean as the standard way of doing business.
- Leaders must participate actively and constructively in the transformation.
- The participatory work force culture Rockwell Collins calls HPWS is essential.
- Clear and frequent communication are essential.
- Continuous improvement must always be encouraged, not just in RPI exercises.
- It is easy to underestimate the effort needed for transformation. Change is even harder in administrative and engineering environments, where it is easier to hide waste and more difficult to envision processes.

All leaders must embrace lean

Kevin Myers, Decorah's plant manager says, "One of the most important things we've learned is that lean means constantly coming back and re-doing. You're never done." Clay Jones, Rockwell Collins President, says, "There will be more change in Rockwell Collins in the next three years than there has been in the last 30 years."

Becoming Lean in the Aircraft Industry

The aircraft industry has been on a long journey toward lean that accelerated in the mid-1990s. Both the commercial- and the defense-oriented sectors of the industry have benefited from the transformation, incomplete as it is.

Boeing Commercial Airplanes

Boeing's Commercial Airplanes organization traces the roots of its lean transformation to the early 1980s when it recognized the need to improve the quality of its products and processes. Commercial Airplanes focused then on continuous improvement and total quality management.

In the early 1990s, Commercial Airplanes began a "5S" program, a program to sort, straighten, sanitize, sweep, and sustain each work area. The 5S program was intended to organize and standardize work areas and processes. Then it began using Accelerated Improvement Workshops (AIW)—the Boeing analog to Toyota's kaizen events—to involve and empower the entire Boeing work force in the transformation. The effort to become lean has gradually become all encompassing. The objective now is to develop a lean enterprise in which all the functions that contribute to the value stream are lean.

Today, a fundamental pillar of Commercial Airplanes' lean production system effort is the concept of JIT. By focusing on time, it can find hidden costs in an inefficient production system. Having materials arrive at the factory just when they are needed for the production process allows the company to minimize the amount of inventory it must hold and store. It also minimizes the cost of obsolescence. In a world of rapid change, parts sitting on a shelf can quickly become obsolete.

In its production systems, Commercial Airplanes strives to apply the right resources and right tools to achieve three key lean principles:

1. *Takt-paced production* describes the rate of assembly in a factory. For Boeing, lean does not necessarily mean doing things faster; it means doing things at the right pace. The customer's rate of demand establishes the pace, or overall takt time. Knowing the takt times of the standard work means that Boeing can pace the work to meet the customer's needs on time.
2. *One-piece flow* is the opposite of batch production. Instead of building many products and then holding them in queue for the next step in the process, products go through steps in the process one at a time, without interruption.
3. *Pull production* means products are made only when the customer has requested or "pulled" it, and not before. This way, Commercial Airplanes does not build products that are not needed. After achieving a predictable pace of production, one-piece flow, and reliable machinery, a company can operate in a pull production environment.

In addition to using takt time, the standard work procedures can ensure that the company knows the standard quantity of materials needed to keep everyone in the process working.

Another important pillar of Commercial Airplanes' transformation is the concept of error-free production. Error-free production means first-time quality. For Boeing, this means:

- Workers stop production when a defect is detected. Doing so prevents defects from traveling on to the next process. The sooner an error is detected, the easier it is to find the cause and solve it.
- Designing reliable processes and machinery means fewer defects occur.
- Human work should be separated from machine work. This means having machines do repetitive and dangerous tasks, while people perform work that requires decision-making and problem-solving skills.

By the end of 1999, Commercial Airplanes' lean manufacturing efforts yielded significant advances:

- Commercial Airplanes made progress toward a smooth and continuous flow of parts with the implementation of lean distribution and point-of-use delivery systems. Point-of-use delivery means the hardware required to build airplanes is delivered directly to the production area that uses it, at just the right time and in just the right quantity. For Commercial Airplanes, this has resulted in a dramatic reduction in inventory levels—by more than $1 billion in 1999.

- Boeing's Spokane, Wash. facility manufactures floor panels. Lean efforts reduced the manufacturing time by 60% and manufacturing floor space by more than 50%. The plant reduced the cost of production, freed up manufacturing capacity, and started a new business—supplying airlines with replacement floor panels for their airplanes.

- Flow-time reduction efforts in the 777 final-body-join area enable Commercial Airplanes to meet a rising demand without investing the millions of dollars needed for a second production line.

- The Frederickson, Wash. plant, where wing parts are built, reduced flow time on its products by 40–50% and reduced inventory levels by 43%.

- The Machine Fabrication plant located in Auburn, Wash. reduced inventory by 60% during 1999. The plant increased inventory turn rates from 4.0 to 6.4, and reduced defects by nearly 50%.

- The Wing Responsibility Center in Everett, Wash. saved more than $3 million in 1999 by implementing visual controls, simplifying the reordering system, and reducing the number of fasteners.

In each case, Boeing credits the employees with the ideas and the commitment to lean with making these achievements possible.

Examples from the Defense Aircraft Industry

The major defense contractors have also used lean concepts to good advantage.

The C-130 line in Lockheed Martin's Marietta, Ga. plant has undergone a 20-year evolution. Probably the oldest aircraft production line in existence—the first experimental YC-130 flew in

1954, the first production C-130 was delivered to the U.S. Air Force in 1956—the line has undergone transformation, especially in preparation for the latest variant, the C-130J.

Bill Kessler, Lockheed Martin's Vice President for Lean Manufacturing and past Director of the U.S. Air Force Manufacturing Technology Program, characterizes the evolution. When he first saw the line, he immediately spotted the need to automate the overhead transport systems that carried fuselage sections and other major components from one side of the plant to the other for assembly. The manual systems wasted a lot of time and manpower. There was also a lot of clutter. It was a typical, traditional line.

Lockheed has leaned out the C-130J line. The overhead transport system that caused work to stop as workers watched slow progress of massive fuselage sections to the assembly point is not there any more. The major subsystems are assembled, easily transportable, near the assembly point. The 5S programs and standard work procedures have resulted in a line that is clean and orderly.

The C-130J has benefited from the application of lean concepts in other ways. Lockheed expects to improve performance and reduce ownership costs by incorporating state-of-the-art technology. Ownership costs may be reduced by as much as 45% and maintenance-man-hours-per-flight hour reduced by 50% or more.

Lockheed Martin's other aircraft lines have benefited as well. The F-16 line has seen an injection of new technology into the product, but at the same time has faced a decrease in production to four planes a month. Nevertheless, with lean production techniques, the company has been able to maintain the same unit costs as when it was producing 25 planes a month.

Lockheed Martin and Boeing's Military Aircraft and Missile Systems Group are in a unique competition for the joint strike fighter (JSF), an affordable, next-generation, multi-role fighter aircraft. There are strict affordability constraints and both companies are using lean-manufacturing techniques to meet the constraints and to gain competitive advantage. The result is a focused demonstration of lean.

Some of the cost and efficiency benefits Boeing has achieved in building its two-concept demonstration aircraft include:

- The time and cost for the design of the forward fuselage, or forebody, were cut in half compared to previous programs. At the same time, Boeing achieved major weight and cost reductions. Assembly began ahead of schedule. Among the lean design and manufacturing technologies Boeing used are advanced 3-D modeling and simulation, automated fiber placement, and high-speed milling. It also used simple, low-cost assembly fixtures. These technologies resulted in designs and a single 3-D database used by the Boeing team across the country. Because of the database, suppliers could start fabrication of parts early. They machined the hardware right the first time. Boeing used the database to simulate assembly processes to avoid costly problems during actual assembly, and to provide shop workers with assembly instructions.
- The final assembly of the first Boeing JSF concept demonstrator began two weeks ahead of schedule. The X-32 forebody, assembled by Boeing Phantom Works in St. Louis, was joined to the mid-fuselage section, assembled in Palmdale, Calif. There were no surprises since joining of the major assemblies had been simulated eighteen months before.
- The crews needed to assemble the Boeing demonstrators were half the size that had been estimated in the plans. Tooling requirements were reduced by 75% over the requirements for Boeing's previous demonstrator, the YF-22 prototype. The tooling costs were less than half those of the YF-22. Overall fabrication and assembly costs were 30–40% below projections. The JSF demonstrator had 80% fewer defects than the YF-22.
- During JSF assembly, Boeing used live video feeds and digital still photography to send images of JSF parts and systems to various sites. Use of live, interactive video feed reduced JSF travel costs by more than $4 million.

Smaller Companies and Plants are Becoming Lean

The effort to become lean is not limited to big automakers or aerospace companies. Companies in many industries have applied lean principles and practices with great success in smaller plants.

Karlee Company

Karlee Company of Garland, Tex. is a recent recipient of the national Malcolm Baldrige Quality Award, given by the U.S. Department of Commerce to companies with the best records for enterprise-wide quality. Karlee is a 550-employee contract manufacturer of precision sheet metal and machined components for the telecommunications, semiconductor, and medical equipment industries. Karlee has applied lean principles as sales have grown. Sales have increased to about $80 million since the mid-1990s at a rate averaging 25% a year.

Karlee has a strong focus on its customers. The company assigns a three-person customer service team to each primary customer to provide ongoing and pro-active support. Since 1996, Karlee has improved customer satisfaction ratings by 32.2% while production volumes have tripled.

Karlee's production is organized into manufacturing cells. Each cell is a focused team, producing products by utilizing lean manufacturing concepts, statistical process control, and Flexible Manufacturing Systems (FMS). The teams also use automated punching, and robotic braking and welding. The vertically integrated manufacturing capabilities include computerized numerical control (CNC) milling and turning for machined components, and complete sheet metal processing. The latter includes plating, painting, and value-added assembly. Integration of value-added assembly includes cabling harness, power supply, and back-plane installation through testing and packaging. Karlee's fabricated products include everything from small brackets to enclosure assemblies. Its machining products range from spacers to large vacuum chambers.

Karlee's integrated operations begin with engineering support through an electronic data file exchange, parallel design support, and 2D/3D modeling capabilities. The operations end with electronic, Just-in-Time, kanban-pull shipping and billing systems.

Karlee uses inventory "turns" as an important metric on how quickly and efficiently its inventory results in a revenue-generating finished product. From 1995 to 1999, the company improved its inventory turns from 9.2 to 15.9. In 1999, Karlee achieved raw goods turns of 13.1 and work-in-progress inventory turns of 28.7. The industry averages are quoted as 7.2 and 9.0, respectively. In

2000, the company went from lead-time assemblies of two-to-three weeks to quick-turn assemblies of one-to-two days.

Green Gear Cycling, Inc.

Green Gear Cycling is a small, 30-employee, company in Eugene, Ore. that makes the Bike Friday®, the world's largest-selling, custom-made, folding bicycle (Stevens 2000). It has $3 million in sales and 17,000 ft of production space. However, the company uses lean-manufacturing principles adopted from TPS.

Green Gear is customer driven, annually building about 2,000 bikes to customer weight, measurements, and equipment specifications, at an average selling price of $1,700. CEO Alan Scholz is quoted as saying, "It's not unusual for someone to call us with plane ticket in hand and say they are going on a trip, (and) can we have a bike ready for them in so many days. We can accommodate those kinds of requests, with a decision-to-buy to riding in three days. We give people what they want when they want it. If you do that, people are willing to pay you for it."

In the 1980s, Alan Scholz and his brother Hanz set out to create a build-to-order, Just-in-Time, world-class manufacturing company. Their goal was a long-term business that would make things of which they could be proud, that did not put a load on the ecosystem, and that would pay good wages and add value to the community.

Green Gear first built a quality $1,000 tandem bicycle, making about 8,000 of them in the late 1980s. In 1992, it started making folding bikes. Sales grew 70% a year through 1997 to about $2.5 million in revenues. Sales over the next two years were relatively flat as the company tuned its management systems to double its growth potential. Recently, sales are at a rate greater than $3 million a year.

Green Gear processes each bicycle through the production system the company developed from the very start. It is a build-to-order, flow-manufacturing configuration organized in a series of cells. In the first cell, a U-shaped configuration, an operator works several pieces of dedicated equipment, all able to run automatically so the operator can multitask. Here, workers cut and shape tubing into frame members before moving the frame parts to a welding cell. The cells are designed so any one cell can do some of the work of the previous or next cell if production runs behind or ahead. The company has a flow motto, "Touch it once, do it now." Once work on a bike has begun, it flows through the process without stoppage at any point.

Takt time, the time between completion of bikes at the end of the process, is adjusted based on how sales are going—another TPS concept based on producing to demand, not projection. In mid-2000, the rate averaged one bike every 1.5 hours across the mix of different models (it takes about nine hours to build one bike), but when a batched order for 50 bikes came in, Green Gear cut the takt time to 27 minutes.

Operating in a one-at-a-time flow system rather than in batches maximizes the chances for continuous improvement. Alan Scholz says, "For us, every bike is a batch, so we have 150–200 chances per month to make process improvements. A small manufacturer operating in a large-batch mode can be put out of business if he ruins just one. If you can make improvements as you find them, you can survive as a small manufacturer." When a quality problem is discovered, the operator switches on a red light and all procedures stop until the production cell is adjusted to eliminate the problem.

Green Gear can offer millions of ways to configure its bikes. It cannot stock parts for all possible variations; so it uses kanban, with parts reordered as they are used and minimum buffer stocks maintained based on vendor response time. Parts are pulled one bike at a time, three days before the ship date established by the customer. The kanban system enables the company to operate at low inventory levels and manage cash flow.

Green Gear has applied lessons from its success with lean manufacturing to other functions—to customer service and sales, for example. Each sales consultant has a customized computer workstation, but with no desk that can become cluttered. This encourages the "Touch it once, do it now" philosophy.

Green Gear practices a "customers for life" strategy. The company believes repeat business will yield $10,000–25,000 for a lifetime customer. Therefore, it provides extra service at no cost when a bike comes in for tire repairs, even replacing a tire for free.

Aeroquip's Van Wert Plant

Aeroquip's plant of 700 employees in Van Wert, Ohio makes metal connectors, fittings, and adapters and joins rubber hoses to them (Bylinsky 2000). Aeroquip hoses, hose assemblies, and quick-disconnect couplings are typically found in critical systems, where they must withstand extreme weather conditions, vibration, abrasion, corrosion, dust, and high operating pressures. Eaton Corp. acquired Aeroquip in 1999.

The plant had some excellent products, but was typical of 1980s factories. Manufacturing was organized by function. Products were sent in batches from function to function. The company had excessive inventories blocking passageways and equally excessive customer dissatisfaction about poor product quality and late deliveries. The plant did not respond well to competition and globalization of markets.

With the help of university professors Jack Muckstadt, from Cornell University, and Dennis Severance, from the University of Michigan, Aeroquip began a long process of transformation that is continuing. Employees were organized into teams to study and change plant operations. One of the most basic changes was the establishment of focus factories—cells of people and machines that concentrate on manufacturing and assembling a specific product, often for a specific customer. Aeroquip's goal now is to be a fast-response organization, in which its customer demand pulls the flow of products through production cells.

The Van Wert managers applied their own version of a kaizen event, called *cell razing*, analogous to barn raising. Teams build, and sometimes rebuild, production cells in a continual search for greater efficiency. Today, 95% of employees serve on two or more improvement teams and advise on all production issues, including the acquisition of new machines. Cycle times have been reduced drastically. For example, Aeroquip has reduced parts finishing from eight days to 24 hours.

The so-called Dynacraft cell, that makes truck parts for the Dynacraft subsidiary of truck-maker Paccar, has adopted a much simpler process for machining and assembling components for truck air-suspension systems. Two workers are stationed at opposite sides of a gravity parts rack. One attaches a nut support to the tub-like part and slides it down the rack. The other immediately puts the part into a stamping machine. Before cell razing, there was no gravity rack. The assembly and stamping jobs at times sat in a stamping queue for 48 hours. Using the flow technique, the cell now processes 700 parts per shift instead of the previous 50.

The Van Wert plant continues to look for new refinements of the company's manufacturing processes. It is building on a ten-year effort that has:

- reduced inventories of parts from 135 days to 45 days;
- increased on-time deliveries from 63% to 98%;
- reduced return rate for faulty component parts by two-thirds;
- and increased operating income by 855% on a gross sales increase of 25%.

EXERCISE

The authors have written this exercise and those in subsequent chapters assuming that the reader can compare his or her company's operations with lean principles and practices. The goal is to help apply lean concepts to the real world. Readers not working in manufacturing companies can apply the exercises to a business or organization with which they are familiar. Almost all the lean principles and practices are as applicable to service companies, government, or even not-for-profit organizations, as they are to the manufacturing industry.

1. Compare the system your company uses with the TPS. Do you think that the approach taken by Toyota would work for your company? If not, why not?
2. In recent years, what changes have your company initiated to become more competitive and gain greater market share?
3. Based on the TPS approach, what changes would you recommend your company make to become more competitive?

REFERENCES

Bylinsky, Gene. "America's Elite Factories." *Fortune*, August 14, 2000.

Cusumano, Michael A., and Nobeoka, Kentaro. 1998. *Thinking Beyond Lean: How Multi-Project Management is Transforming*

Product Development at Toyota and Other Companies. New York: The Free Press.

Goldman, Steven L., Preiss, Kenneth, and Nagel, Roger N. 1997. *Agile Competitors and Virtual Organizations.* New York: John Wiley & Sons, Inc.

Hounshell, David A. 1984. *From the American System to Mass Production, 1800-1932.* Baltimore, MD: The Johns Hopkins University Press.

Jordan, James A. Jr., and Michel, Frederick J. 2000. *Next Generation Manufacturing: Methods and Techniques.* New York: John Wiley & Sons, Inc.

Liker, Jeffrey K., Editor. 1998. *Becoming Lean: Inside Stories of U. S. Manufacturers.* Portland, OR: Productivity Press.

NGM Project. 1997. *Next Generation Manufacturing: Framework for Action.* Bethlehem, PA: Agility Forum.

Preiss, Kenneth, Goldman, Steven L., and Nagel, Roger N. 1996. *Cooperate to Compete: Building Agile Business Relationships.* New York: Van Nostrand Reinhold.

Shook, John Y. 1998. "Bringing the Toyota Production System to the United States: A Personal Perspective," in *Becoming Lean: Inside Stories of U. S. Manufacturers.* Liker, Jeffrey K. Editor. Portland, OR: Productivity Press.

Spur, Guenter. 1991. *Vom Wandel der industriellen Welt durch Werkzeugmaschinen* (The Transformation of the Industrial World brought about by Machine Tools). Munich, Germany: Carl Hanser Verlag.

Stevens, Tim. "Pedal Pushers." *Industry Week,* July 17, 2000.

Womack, James P. and Jones, Daniel T. 1996. *Lean Thinking: Banish Waste and Create Wealth in Your Corporation.* New York: Simon and Shuster.

BIBLIOGRAPHY

Boeing Commercial Airplanes Group.
http://www.boeing.com/commercial/initiatives

Boeing Military Aircraft and Missile Systems Group.
http://www.boeing.com/defense-space/military/jsf/

Green Gear Cycles, Inc.
http://www.bikefriday.com/index.htm

Karlee Company. http://www.karlee.com

Lean Aircraft Initiative. http://lean.mit.edu/public/index.htm

Lean Enterprise Institute. http://www.lean.org

Lockheed Martin. http://www.lmaeronautics.com/
fighter_programs/jsf

MIT International Motor Vehicle Program. http://
www.mit.edu/afs/athena.mit.edu/org/c/ctpid/www/impv.html

MIT Leaders for Manufacturing Program.
http://lfmsdm.mit.edu

Next Generation Manufacturing Report.
http://www.dp.doe.gov/dp_web/public_f.htm

NIST's Baldrige Awards.
http://www.nist.gov/public_affairs/baldrige00/Karlee.htm

NUMMI. http://www.nummi.com

Rockwell Collins. http://www.collins.rockwell.com

Chapter Three

Lean Enterprise Principles

It is a natural step to take the simple prescription of lean manufacturing and apply it across the entire company and beyond. Take any process:

- Focus on the intent of the process.
- Eliminate every part of the process that does not contribute to meeting intent.
- Examine the remaining parts to determine whether they contribute value.
- Eliminate those that do not contribute to value.
- Work continually to lower the costs of the remaining ones, make them timelier, and improve the quality of their results.

If you can make a manufacturing process lean, you can make any business process lean. If every process within a company is lean, then by definition, it is a lean company. Simple.

Well, it is not as simple as it seems.

In fact, it is anything but simple. A lean company is an integrated company where people and processes interact, often in unspecified ways. The totality of these people and processes in a lean company is different—fundamentally transformed— from those of traditional companies. People do their work differently. Decisions are made differently. The company uses technology, knowledge, and decision support systems differently.

> If you can make a manufacturing process lean, you can make any business process lean

The Lean Aircraft Initiative (LAI) is a cooperative effort of MIT, the U.S. Air Force, and many large contractors. It has struggled with the question of what really is a lean company. Surely, it is a company where all processes are lean. However, it is a lot more.

The LAI described a lean company in its Lean Enterprise Model (LEM). The LEM is a behavioral model that provides a benchmark of attributes for a lean company. A company that wants to be lean wants to look like the company described by the LEM. The LEM is based on two meta-principles, four enterprise principles, and 12 overarching practices. The LEM does not provide a recipe for becoming lean, but a set of targets toward which any lean initiative should lead.

DRIVERS OF TRANSFORMATION TO THE LEAN ENTERPRISE

The automobile industry was driven to become lean by rapid changes in the market and global economy. It had to build more competitive products at lower, more competitive costs so it could survive. Similar forces drive every industry. Executives face a set of dilemmas demanding solutions today and a series of global drivers posing more challenges tomorrow.

Dilemmas of Corporate Executives

As a corporate executive today, you constantly have to balance many issues at once. Examples are:

- Your vice president of human resources (VP-HR) may propose an education and training program that she wants to couple with incentive compensation. The motivation is to prepare your most qualified employees to be immediately productive as your company adopts new processes and technologies. That way you can retain them, avoiding the costs of termination and the expense of hiring new employees with the needed skills, while maintaining work force loyalty and morale. But at the same time, your vice president of operations may develop a staffing plan to meet your cost targets during slack times. Part of the plan may require laying off some of the same employees that the VP-HR wants to re-educate.

- Your vice president of engineering may propose a costly new facility incorporating advanced processes to give you cost and competitive advantages today. But your chief financial officer (CFO) may worry forcefully that the investment will not be depreciated before these wonder technologies are made obsolete by the next ones.
- Your chief knowledge officer may argue that while it is impossible to put a dollar value on your company's knowledge base, it is a big differentiator between your company and its competitors. But, as soon as he ends his case for tight control over your intellectual property, your vice president of strategic alliances may propose a knowledge sharing agreement with one of the industry's major suppliers. She may argue that the agreement is necessary for gaining access to the knowledge you need to be competitive on your next big major projects.

Your company cannot do everything, of course. It may be good at many things, but it cannot afford to be the world's expert on everything that goes into a complicated product. On the other hand, the company cannot afford not to have access to all the competencies when it needs them.

You want strategic alliances that lock in long-term relationships with the company's suppliers and customers. However, those suppliers and customers may be in play—candidates for mergers, perhaps even with your competitors. Their technologies may prove inadequate in the future. They may not be able to match your transformation to the lean paradigm. Similarly, how can you have a long-term relationship with a customer who is being romanced by competitors with better delivery positions and financing arrangements and who might merge tomorrow with your competition's captive customer?

In the background, of course, there is the continuing dilemma—the "herding cats" dilemma—of simultaneously satisfying customers, employees, stockholders, the governments of the countries and localities where the company does business, and the people in the communities where it operates.

These are tough dilemmas. However, this is just part of the environment within which your company operates, hopefully as a lean enterprise.

Stakeholders

The company must satisfy many stakeholders to succeed. One way to understand this is to think of stakeholders as separate groups of "customers." Who are these people?

- Paying customers—clearly, the consumers who pay for your company's products are an important group of customers. If they do not see value in the offerings, there is no income, no profits, and no business. This book puts strong emphasis on these customers.
- Investors—the same as paying customers are investors, the people who have put their faith, and their money, in your ability to provide value in return. Usually their metric for value is financial—real or potential return on their investment. Investors are not a monolithic group. A company should segment its investors just as it does its market to understand what value it must deliver to them. The company may have owners who are active in running the company—or those who are passive. Investors may be individual shareholders, large or small. They may be managers of mutual funds, representing thousands of individuals. They may be managers of pension funds with the fiduciary responsibility of the livelihood of millions of senior citizens. Each investor segment has its own criteria for the combination of returns and risks that represent acceptable value.
- The work force—the nature of employment is changing. Qualified employees who can contribute to your company have greater independence than ever before. You must deliver value to your work force, or they, like the paying customers, will walk. This is the result of: the higher value of their knowledge; a better understanding of the dynamics of an employment market in which neither employees nor companies can assume a model of long-term employment; and the tight labor market.
- Suppliers and partners: your company depends on its suppliers and on partners in its joint ventures. They, too, have many choices. Most suppliers have many product lines and many customers. They are not dependent solely on their relationship with one company. Indeed, they must see sufficient value

in the relationship with a company to justify their investment in it. You have to sell them.

- Government—your company does not operate in a societal vacuum. Every government jurisdiction in which it functions will judge the company on the value it brings to the public. Again, government is not a monolith. The water district may be a supplier. The local environmental protection organization may be a paying customer, or it may be a partner, or it may be an adversary. Schools and colleges supply entry-level employees and then help retrain them as needs change. A jurisdiction that does not see value in your company's participation in its community will, at best, tolerate it. Given a choice, the jurisdiction will favor companies that provide it with the best value in return.

Global Drivers of the Future

Not only must companies deal with today's dilemmas; they also have to prepare for a future that is a juggernaut looming down on them. The Next Generation Manufacturing (NGM) project identified the closely coupled forces (see Figure 3-1) that are shaping the future (NGM Project 1997):

- rapidly rising customer expectations;
- globalization of markets and competition;
- pace of technology change;
- global availability of advanced technology and competitive practices;
- global skill-based competition;
- and environmental responsibilities and resource constraints.

Rapidly Rising Customer Expectations

Levi Strauss invented jeans and was the premier supplier for millions of people. It seemed to be a company that would hold that position forever. One of the most respected companies in California, it was successful, with good work force relationships, and seemingly had an unending franchise on ubiquitous blue-denim pants. Yet in early 1999, Levi Strauss was forced to close many of its U.S. plants as it became a victim of customers' expectations for

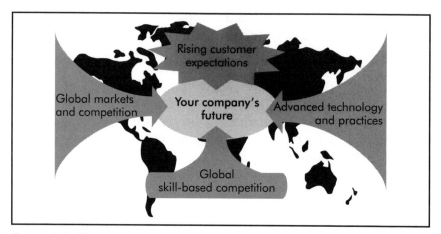

Figure 3-1. The Next Generation Manufacturing Project identified coupled forces shaping the future.

different styles, different fabrics, trendier brands of equal quality, and lower prices.

The new Ford Focus® is an entry-level car. But it is very different from the 1980s entry-level Escort®. It has standard equipment features that were optional only a decade ago, and did not exist 25 years ago. Many mid-priced cars now come with service features, such as 24-hour-a-day roadside assistance, once only the province of luxury cars. GM's OnStar℠ technology provides access to a central-help facility as an option on most of its vehicles and standard on a few. Cadillac is developing a night-vision system, demilitarized technology for seeing well beyond the reach of today's headlights. All this is transforming the car into a sophisticated information appliance, with each new feature appealing to the customers' divergent demands for drive-ability, comfort, safety, and panache.

End-users are quite intolerant of inadequate functionality, late delivery, or shoddy quality. They are an instant-gratification generation, having grown up expecting near-perfection at an affordable price.

People who succeed in selling products to end-users are aware of the need for customer satisfaction. They know that, if they sell an inadequate product, they will not get a second chance with that customer. They know that if they make one mistake in quality, they may be tainted by rapidly spreading word-of-mouth or by a blunt Internet chat-room discussion. They know that if they sell a poor quality product, their customers will hound them continuously. Moreover, they know if they cannot deliver the goods, someone else will.

As the end users grow more demanding, so too do the retailers and distributors who sell to them. These businesses know that there is no pipeline, no shelf space, and no mind share, for inadequate or over-priced products. Retailers and distributors demand ever more of manufacturers. As manufacturers respond to higher expectations, they will in turn put more pressure on the supply chain. Delivery of defective parts or poor product support by a supplier will quickly reflect back on the manufacturer's profits and eventually lead to financial penalties, or worse, for the supplier.

Customer anger can create a backlash at both the manufacturer and the supplier. The backlash on the manufacturer to the supplier is well-illustrated by reactions to the defects in Firestone tires mounted on Ford Explorers®. However the investigations into design and production defects end, both companies will live for years under skeptical scrutiny by wary customers.

In other instances, poor performance by distributors and service providers can reflect on manufacturers. Many lean companies have looked to the all-pervasive expansion of the Internet as a way to reduce dependence on perceived weak links in the chain linking the manufacturer with its customer. Dell is a leading example of this, with much of its contact with customers taking place directly via the Internet. More traditional manufacturers, such as the automotive giants, are jumping on this bandwagon.

Globalization of Markets and Competition

Globalization is a story that is being repeated in industry after industry. The automobile is a global product. So are airliners, boom boxes, rice cookers, and designer jeans. Whatever you make is potentially a global product, too. You may never know how your product got to Kurdistan. You may never know that your supplier's supplier is in Chile. Your product is everywhere, your production system is everywhere, and so are you.

There is profitable demand for high-quality manufactured goods in nearly every country. Even countries with high poverty rates have some capital formation, and there are growing numbers of people with middle-class incomes and aspirations. Furthermore, knowledge of products and their use for wealth-generation in more affluent countries drives demand even in the face of punitive fiscal restraints. The trick is to locate these regional and national markets and then find the right way to reach them, profitably and without blundering into cultural or legal restraints.

If markets have become global, so too have competitors. Your competitor for the electronic instrumentation market in Bangalore may be Agilent, the Hewlett-Packard spin-off, or a little company from Boston's Route 128, or an indigenous division of Tata Industries, or a start-up from Taiwan or Israel. Tomorrow, that competitor may be a company from Bandung or Riga. You will never have a market anywhere in the world sewn up for long before a competitor tries to unseat you.

Markets have become global, so too have competitors

There are profits to be made across the globe. However, when your company competes all over the world, you also take on new risks. Global competition is sure to be buffeted by unforeseen shocks in the global economy. Globalization, in the large, is proceeding inexorably. On a country-by-country basis, local economies suffer normal cycles. They suffer from nationalist egos, bureaucratic mismanagement, currency imbalances, and natural disasters. Minute by minute, day by day, though, globalization is a dance in which the local economy may take two steps backward for every three steps forward.

Pace of Technology Change

Transistors replaced tubes in computers. Integrated circuits replaced discrete transistors. Microprocessors replaced multi-chip processors. Each time, cost/performance curves changed dramatically. Surface-mount technology reduced costs. Line widths etched on semiconductors go from two microns to one, from one to a half-micron, from a half-micron to 0.18 microns. Each time there is a ripple effect in cost/performance ratios. Copper replaces aluminum as the electrical connector in integrated circuits. There is no let-up in the pace of technology change. New technologies make it possible to build the electronic circuitry needed for a powerful PC on a single chip. New technologies are maturing and supplanting old ones on an ever-reduced cycle. Companies that build computers are transformed by this continuous torrent of technology change. So are the companies, and people, that use computers.

Changes in technology are most evident in computing and communications. The impact of some new technologies is incredibly swift. The picture of dozens of sightseers on the Great Wall of China talking in a score of languages on their cell phones is witness to proliferation in Asia of cell phones as a way to overcome inadequate wire-based phones.

Changes in other industry sectors may not seem to come quite so fast, yet the level of innovation in the automotive industry, the pharmaceutical industry, and many other industries has been the highest in history. That pace of change must be managed. For example, important technology advances in the personal computer industry show up every three months or so. Should I replace my PC now or wait for three months for a PC that includes, at no additional cost, the next technology upgrades? Your company may not have to deal with technology advances that come so quickly, but the issues are similar. When should your company make a multi-million-dollar advanced technology investment? When should it commit to the generation of technology beyond?

Global Availability of Advanced Technology and Competitive Practices

Information about ideas, technologies, and business ventures is available ubiquitously and globally. The Internet makes it harder and harder to maintain artificial restrictions on the flow of information. Companies that can convert this sea of information into useful, relevant knowledge faster than their competitors are the companies with a competitive advantage.

Anyone with a passport can go from his or her workstation to any of the three largest cities in more than 150 countries in 36 hours. In those cities will be people who went to the same university system, or who may have worked in the same company, or worked for a respected competitor. Because of these common experiences, these individuals become peers as world citizens. Loose networks of entrepreneurs span the world. Advanced technology flows across those networks.

Some of the new competition is as technologically advanced as traditional competitors. Taiwan has developed new cities built around R&D resources to mimic Silicon Valley and Route 128. Many technology leaders in these new cities "time-share." They spend as much time in Austin or Santa Clara or Framingham as they do in Taiwan.

The Internet is a primary tool for worldwide communication of advanced technology. It was born of an open culture intended to facilitate sharing of knowledge. The vision of communities that flourish through shared knowledge remains a motivator for much of the best development of Internet technology. That vision of a community thriving by sharing knowledge shows up in the many Internet sites where people with common interests exchange information. A lot of it is hobbyist information, but much of it is professional. Bio-engineers discuss the best way to design computer interfaces for the disabled. Consultants trade specialized knowledge of contracts and intellectual property. An earnest engineer in Pakistan asks a question. Within a few hours he, and everyone else on the Internet gets 10 or 20 answers that, in combination, give him a better solution than any he could have developed working alone over several days.

For an additional modest investment, an Internet user can gain expert knowledge on nearly any subject through subscription repositories on nearly any subject imaginable. Trade and professional journals, handbooks, and other databases and repositories of knowledge are easily accessible from any PC connected to the Internet. With the ubiquitous availability of cellular and satellite telephony, there are few places on earth where someone with a laptop cannot use these sources.

To be sure, there is much information that is proprietary and kept more or less in confidence. However, as anyone who surfs the Internet knows, incredible amounts of specialized knowledge are available to someone who is patient and persistent. Knowledge can be found by the clever with a simple search engine. Individuals who are really clever can build an intelligent agent capable of searching public sites worldwide for specific information. Basic search results are widely circulated.

For specialized or proprietary knowledge, a well-crafted search will identify the company with the best process or the best technology or the best measurement system. Then, you can deal directly with the best source of the knowledge you need. The information may cost you money, but you gain an advantage from knowing how and where to get needed information without wasting large amounts of time doing a search.

There is no need for trial-and-error in isolation or for mastering "baby steps," before moving incrementally to advanced production techniques. A company can learn, and its upstart competitors in Uzbekistan can too, from the established companies almost overnight and then start improving their processes. Competitors can learn just as the Japanese did when they adopted Western ideas of mass production and Deming's ideas on quality after World War II. Over many years, the Japanese evolved those ideas into leadership with lean production. Your competitors will evolve similar, innovative business models to world-class maturity while compressing time from years to months—as we have seen in the growth of Chinese manufacturing companies like V-Tech in the past decade.

Global Skill-based Competition

Countries all over the world are investing in advancing the skills of their work forces. These nations are doing this at a time when high-value skills need not be co-located in the enterprise. They are also doing it at a time when the U.S. educational system is not producing enough highly skilled people to sustain U.S. high-technology industries. The global availability of well-educated people places less-educated work forces, even in developed countries like the United States, at a disadvantage. U.S. companies are turning to immigrants or outsourcing their needs offshore.

All countries are seeking to upgrade the skills of their citizens. There is more intense competition at all skill levels. For example, in 1980 the government of Singapore initiated a training and education program to increase by ten-fold the number of people who could work in information technology industries. This goal was achieved within a decade. Singapore continues to build on this base as it has moved away from low-value assembly jobs to high-value software and systems integration work.

In other countries, literate populations with math skills are finding ways to compete in global skill markets. This is especially true as more of the value of manufactured goods lies in software embedded in products and in software that controls manufacturing processes. India is a country of nearly one billion people—many well-educated, under-utilized, and ambitious to better their conditions. India is using this strongly motivated talent pool to build a strong software export industry. It is no surprise that one of Hewlett-Packard's top software development groups is in India or that there is a growing corps of Indian entrepreneurs whose companies link Silicon Valley and India.

The opening of China to free markets since the accession of Deng Hsiao-peng has introduced even more educated workers onto the global labor market. A manager, on assignment in Beijing for his multinational company, finds the quality of the Chinese work force, including managers, equal to, and maybe exceeding, that of his company's California work force. Other countries, like Sri Lanka and the Philippines, are trying to mobilize educated populations. Still other countries, such as Myanmar and Cuba, with higher literacy rates than the United States, have populations that will become quite significant in their regions when artificial, government-imposed constraints and embargoes are relaxed.

The breakdown of the Soviet block led to a free market for large numbers of highly skilled people. Other areas of the world have well-educated, but underutilized, populations. The new reality is that these people can and do compete in the world market. Companies like Asea Brown Boveri (ABB) expanded in the mid-'90s primarily by opening facilities in Eastern Europe and Asia. Residents of the former Soviet Union have emigrated to Europe and North America, where they are finding their technical skills in great demand.

Environmental Responsibilities and Resource Constraints

As demand builds and more and more countries are industrialized, environmental responsibilities and resource constraints increasingly will be important factors.

There is a continual tension among competing needs. The need to improve living conditions of the world's less affluent people competes with the need to sustain living conditions in developed nations. Both needs compete with the need to maintain or improve the natural environment for the benefit of all. We are plagued with doubts that the earth can provide needed resources. Are there enough petroleum and other energy resources? Many who study industrial pollution of groundwater, rivers, even the ocean, ask if there is enough water. The proliferation of little plastic water bottles speaks to fear of water pollution. As farmland is converted to industrial use, others ask if there is enough arable land to feed the world's growing population.

The balance between industrial production and air quality can be especially difficult to achieve. High temperature and high humidity "bubbles" that significantly change the local microclimates over industrial developments have been noted for decades.

Intelligent use of energy reduces costs and improves profits. Intelligent re-use of water also reduces costs and improves profits. Intelligent land use planning minimizes the waste of time and energy in commuting, or the waste of agricultural land for concrete structures. Co-location of facilities that use each other's wastes as raw materials reduces transportation costs and improves profits.

Other forces, usually imposed by government, push manufacturing companies to reduce adverse environmental effects. In Europe, automakers must use materials that are 95% recyclable. In the U.S., there is pressure to increase recycling from 85% to 90% or higher.

The result of these factors is a focus now on sustainable development, the development of a manufacturing industry bringing benefits to the greatest number of people while having a neutral, or even a positive, effect on the environment.

Companies are responding. There is a growing move toward making recycling easy. For example, Hewlett-Packard provides a prepaid United Parcel System (UPS) shipping label for return of spent laser printer cartridges. IBM recently announced a personal computer recycling program accessible to home and small-office users.

THE LEAN ENTERPRISE MODEL

The Lean Aircraft Initiative's Lean Enterprise Model (LEM) describes a company that can solve today's dilemmas and respond to global drivers of the future. The model describes the attributes, not the functions, of a lean enterprise. It is a systematic view of how a company should organize and operate. The model is not a complete description of an enterprise, since it does not deal with specific operational and functional strategies. However, the LEM principles guide operational strategy, and the LEM lists the practices that should be used across all functions, and provides some criteria for investment decisions.

The Lean Meta-principles

At the apex of the LEM are two meta-principles, two pervasive characteristics of the lean company. They provide litmus tests for any action an enterprise takes. (See Figure 3-2.)

- Does the action improve the company's capability to respond to change?
- Does the action reduce the resources required to achieve the company's intent?

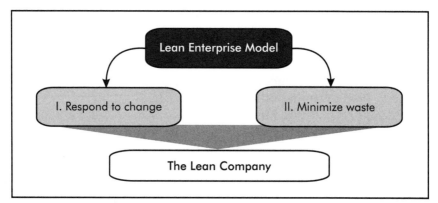

Figure 3-2. The apex of the LEM consists of two meta-principles.

I. Meta-principle: Respond to Change

Everything is changing—now! Today's common wisdom is right for today, but it may be wrong for tomorrow. The lean company must be prepared for change. It should be prepared not just for the changes that can be predicted, such as technologies resulting in faster, cheaper microprocessors. The company also should be ready for unpredicted and unpredictable changes, like an earthquake that disrupts the flow of parts. A short list of change considerations includes customer need and demand, the work force, the shareholders, natural disasters, geopolitics, processes, regulation, and management.

Everything is changing— now!

Changing customer needs and demands. Demand is based on what customers need and on what they want. Changes in demand may be fashion statements. Or, they may be results of changes in basic attitudes—for example, toward specific environmental protections. Or, they may reflect changes in consumer confidence levels, interest rates, or emergence of conceptually competitive products. They may simply indicate changes in what customers need as their lifestyles change.

Change in the work force. Some demographic changes are simple and obvious, driven by the demand for equality in gender and race. Some are subtler. For example, in California there is no majority ethnic group and recent immigrants continually are introducing new ethnic cultures into companies. Longer life spans are bringing about an aging work force. The role of labor is changing as automation and machines replace manual labor, and as work force knowledge, skills, and judgment must increase to make complex decisions.

Shareholders become more sophisticated as their demands change. Shareholders vary between having patience with accretion of long-term value and desiring short-term gains. Their emphasis on societal goals shifts as social issues gain or subside in prominence. Their attitudes fluctuate between optimism over economic growth scenarios and pessimism when things look gloomy.

Natural disasters cause change. An earthquake in Japan or floods in England can disrupt the supply of manufactured parts to plants throughout the world and even create regional economic woes. A hurricane in Central America can wipe out developing markets.

Geopolitical changes can affect businesses. A change in government can open a country as a market or, conversely, can severely limit market opportunities. Conflicts between countries and within countries can cause scarcities of natural resources. When geopolitical change is compounded by radical, religious, or cultural reform, the populace's demand profile can change dramatically.

Changing manufacturing processes. There are changes in manufacturing itself. New materials. New technologies. New processes. Some are incremental, such as a shift from milled metal parts to near net-shape parts or injection-molded plastic ones. Others are more dramatic, such as GM's shift from steel to aluminum, or Boeing's move to digital prototypes. New concepts, like designer materials formulated for specific product applications, or fabrication at dimensions measured in nanometers, promise fundamental structural change for major enterprises.

Regulatory changes. The regulatory environment changes as more is learned about the beneficial or harmful effects of materials and processes, as regulatory techniques are changed from those that impose specific mitigations to those that specify intended outcomes, and as new monetary, environmental, and business regulations are imposed.

Changing management techniques. Even our understanding of management is subject to change. The management expectations, techniques, and styles of the 1960s seem archaic to baby boomers. Those of the 1980s seem archaic to Gen-Xers. Those of the past decade will soon seem archaic to the so-called Millennial or Gen-Y generation.

This dynamic environment means that the decision-makers in a manufacturing company every day are faced with changes affecting the profit and loss, perhaps even jeopardizing the life of the enterprise. There is an important and fundamental distinction between two types of innovation. One type, sustaining innovation, fuels improvements in an existing product and business model. These are the innovations allowing a company's next product to be better, faster, or cheaper, based on today's business model. The other type, disruptive innovation, creates a whole new product or business model. New and unknown competitive entrants often use disruptive innovation (Christensen 1997). These competitors' products, on first examination, may not seem to threaten an established product line. The results though can be devastating if either the capabilities or unit cost of the new product fails to meet customer needs (as shown in Figure 3-3).

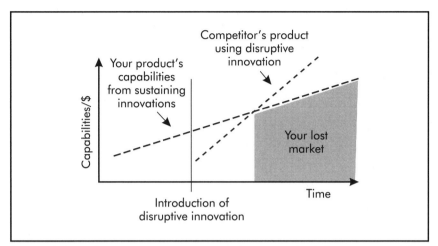

Figure 3-3. A disruptive innovation can destroy today's business model.

Innovation and change come from all directions. They are major and minor, recognizable and subtle. They may come with years of warning. More likely, they will be disruptive and come with no warning.

Time is an explicit variable for the modern manufacturing company. It instills a sense of urgency, a need for quick, crisp decisions determined by answering the following questions:

- For the market-oriented, the significant question is, "how long will the window of market opportunity be open?"
- For the technologist, the question is, "how soon will today's materials and technology become obsolete?"
- For the operations person, the question is, "how soon before a better process is found?"
- For the financially oriented, the important question is, "will we be able to recover our investment before the next change hits us?"

Once, the time constant for global competition was measured in the months and years it took sailing ships to cross the ocean. Then, it was measured in the days or weeks of steamship travel. Then, it was recorded in the minutes and hours of intercontinental telephony and air flight. That is ancient history. Today, new knowledge or new data is accessible anywhere in the world within seconds after its creation. The Internet and cell phones mean that new design techniques or real-time shop floor data are instantly available on Denali, in the Tasman Sea, and in the Sahara Desert, let alone in Toronto, Milan, and Novosibirsk.

Nothing is stable about a manufacturing enterprise. No static model can describe it. A lean company is one with the self-knowledge that it is always in a state of flux due to the dynamic environment in which it operates. A lean company acts swiftly and effectively as soon as the environment presents it with challenges and opportunities that require it to change.

II. Meta-Principle: Minimize Waste

The second meta-principle embodies the original idea of lean. Minimizing waste, of course, is the mantra of traditional lean production systems. In the lean enterprise, waste is defined broadly, measured not just by the cost of a unit process. Waste includes:

- unnecessary expenditures;
- results that do not meet the intent of a process, and therefore must be eliminated;
- costs of maintaining obsolete expertise;
- opportunity costs of cumbersome decision processes;
- rework required when one process is changed without considering the impact on other processes.

Business process reengineering (BPR) is a waste-reduction method. When done well, it focuses on the intent of a process. Once the desired features, quality, and cost of the outcome of the process are understood, BPR looks first for activities that do not contribute to achieving the outcome. The most obvious sort of waste is of time, energy, and other resources that lead to nothing. Trimming unproductive activities may be enough to transform a traditional process into a lean one.

Early in IBM's transformation, it eliminated roughly 90% of the routine reports required from its field-service organization. Most of the reports did not contribute to the process of managing the delivery of services to customers. The reports were eliminated with little efficacy of the traditional service processes, saving the costs associated with preparing them. The resulting immediate release of resources was applied directly to customer service. IBM's result was a more lean process and a more lean organization.

A deeper look at processes occurs when the question is: "Is there a different way to achieve the intent of the process that uses fewer resources?" This is the question that leads to:

- the scrapping of entire processes,
- combining processes, and
- substituting alternative processes.

At the enterprise level, this is the question that leads to the adoption of alternative business models.

As IBM's transformation progressed, the business model describing service delivery changed. The company increased its emphasis on automated tools that permitted remote problem analysis and enabled customers to do much of the service previously done by IBM's field service technicians. Most routine service activities that technicians did 15 years ago have been eliminated, freeing the service organization to perform more specialized, higher-value services.

The first meta-principle affects the second and promotes the value of time. A waste of time in unit processes translates into loss of competitive advantage, loss of opportunity, and the inability to respond to change. Waste of time in the coordination of processes into systems can be especially devastating. The traditional product and design processes used in the U.S. automotive industry were particularly wasteful of time, leading to product development cycles of a decade or more.

Nowhere is this situation better described than in a book by Richard E. Dauch (Dauch et al. 1993):

> "About four years ago, after work began on a new model, the engineering documents supervisor would fill a van with layouts and detail drawings—some on Mylar and others printed on faded brown and blue—drive a dozen miles to the dismal lair of manufacturing planning, dump the whole mess unceremoniously at the feet of the receptionist, mumble 'prints for the '65,' and flee back to his ivory tower.
>
> "Summoned by a telephone call, a perspiring ex-mechanic would be muttering to himself even before

he stooped to retrieve the wads of paper that would sour his life. These manufacturing people felt about product engineers the way an infantryman feels about a commander who orders him onto the battlefield while cowering in a bunker out of artillery range. Those who have not experienced it cannot appreciate the fury induced by this system. When a vehicle turned out well, you can be sure success came out of the hides of those plant rats."

Reengineering of development processes, using lean principles, has reduced development cycles from years to months. It is a significant contributor to the re-emergence of the U.S. auto industry—and of other industries as well.

Lean Enterprise Principles

Under the meta-principles, the Lean Enterprise Model (LEM) has four enterprise principles (see Figure 3-4). These principles describe the next layer of behavior for the work units within the enterprise.

A. The Right Thing, at the Right Place, at the Right Time, and in the Right Quantity

The lean company places great emphasis on high-quality execution of any process it puts in place. Assuming the processes are chosen and designed to optimize leanness of the company, the right resources, and only the right resources, need to be where they are needed, when they are needed. The prototype example of this principle of action is Just-in-Time (JIT) delivery of parts to a vehicle assembly line—delivery of the right parts just as they are needed for an individual, customer-specified vehicle.

This principle of action drives unit manufacturing and business processes. It also drives information systems providing the knowledge workers need as they need it. In addition, it drives the decisions systems, so that decisions are based on up-to-date conditions and don't introduce delays in responses to customer needs.

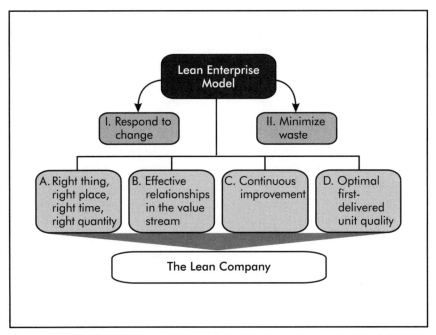

Figure 3-4. The four enterprise principles of the Lean Enterprise Model (LEM).

An important aspect of the Just-in-Time concept with the right resources in place is the need to have people with the right skills and knowledge in place when the process needs them.

B. Effective Relationships within the Value Stream

The value stream from the supplier of raw materials to the satisfied customer for any product and support service likely involves many people, work units, and companies. The value stream flows through an extended enterprise. If you are the manufacturer, you want all elements of the value chain working smoothly. You do not want them in contention, wasting time, effort, or money because of unclear product specifications, business arrangements, or communications.

Effective relationships will require well-defined, formal specifications and agreements. They also require systems compatibility and even a compatibility of approach by all contributors to the value stream. Finally, not every eventuality in the development of a process can be defined in advance. Effective relationships will depend greatly on mutual trust and mutual problem-solving skills, as every contributor in the value stream responds to unanticipated events with agility.

C. Continuous Improvement

As discussed in Chapter 2, a fundamental tenet of lean production systems is that every worker, including each of the company's managers and employees, is constantly seeking ways to improve the process on which he or she is working. An improvement may be a change leading to reduced costs for material, energy, and labor, and reduced labor fatigue—while maintaining the quality of the output. An improvement may be a change leading to greater quality at no additional cost. An improvement may not change unit cost or quality, but lead to an earlier completion of the worker's task or better flow from one process to the next.

Continuous improvement requires a mindset that permeates the enterprise, that questions the status quo, that is observant and creative, and that can work on the boundary of what works now and what might work better. It requires management that encourages continuous improvement initiatives, even when those initiatives involve risk.

D. Optimal First-delivered Unit Quality

It is imperative that the first unit of any product delivered meets the quality needs and expectations of the customer. Each element of the value stream must view all the downstream elements, as well as the ultimate end-user, as customers. When they do that, the enterprise will be assured that the designs, materials, manufacturing processes, and delivery channels are right the first time. If they are right, the waste of rework will be minimized in each step of the product cycle.

The imperative for the quality of the first delivered unit is so important that it has spawned a number of methodologies and tools, such as the Total Quality Management (TQM) and Six Sigma methodologies.

EXERCISES

1. You have a network of friends who have dreamed of going into business together. One day, you send them an e-mail outlining your idea for a "frazit." They agree that, if you can be first to market, the "frazit" could have worldwide appeal. Their estimates are that you could sell a couple of million at $500 apiece. Together, they can lay their hands on $1 million to invest. So now you get serious. How would you use the lean meta-principles and lean enterprise principles to help structure your new company?
2. How would you allocate the $1 million, using lean principles, to maximize your return?
3. As you are developing your "frazit," you learn at last week's trade show that someone else is coming out with a competing "witchit" that has some very appealing features. What changes will you make in strategy to meet the competition?

REFERENCES

Christensen, Clayton M. 1997. *The Innovator's Dilemma: When New Technologies Cause Great Firms to Fail*. Boston, MA: Harvard Business School Press.

Dauch, Richard E. and Troyanovich, Jack. 1993. *Passion for Manufacturing*. Dearborn, MI: Society of Manufacturing Engineers, pp. 120-121.

NGM Project. *Next Generation Manufacturing: Framework for Action*. 1997. Bethlehem, PA: Agility Forum.

BIBLIOGRAPHY

Lean Aerospace Initiative: http://lean.mit.edu/public/index.html

Chapter Four

Overarching Lean Practices

The Lean Aircraft Initiative's Lean Enterprise Model (LEM) describes the behavior of a prototypical lean company. The Lean Meta-principles and Enterprise Principles discussed in Chapter 3 provide basic standards to judge every activity of the lean enterprise. They have the value of being succinct and direct, but open to much variability in interpretation.

The LEM goes further by describing 12 overarching practices that narrow the interpretation of the principles, but that still apply to the enterprise's every activity (see Figure 4-1).

These overarching practices apply to management policies and organizational relationships within and outside a company and throughout the entire extended lean enterprise. They also apply to lean relationships within the company. This dualism pervades the discussions of each of the practices.

1. FOCUS ON THE CUSTOMER CONTINUOUSLY

The first rule of the lean company, and indeed of any modern business, is to make a profit and increase the value of stakeholders' investment. Profitability depends critically on the response of paying customers to value in the products offered them. Success requires a continuous effort to meet customers' expectations, which means that throughout the company, every activity should serve the cause of providing customers with products and services that provide them value, as they measure value.

Success requires a continuous effort to meet customers' expectations

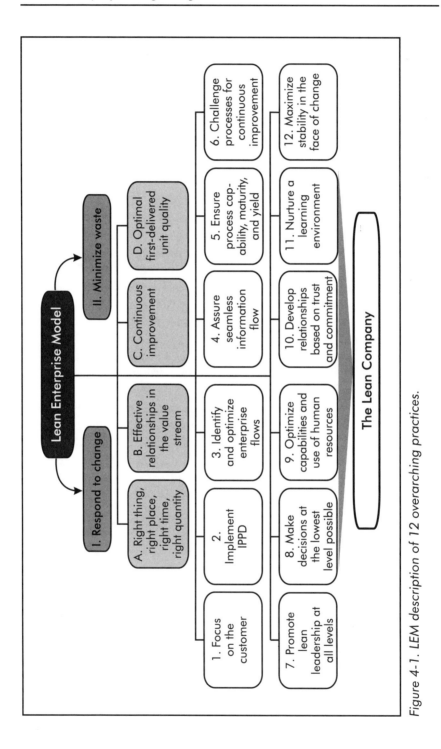

Figure 4-1. LEM description of 12 overarching practices.

For most customers, value is defined as a product of service that meets their expectations for outcomes with some combination of greater functionality, faster delivery, and faster response to service needs. Their definition also includes lower initial and life cycle costs. Many 21st-Century customers will want the outcome to be some form of memorable experience (Pine and Gilmore 1999). The specific combination will depend on a product or service meeting the particular customer's needs. You must provide functionality, quality, and reliability, of course, but you also must provide accessibility, usability, maintainability, availability, and disposability—all with enough benefits to justify the price.

Value may not be perceived by customers in the same way as it is by employees. Customers who need a cheap widget for a few weeks may not value a multi-function widget that will not wear out in a century. Similarly, employees may see a product as a utilitarian throwaway, while the customer may find more lasting value in the product. Emphasis on the customer and understanding his or her needs means employees must view their work as a paying customer would view it.

Employees should focus on two important aspects of customer value:

- First is the dynamic definition of value. Tomorrow's customer may see today's value as inadequate, or even irrelevant.
- Second, customers expect a product to give value reliably throughout its entire service life. The service life that counts is the one defined by the customer.

The Dynamic Nature of Customer-defined Value

Customers demand choice. To put it more accurately, they demand to be given what they want, not what the manufacturer chooses to sell. Everywhere in the world, customers demand high-quality products that meet their requirements and fit their pocketbooks. In addition, they want those products when they want them—not before, not after. Competitors from every country vie for customer attention in every industry sector.

In the automotive sector, Henry Ford told his customers 80 years ago that they could order any color of Model T they wanted—as long as it was black and had a 20-horsepower, four-cylinder engine—

but, oh, by the way, they could purchase an optional electric starter. For nearly two decades, there was no viable choice if customers wanted an affordable and reliable automobile. Today, the Thai banker who drives a red Boxster® between Bangkok and the beach on the Gulf of Siam, is demanding—not just about color and style, but also about handling, acceleration, braking, and reliability. She is just as demanding as the American engineer who drives a white Excursion® from Silicon Valley to the ski slopes of the Sierras.

The effects of diverse and rapidly shifting customer demands are remarkable. Once the auto industry could design for model runs of a million or more vehicles spread over several years; now a market for 50,000 vehicles of a given model is considered to be substantial. Once it was okay for a new model to take 5-10 years to go into production; now GM has an 18-month target because customer attention spans are so much shorter.

The simple lean-production paradigm was easy to apply when the same basic product was churned out year after year. One could continuously improve the design and manufacturing processes to squeeze out any excess costs. The new view of mass customization is that the waste reduction principle should be applied simultaneously both to the base platform and to its adaptation to new uses.

A company should know its customers well

The ever-changing demands of customers mean that a company should know its customers well. The focus on the customer is, first, the Just-in-Time (JIT) principle—to provide products and services to customers who want them, when they want them, at a price they are willing to pay. To do that, a supplier must have the right functions in its products and services—the functions customers want, and in forms they can use comfortably.

Reliable Delivery of Value

The focus also must be on providing products and services that meet the customers' value expectations throughout their entire service life. Reliability and availability start with on-time delivery of the offering. It is not enough to deliver value at the time of purchase only. A product must deliver value for as long as the customer expects it to do so. It must be available when the customer needs it or wants to use it.

There was a time when middle-class customers expected their new cars to last for three or four years. When the cars began to burn oil and show rust, the customers turned them in for flashy new models. Today, it is common for customers to talk of their 12-year-old cars with more than 200,000 miles and to muse about replacing them in a few years. Every part in those cars must wear gracefully for decades, not break unexpectedly or catastrophically. Each part must be easily replaceable on a quick visit to a service bay.

Customers have found value in the world's fleet of Boeing 727s, long after they passed the service lifetime that Boeing first projected. In this case, value has come from the maintainability of the plane and its flexibility to accept upgraded components.

Similarly, every part in a company's products must be reliable throughout the service lives of the products. The care employees take as they design and produce even the smallest parts will affect the customers understanding of how well a company delivers value.

2. IMPLEMENT INTEGRATED PRODUCT AND PROCESS DEVELOPMENT

Integrated Product and Process Development (IPPD) is the concurrent, coordinated, and systematic development of a product and the processes by which it is made. Many approaches to IPPD are in use. Each has one common objective: avoiding costly redesign and unanticipated problems during start-up and in production. IPPD also avoids compromises that degrade the performance of the product. The idea is to minimize, or even eliminate, costly engineering change orders once production is started. The key is to put in place the right processes that can be implemented:

- rapidly,
- concurrently,
- interactively,
- iteratively,
- and with the customer and entire supplier base.

A company's IPPD management strategy is the foundation for the relationships within the company and across the extended enterprise that leads to successful products. The strategy must include close and empowered relationships within and among the work force, customers, partners, and the supply chain. The IPPD strategy will set the tone and style for the multiple activities necessary to create needed quality processes, capabilities, and competencies. IPPD is inherently team-based.

Integrated Product Teams (IPTs), alluded to in the last section, are composed of people who possess the core and support competencies required for designing and producing the product. Some competencies come from within the company. Others must come from partners' experts, companies in the supply chain, or even from customers. IPTs should include anyone involved in carrying out their own function, be it design, fabrication, tooling, testing, product support, field service, training, environmental disposition, or any of the other activities across the life cycle of the product. It is essential to include the supply chain into the team at the earliest appropriate time.

IPPD is the core of Rapid Product and Process Realization (RPPR) in any integrated 21st Century manufacturing environment. RPPR is discussed further in Chapter 6.

3. IDENTIFY AND OPTIMIZE ENTERPRISE FLOWS

There is an international consensus that the organizational building blocks of a lean company are teams of people (Jordan and Michel 2000). Each person embodies one or more of the individual core competencies. The teams should possess definable core competencies, which in turn define core competencies of the company. The teams are responsible for specific activities contributing to meeting enterprise objectives. The company should team with other companies that possess complementary-core competencies. The consensus then is that lean companies look more and more like networks of globally distributed teams that aggregate several core competencies and work together to achieve and optimize operational and strategic goals (see Figure 4-2).

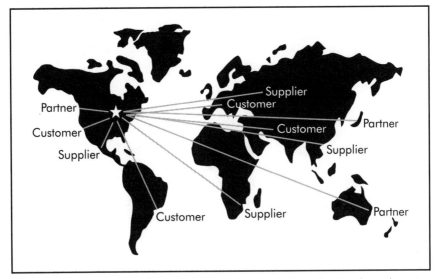

Figure 4-2. Lean companies look like networks of globally distributed teams.

Flows in the Team-based Lean Company

Suppose there is a spark—an idea for a product. Your company decides to manufacture the product. Then the customer buys and uses it. Finally, the customer recycles or disposes of it. To create such a product requires an extended enterprise with capabilities that:

- do initial conceptual designs;
- acquire raw materials;
- acquire parts;
- fabricate subassemblies;
- assemble finished products;
- provide service;
- and recycle or dispose of the product.

Within the extended enterprise are flows that have value and contain products, materials, and knowledge. Their contents flow back and forth across organizational boundaries. The flows can be smooth, with little energy loss as they move from team to team and organization to organization, or they can be turbulent, with energy-wasting swirls and eddies. A lean enterprise will seek to identify the flows and then make them as efficient and smooth as possible. Part of the task is to eliminate flows through high-impedance channels in favor of those through low-impedance ones. Another part of the task is to reduce the impedance within channels.

The Flow of Value

How does a product get to the customer? Several years ago, a simple model of production systems, the *value chain,* gained prominence (Porter 1998). Each function in the chain, from product concept to delivery, is a link in the chain. The following model suggests a dynamic variation, the *value stream* (see Figure 4-3).

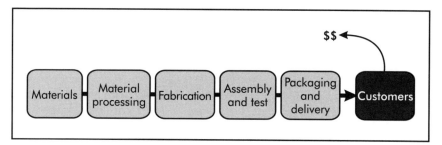

Figure 4-3. A model of a conventional value stream.

The value stream is the increasing creation of value as a product moves through a sequence of activities. Typically, the value stream takes raw materials and, successively turns them into processed materials, parts, subsystems, and assembled products. It then distributes the products to customers, services them, and perhaps even recycles or disposes of the products at the end of their service life. Each activity adds value to the product—or should.

The value stream model is important because it provides an organized way to think about product realization as a series of activities with defined interfaces. The activities can be evaluated based on cost and the value added to product realization. Cost can be measured in financial terms, by the time delay the activity introduces into the stream, or by the cost in human resources that could be applied elsewhere. Any activity where the creation of value cannot be clearly articulated is a target for examination, modification, and perhaps elimination.

The value stream model (Womack and Jones 1996), coupled with the analytical techniques of Value-Stream Mapping[SM], continues to be a powerful tool, although the underlying notion of a stream of sequential activities requires elaboration.

IPPD seeks to maximize concurrency and minimize the time necessary for a product to move from concept to launch. IPPD enables a company to perform as many activities in parallel as it can and further improve cost and quality objectives. This means that a core value stream can exist that has a number of tributary streams such as the arterial system in the human being (see Figure 4-4).

Each tributary stream is a value stream enabling some downstream activity in the core value stream. For a complicated product in a time-sensitive competition, each tributary stream itself has many tributaries. Again, the value stream defines the value of all efforts—ensuring that every activity, in every tributary, adds value to the product. Properly done, such an approach focuses all activities to assure that the value customers seek is achieved.

Even this model is insufficient, however. Overlaid on the linear sequences of activities of the value stream and its tributaries are the interactions of parallel activities and tributaries. An activity in one tributary stream affects the value of many activities in other tributaries, both serial and parallel activities.

While optimizing the value of each activity is important, optimization must be approached from the customers' point of view. Often, customers assess this value in terms of life cycle costs. Focusing on optimization of a single process as a stand-alone activity may lead to higher, rather than lower, life cycle costs. The integration of several related processes could very well result in lower support costs and, thus, in lower life cycle costs.

The Flow of Materials

The fundamental idea of manufacturing is conversion of raw materials into fabricated parts that are assembled into finished products with an intrinsic value. Products are distributed, used

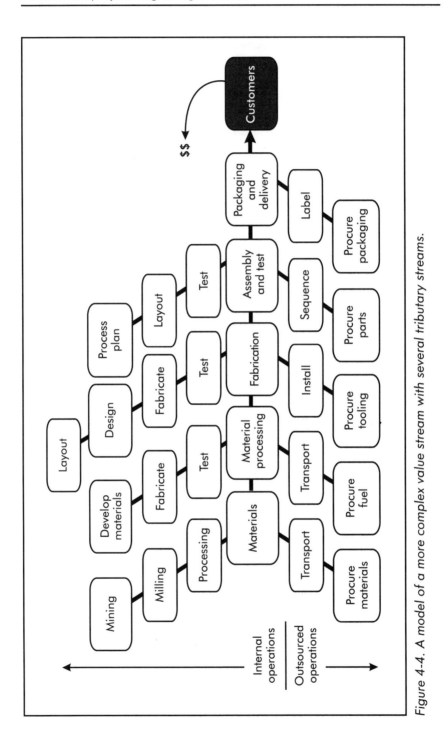

Figure 4-4. A model of a more complex value stream with several tributary streams.

by customers, and then recycled or otherwise disposed of. Therefore, the notion of the flow of materials is a natural one. We could use Figures 4-3 or 4-4 just as easily to describe this flow as the flow of value in a production system.

In ideal lean systems:

- Flow means materials are never held in inventory. A company is either actively processing them or moving the materials to the next process. Lean minimizes transit time from operation to operation and from process to process.
- Flow should not happen unless a customer wants the product that results from the flow. If the customer does not want the product, then the flow is wasted. So-called "pull" (kanban) systems trigger material flows so that the amount of material pulled through the production system matches demand as demand occurs, activity by activity.

Modern logistical systems embody the idea of Just-in-Time (JIT) delivery of required materials. Delivery occurs when and where an activity requires materials. In practice, small buffer stocks are maintained as a protection against unpredictable changes or delays. In essence, however, all materials should either be moving to a workstation or be worked on.

Flow is measured by metrics such as flow efficiency. *Flow efficiency* is the ratio of time required to perform one operation on a product divided by the sum of that time plus the transit and wait time to the start of the next operation (see Figure 4-5). The flow efficiency of a production system is improved when transit and wait times are reduced. If they can be driven to zero, flow efficiency will go to 100%. The work should enter the activity at the precise time scheduled for that activity, and there should be no delays while the work is in process, especially if several operations are performed at a single workstation.

The MIT Lean Aircraft Initiative surveyed 17 companies to compare flow efficiency in three sectors: airframe, electronics, and engines (Shields 1996). The results showed that there is great variation in the sectors. On further analysis, the MIT group found that in job shops flow efficiency averaged about 1%. However, shops that had adopted the lean practice of in-line processing averaged nearly 20%.

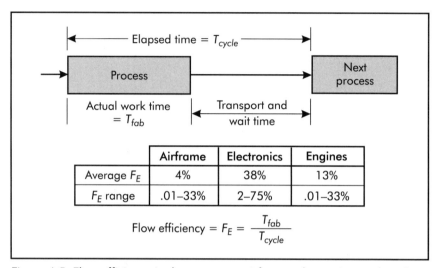

Figure 4-5. Flow efficiency in three sectors: airframe, electronics, and engines.

Proper preparation of materials for the next operation is important. Flow can be optimized when materials are prepared properly for their specific uses in the subsequent operations.

The Flow of Knowledge

Intellectual content, or knowledge, is the competitive discriminator among products (Thurow 1996, Drucker 1995). Companies that formerly competed using energy, now compete using knowledge. Other things being equal, someone is most likely to buy the "smartest" product from a company that knows a customer's needs well enough to anticipate those needs. Other things being equal, a customer is likely to buy a product made by a company with the smartest, most efficient, and timely processes.

Knowledge is data and information combined with human thought to produce useful decisions. More refined knowledge becomes wisdom when the user has the capacity to judge soundly and deal broadly with facts and knowledge. For a given activity, knowledge conveys both when and how to act to produce desired results.

The shift to knowledge-based competition is already symbolized in the term *knowledge worker.* Originally, this term referred only to the white-collar worker who kept track of the company's business and administration. The term has now spread to nearly all occupations and activities. The blue-collar work force now spends less time on manual activities than it does on acquiring and manipulating data, turning it into knowledge, and making operational decisions.

Just as materials should flow to an activity Just-in-Time, so too should knowledge. Knowledge required in an activity must be available when it is needed and in a form such that the activity does not waste time and efforts to make it useful. It is equally important that the activity not waste its resources fending off unneeded knowledge.

Knowledge flows over the activity network of the extended enterprise (Figure 4-2). A company may be able to organize material flow into linear or parallel systems (as shown in Figures 4-3 and 4-4), but the source of the very knowledge needed in a given activity may reside in several places in the network, such as:

- the team members conducting the activities;
- in other activities that may or may not be part of the value stream;
- in corporate-knowledge bases;
- and in repositories outside the enterprise.

4. ASSURE SEAMLESS INFORMATION FLOW

The purpose of a company's information system is to convey knowledge so people and processes can make decisions and act efficiently and effectively. The information system must be structured so that the company can be a part of one or more dynamic extended enterprises. The system should be adaptive, responsive, transparent, lean, and able to respond quickly to changing business needs. If the lifetime of a business system is less than two years, but it takes upwards of two years to create it, the company will not survive.

The challenge is to have information available no later than when it is needed. The system should provide seamless integration of a company's business and manufacturing processes, equipment, and people, including customers and suppliers (see Figure

77

4-6). The company's information system should provide transparency; that is, the presentation of data, information, and knowledge to users in clear, intuitive, and unambiguous ways.

At its most idealistic, this network model makes the data, information, and knowledge of the extended enterprise available in real time to everyone in the enterprise. Ideally, it would make this information available in ways fitting naturally into each individual's cognitive and decision-making processes.

In reality, of course, not everyone needs, wants, or should have access to everything available. In reality, no one has the time or

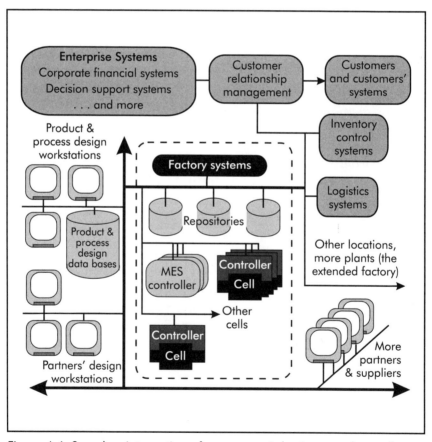

Figure 4-6. Seamless integration of a company's business and manufacturing processes.

capacity to use everything that could be available. Consequently, the knowledge made available to each activity should be filtered to match its needs.

Function modules (applications found on servers) must have the capacity for easy and rapid incorporation into reconfigured information systems, no matter what processor they run on. Systems will be lean if the function modules can be plugged into the systems and immediately begin to perform their intended functions. Plug-and-play systems must be totally compatible with the semantics and processes existing at the module interfaces so modules can function seamlessly and assure an effective behavior of the system. Often, plug-and-play systems use object-oriented and functional-component software that can be reused. Some systems are augmented by agent technologies that give software objects the ability to act autonomously in carefully crafted situations. The technology of the World Wide Web provides easy access to data and information from anywhere in the world.

5. ENSURE PROCESS CAPABILITY, MATURITY, AND YIELD

A lean company is a finely tuned organization, much more than the sum of its processes, but fully dependent on each of its processes to do its specified job. Each process should be lean, able to adapt to change, and generate little or no wasted effort.

Each process has to have the capability to produce its desired results in a reliable and trustworthy way. Downstream activities must be able to rely, unquestionably, on those results. Not only must the basic functionality be there, but so must the capability to vary the process as circumstances change. For example, not only should a welding cell be able to perform the welds on the body of two-door SUVs, it should be capable of doing them on the bodies of four-door SUVs, or two-, three-, or four-door pick-up trucks, with minimal reprogramming or change over time.

Every process should undergo qualification to demonstrate its maturity. Processes undergo a learning curve. They start as bright ideas in the research labs or are proposed by innovative process engineers. Then, they are subjected to paper studies and committee reviews. They move to a pilot test. Finally, they are implemented for routine operations. A well-qualified process is one that can be reliably characterized for standard work procedures.

Often there is a need to move quickly to implementation. At times, a monetary incentive is provided to speed up the process. Yet, if a company implements a new process before the bugs are worked out, time and money will be wasted because of the rework required to correct the faulty process and its flawed results. The goal of the lean company, of course, is to have the first part of the process right, minimizing scrap, rework, and in-process repair.

The qualification of a process may come through modeling, simulation, operator training, and rapid prototyping. It may require hybrid prototyping, where input to a simulation comes from other live activities.

Yield is measured by the number of acceptable pieces made, divided by the total number of pieces processed. Ideally, a process will yield a perfect result every time. A 100% yield often is not possible, but it is approached more frequently as companies apply Six Sigma and similar quality programs. The objective is to develop a process that yields right results the first time and every time it is employed in production. In many cases, yield is not defined just as the ratio of the number of perfect results to the number of attempts to use the process. It is also defined as the number of perfect results per unit of time. Both measures are important. The first says no effort is wasted on unusable results. The second says no time is wasted in obtaining the results.

In lean production, the time when the process is performed depends on the *takt*, or synchronization time. The process gives reliable results at the time it is needed to maintain flow. It is equally important that this be a fast process. Attention to process maturity, or getting things right the first time, can pay big dividends. Chrysler ramped up to full production of its 2001 minivans in 25 days, in comparison to the 100 days it took for its predecessor model. Chrysler estimates the bottom line impact at $500 million.

Many processes are performed outside the company and involve suppliers. They, too, need to be incorporated in maturity models or other process evaluation techniques. A certification procedure must be applied to give meaning to the process evaluation.

6. CHALLENGE EXISTING PROCESSES FOR CONTINUOUS IMPROVEMENT

However well-designed a process is, there is *always* room for improvement.

Continuous improvement is a fundamental concept in lean production systems. It applies to the company's systems and processes as well. This overarching practice symbolizes a major difference between the cultures of traditional and lean enterprises.

Continuous improvement is the result of a mindset, an attitude held by each person in the organization that says, "There must be a better way." Continuous improvement requires restless minds operating today's processes as well as they can, while seeking changes that will make tomorrow's results even better.

At the detail level of running a company, the people closest to the work often know best how to improve it. They see the things that slow them down, interrupt the flow of their work, and divert their attention. They see warning signs before processes and equipment break down. Often, they are the ones who must patch the faulty processes. In a lean company, employees anticipate problems, and then look for solutions on their own initiative.

> However well-designed a process is, there is always room for improvement

In some companies, especially ones with tight hierarchical supervision and control, employees find it difficult to affect processes. They do not try to improve things. They are content to do them the same way they have always done them. After all, they think, the foremen, managers, and executives will tell them if there is a better way. If they do not look for things to improve, if they do not even ask questions, they will not find a better way—at least not until the process breaks down completely.

Clichés capture these attitudes. "If it ain't broke, don't fix it." To a great extent, the attitudes are the result of conservative human nature. As the Thai saying goes, "The little ones do because the big ones do." The lean company breaks this mold by demanding improvement in all processes at all levels. The lean company adopts continuous improvement as a defining cultural statement and demands that the entire work force internalize it.

The challenge can be a little one. How can we get rid of the burr resulting from drill wear? Or, the challenge can be big. Is there a way to reduce the number of unit processes to fabricate a vehicle fuel pump? Finally, the challenge can be huge. Is the business model developed for this year the right one for next year? Employees must be willing and encouraged by the company to ask these questions.

It is not enough to ask questions. Each employee must be willing, and encouraged, to propose immediate solutions to eliminate problems. Furthermore, everyone should be encouraged to implement small improvements on his or her own. If the challenge and solution affect other people or groups, employees should be encouraged to initiate discussions and participate in team efforts to resolve the challenge.

The questioning needs to be enterprise-wide, including suppliers as well. The supply chain should be managed sensitively, so employees can question supplier practices in ways that lead to improvements. It is a two-way street, of course. A company should encourage employees to listen to suppliers for ways to improve the company's processes.

7. PROMOTE LEAN LEADERSHIP AT ALL LEVELS

Corporate management has the responsibility to lead the whole company. Yet in a lean company everyone will be asked to lead at some times and follow at other times. Leanness should be a factor in each leadership act an employee initiates—for example, in gathering support for a solution to a challenge. Furthermore, acts of leadership should be lean.

Leadership is a set of behaviors that causes others to achieve results. Leadership is a very human thing, varying with the individuals involved. It is relational, depending on the relationship between those who choose to lead and those who agree to follow. The relationship depends on the situation. It occurs in the context of a specific need and involves unique individuals, who have some common and differing goals. The best leadership is the leadership that works now.

In traditional companies, *leadership* is often a synonym for *management*, the people at the top of the organization chart. Many lean companies, however, cannot be described hierarchically. They are networks of core competencies embodied in individuals and small teams. In a knowledge-based competition, these people and teams will be the legitimate leaders for their competencies. Some, of course, will contribute leadership only in their narrow specialty, or by taking the initiative in meeting their particular challenges and tasks. Others assume broader technical and motivational leadership roles within the team.

A competitive, extended enterprise requires great leadership at all levels, from the smallest temporary team through foremen, line management, and staff, to corporate executives. Employees at all levels may need leadership training. Part of that training should put major emphasis on how to incorporate lean concepts into leadership.

Lean leadership is Just-in-Time and just enough. Each employee needs to know when to exert leadership to accomplish a goal. The employee also needs to know when to let go of a leadership role when it is better assumed by someone else. The successful lean company will require great leaders and equally great followers. It needs informed followers that recognize and are guided by the leader for specific competencies.

> **Lean leadership is Just-in-Time and just enough**

Leaders and followers flow dynamically within a team, a company, or an extended enterprise—always seeking the best decisions and the most effective actions with the smallest overheads. One moment the team leader may be a follower of the person with a specialized competence. The next moment, leadership will shift to another team member, perhaps with the team leader serving as the facilitator of the shift. The entire work force, including executives and managers, must become comfortable with transitory, reciprocal sharing of power and influence.

Lean leadership requires a degree of sensitivity, even a denial of ego that can result from power sharing. The work force may have to be taught how to deal with this challenge.

8. MAKE DECISIONS AT THE LOWEST LEVEL POSSIBLE

In traditional, hierarchical organizations, decision-making is often a high-overhead process. A team of employees may identify a better, cheaper way to mold pump housings. The foreman, after being convinced by the team, takes an idea to the line supervisor. The line supervisor takes it to the plant's process engineer. The process engineer goes to the plant manager. The plant manager takes the idea to the manufacturing vice president's staff. The VP's staff will take it to their boss, who will bring it to the financial vice president. If there is disagreement, the proposal will go to the senior vice president of operations to resolve the conflict. Once a decision is made, it rattles back down the chain, finally reaching the team for implementation.

Decisions made this way are costly. They take the time and energy of many people. Often, these people do not have direct knowledge of the subject and must spend time studying it. Decisions made this way are also costly because of the elapsed time it takes to make them. By the time a decision reaches the implementation team, the competition may have introduced a product that closes the initial window of opportunity. By making decisions at the lowest level consistently, a lean company can avoid the involvement of unnecessary people and the resulting waste of time and money.

Information technology has made it possible to transfer knowledge instantaneously across levels and to aggregate data automatically. Consequently, it is easier for teams doing the work to obtain all of the data and knowledge they need for decisions. At the same time, executives more easily can obtain information they need for strategic decision-making. A lean company is a flat organization, not bound by traditional span-of-control arguments, but organized with minimal management control needed for the job. In practice, this means many companies can reduce the number of management levels in an operating division from nine to three, for example.

9. OPTIMIZE CAPABILITIES AND USE OF HUMAN RESOURCES

The dynamics and uncertainty of the future will continue to challenge the company's work force for quick, flexible responses. Companies will be forced to adjust the size and skill sets of their work force. They will be forced to do so by external and internal partnerships, with requirements for structure and control in extended enterprises, and to take full advantage of rapidly changing technologies.

The need for speed and innovation requires companies to use and reward the knowledge of every employee. Companies that give teams of employees the autonomy to make their own operational decisions depend on these teams to dig deep and do the necessary homework. Workers are expected to exceed their commitments, and to respond with whatever extra efforts are required to overcome new conditions. This is a discretionary effort—the effort that goes beyond the minimum needed just to hold on to a job.

Three needs will be dominant forces in the workplace for manufacturing in the next decade:

- the need to employ the best knowledge for all decisions—whether they be strategic decisions, product decisions, or operational decisions—in the manufacturing cell or within business processes;
- the need for a rapid response once a customer articulates a need;
- the need to meet tighter and tighter cost constraints forced by unremitting global competition.

Lean companies are responding with new ways to organize the workplace and new understandings of the nature of work, management, leadership, and employment. Employees in lean companies are knowledge assets, not physical assets. They are not subservient to management, but partners in leadership.

Companies striving to eliminate waste and improve profit margins work hard to identify their core competencies. They build on the existing competency base. Ideally, each project they undertake extends that base to a higher level. Knowledge begets more knowledge, and skills beget more skills. As a company becomes known for its particular strengths, it attracts the best people in those disciplines. Eventually, the company's core competencies dominate its product and process development projects. People are valued for their core competencies, their abilities to get things done using their skills and knowledge.

Most job descriptions and performance plans, even procedure manuals, provide caricatures of real work. They describe the minimum needed to get the job done, giving more or less detail on how to do the job. When people are treated as physical assets ("We need a pair of hands in the process, so I guess we have to hire someone."), they tend to do just the minimum. Since they are not being paid to think, they do not. Since they do not have much ownership in the end product, they do not have the motivation to do more than the minimum. They do what they are told, just well enough to continue being paid. But, most people can do much more. They can add value by finding ways to do their jobs better, faster, and cheaper. They can solve problems when they first appear. They can initiate independent, although disciplined, thoughts, decisions, and actions.

Lean companies will nurture the capabilities of people to add value through merit-based compensation that rewards right-the-first-time quality and high throughput, and through training and education that augments and reinforces knowledge and skills.

10. DEVELOP RELATIONSHIPS BASED ON TRUST AND COMMITMENT

The market imperative is for rapid responses with the right products, in the right places, at the right times. Emerging information technologies enable collaboration. Knowledge retrieval and delivery technologies make it possible to form teams to combine human and machine intelligence in natural ways. It permits greater fluidity among the enterprise's work units. The result is further extrapolation of today's trends toward team-based organizations.

Teaming is sharing power and responsibility among the people in a small group. *Partnering* is teaming among larger groups and organizations. Sharing power is hard. People who have power are confident that they do the right things with it. If they share it, they must trust that the other person will use the power as effectively as they could. They have no choice, though. Global competition requires more responsiveness and performance than one person can achieve. No one person is quick enough to master all of the details to make the right decisions in a timely manner.

General Electric's CEO, Jack Welch, provides an excellent example of the importance of trust in the following passage (Tichy and Sherman 1993):

"Trust is enormously powerful in a corporation. People won't do their best unless they believe they'll be treated fairly, that there's no cronyism and everybody has a real shot.

"The only way I know to create that kind of trust is by laying out your values and then walking the talk. You've got to do what you say you'll do, consistently, over time.

"It doesn't mean everybody has to agree. I have a great relationship with Bill Bywater, president of the International Union of Electronic Workers. I would trust him with my wallet, but he knows I'll fight him to the death in certain areas, and vice versa.

"He wants to have a neutrality agreement in GE's nonunion plants. He wants to recruit more members for the union.

"I'll say, No way! We can give people everything you can, and more."

Trust has a dominant role in lean extended enterprises. Trust is essential for any kind of teaming. The problem is that trust is elusive. It is often visceral. We know it when we feel it, we know it when it is not there, but we cannot say why. Trust is one of the central dilemmas for modern business (Smith and Berg 1987). People are continually faced with situations that require trust. However, they find it difficult to trust someone unless they already have developed a trust relationship with him or her.

Individuals want to know how others will respond to them before they trust the other people. There are parallels in business. Business people want to know that partners will honor commitments, but not just to the letter of a contractual agreement. They would like partners who act in a spirit of loyalty to achieve common goals. They want partners who will respect integrity, yet who will help with unexpected problems. They want partners who will recognize their own weaknesses and get help. Business people need partners they trust. They must feel comfortable explaining to partners the abilities of a businessperson's company to perform within the team or an extended enterprise. They need partners who trust them enough to reciprocate.

Trust has a dominant role in lean extended enterprises

The lean company must work in trustworthy relationships if it is to maximize its responsiveness and minimize wasted effort. Two companies that do not have a trust relationship will spend months, or years, writing protective contracts. They will waste time better spent on moving the product ahead. Managed supply chains, such as those developed by Chrysler in the late 1990s, provide one model for trust-based alliances. Suppliers can be assured of a long-term relationship—not limited to a single part for a single-vehicle platform—as long as they are trustworthy partners. Other forms of strategic alliances also reduce the overhead costs of trust building.

You need to be able to establish trust quickly if you, your co-workers, and your partners are going to address market opportunities in a timely manner. You need to create a vision for your company's roles in a collaborative extended enterprise. Then you need agreement with your co-workers and partners on a common set of goals and metrics of success. You need a shared risk and reward agreement.

Ideally, when partners are trusted in an extended enterprise, it is because everyone shares a common set of ethical business practices. An understood set of ethics is just a starting point for trust. Trust is iterative. Experience builds it. A businessperson trusts a partner who gives consistent, predictable results using understandable, workable processes that yield products of the same character and quality.

The extended enterprise may not have the luxury of engaging in relationships only with those who already have proven themselves by long-term association. Competitive pressures may require greatly reduced time to develop a trusting relationship—maybe one reduced by orders of magnitude. Companies are turning to pre-qualification, benchmarking, and trust agents or brokers, as ways to accelerate the trust process.

11. NURTURE A LEARNING ENVIRONMENT

Each change requires some learning. The learning may be individual or it may be institutional. A company may have to learn how to do something new. Its employees will always be learning new things. The company needs to encourage questioning and learning at all levels. It must become "a learning organization" (Senge 1990).

A company must be learning-focused, or filled with people who are always learning, individually and as groups. The individual, the teams, the company, and the larger community collectively share responsibility for continuous learning. Ultimately, individuals have to take the initiative to acquire needed knowledge. Individuals have to carry motivation and the ability to learn within themselves.

A recent survey of U.S. manufacturers correlated the hours of formal training per plant employee with a number of factors (Owen 1999). Productivity per employee, measured by revenue from products shipped, increased by one-third when employees received more than a week of training. On-time delivery rates increased from 90% to 98% as training increased. The manufacturing cycle time for companies that provided more than two weeks of worker training was half that of companies with a day or less. Companies with longer training periods had an inventory turn-rate that was nearly twice that of companies with the least training. Bottom line: companies that supported greater training better met the time pressures of global competition.

12. MAXIMIZE STABILITY IN A CHANGING ENVIRONMENT

The 21st Century will be one of turbulent change, both at the enterprise level and at the factory level. Toyota and other early pioneers of leanness found that the more stability they built into the production system, the better able the system could withstand change without undue disruption in the workplace. By using the techniques of lean production, Toyota was able to have both order and transparency. When a product change occurred, most of the activities were familiar, and the ones that were not were clearly defined and easily adaptable.

A company faces change in all areas, not just on the production line. It cannot hide its head in the sand and deny change. Rather, it needs to respond to change with the least effort. A company should make only the changes that respond to

A company faces changes in all areas, not just on the production line

changing market conditions. It should not make changes capriciously, because it recognizes that every change incurs costs. The cost of change is discussed in Chapter 7.

Maintaining stable and trusting relationships is hard in the face of change, but the lean company makes strong efforts to maintain them with its customers, partners, and suppliers.

For the work force, 21st Century companies inherently will be less stable than their predecessors because they are tied to transitory market conditions. Only rarely can companies offer lifetime employment. Companies, individual workers, and public institutions share the responsibility of employment stability. Among this shared responsibility are the following factors:

- Career management—everyone in the work force has to be an entrepreneur in his or her own self-interest. Each needs to identify, develop, and market personal core competencies. Personal security comes from one's employability, not one's present employment.
- Education and lifelong learning—while companies may continue to educate workers on company-specific processes and technologies, they should expect a high level of knowledge in the work force. Much of the knowledge that companies require of a worker needs to be gained through his or her initiative. Workers will depend on public institutions (schools and colleges) and public access (the Internet) for this store of knowledge.
- Lifetime resource planning—given instability in employment, workers have to control their long-term financial planning—planning that will give them the financial ability to maintain their chosen lifestyles during retirement.
- Communications—the familiar hierarchical model of bosses directing employees is shifting to one of teams of specialists working together to meet shared goals. This means workers have to communicate well, with clarity and honesty, and develop a culture of trust-based relationships. Some companies may be strong enough to do this from within, but most will need the support of the societal institutions to help build work force communications skills.
- Change skills—people who have not had to change jobs very often have difficulty in coping with change. (Dealing with

Change is discussed more in Chapter 7.) There is a certain skill in responding to the unknown. Change without practice and not having coping skills is painful, even devastating. As the pace of change increases, a company needs to help employees see the stability of its values, strategies, goals, relationships, and practices. At the same time, the company must be aware of the work force and the community, so that workers can be confident of finding employment even when there is change.

ASSESSING A COMPANY'S LEANNESS

Transforming a company into a lean enterprise is a continual process, a journey without a fixed destination. The boundaries of leanness continue to move forward, so that there is always a next step.

Where is your company on this journey? Are you just starting? Have some of the changes you have made in recent years taken you a little way on the path? Or, are you fully involved in the transformation process and right on the frontier of the possible? To answer these questions, you need a tool to help you assess where you are.

You can assign metrics to a company's activities that relate them to strategic goals. While these metrics also may drive a company toward leanness, they have the corporate strategic goals as their primary focus. They do not measure lean attributes. Another approach is to assess the degree to which the lean culture has been internalized and is observed by the people of an extended enterprise. The assessment can be used as a guide to the success of lean efforts and to areas that require more attention.

Is Perception Reality?

An assessment technique, directed toward overall lean transformation, is an adaptation of concepts found in the Capability Snapshot®. This tool is used to assess the perceptions held by different groups of stakeholders of the company's customer satisfaction, operations effectiveness, organizational agility, and innovation opportunities. Typically, stakeholders who contribute to the assessment are customers, board members, executives, managers, supervisors, employees, suppliers, and investors. Some companies may seek input from the communities where they operate.

The Capability Snapshot gives a company a way of identifying mismatches in perception among the stakeholder groups—reducing, for example, the possibility of the corporate leadership falling prey to hubris. It also identifies perceived weaknesses for the company. Sometimes the weaknesses are obvious to all. At other times, they are subtler. In either case, the assessment is a pointer to an area that may require management attention.

Perception is reality to the perceiver. Yet, it may not be objective reality. In addition, it may not be someone else's reality. However, it is the reality in the world in which the perceiver lives and works.

Transformation into a lean company ultimately depends on developing a corporate culture where all stakeholders embrace lean principles and practices. Since corporate cultures are subjective, perceptions of stakeholder groups can provide an assessment of internal leanness from their vantage point. These assessments are snapshots, with the first one forming a baseline. Subsequent snapshots will show progress from the baseline, or in the worst case, whether a company strayed from leanness.

Assessing Perceptions of Leanness

The Lean Enterprise Model (LEM) provides a framework for assessing perceptions of leanness. Referring to Figure 4-1, items A-D, one can build assessment questions around each of the principles and overarching practices. The following questions should probe both perceptions of a company's position on the spectrum of leanness as it exists now and on perceptions of trends. Is a company perceived as being lean now? Is it perceived as becoming more, or less lean?

The trend is important. Before its merger with Daimler Benz, Chrysler was thought to be the most lean of Detroit's Big Three automakers. There is significant evidence that, in the aftermath of the merger, Chrysler lost its focus on leanness, so that its unit costs rose rather than continuing to fall.

As with the Capability Snapshot, the goal is to develop a 360-degree assessment that takes into consideration several different points of view. The questions used should be tailored to the group whose perceptions are sought. Although the subject matter should be comparable for each group, the questions asked, for example of customers, should reflect the customer viewpoint. Questions asked of the work force should reflect its viewpoint. Questions asked of suppliers should reflect theirs. And questions asked of equity stakeholders should reflect theirs.

Example: Assessing the Lean Meta-principles

The two lean meta-principles provide the defining characteristics of the lean enterprise: responsiveness to change and minimization of waste. These two characteristics will manifest themselves differently to different stakeholder groups. The responsiveness to change and the minimizing of waste might be assessed by using the multiple-choice questions in Tables 4-1 to 4-5. Each is targeted to a stakeholder group.

If the average number for the stakeholder groups on both of these questions is close to 5.0, you have a company that everyone agrees is lean. If the average is close to 1.0, the company has a long way to go. If the average varies widely by stakeholder group, you need further analysis to understand why, and then develop a plan to correct the imbalances.

In Appendix A, 18 pairs of survey questions cover perceptions of lean meta-principles, lean-enterprise principles, and overarching practices. As above, each question is stated five ways, appropriate for customers, managers, workers, suppliers, and investors.

The first question of each pair probes the current state of a lean principle or practice. The second one addresses the trend for that principle or practice. These questions should be answered with quick, on-a-scale-of-one-to-five, answers that can be tabulated automatically and analyzed statistically. In practice, respondents should be given an opportunity to elaborate on numerical values if a question strikes a passionate chord.

As with opinion surveys, the survey must be conducted in a manner that will protect the individuals and the information with confidentiality. This may require the use of an agent outside the company.

Table 4-1. Survey of customer perceptions of the lean meta-principles

Lean Principle or Practice	Question	Choose One Answer by Number				
		1	2	3	4	5
1. Respond to change	What is the company's response when you come to it with a new requirement?	Very poor	Poor	OK	Good	Very good
2. Minimize waste	How efficiently does the company handle its transactions with you?	Very inefficiently	Inefficiently	OK	Efficiently	Very efficiently

Table 4-2. Survey of executive perceptions of the lean meta-principles

Lean Principle or Practice	Question	Choose One Answer by Number				
		1	2	3	4	5
1. Respond to change	What is your company's response to changes in customer needs?	Very poor	Poor	OK	Good	Very good
2. Minimize waste	How many areas in the company have activities where there is obvious waste?	Most areas	Many areas	Some areas	A few areas	Almost no areas

Table 4-3. Survey of employee perceptions of the lean meta-principles

Lean Principle or Practice	Question	Choose One Answer by Number				
		1	2	3	4	5
1. Respond to change	Is your work more or less difficult when the company responds to changing customer needs?	Much more difficult	More difficult	No significant difficulty	No more difficult	Easier
2. Minimize waste	How wasteful is the company in the activities you see in your daily work?	Extremely wasteful	Very wasteful	Somewhat wasteful	Occasionally wasteful	Almost never wasteful

Table 4-4. Survey of supplier perceptions of the lean meta-principles

Lean Principle or Practice	Question	Choose One Answer by Number				
		1	2	3	4	5
1. Respond to change	How easy or hard is the company to work with when it has to change its orders from you?	Very hard	Hard	Somewhat hard	Easy	Very easy
2. Minimize waste	How much wasted effort is there when you work with the company?	Extreme amount of waste	A lot of waste	Some waste	Occasional waste	Almost no waste

Table 4-5. Survey of investor perceptions of the lean meta-principles

Lean Principle or Practice	Question	Choose One Answer by Number				
		1	2	3	4	5
1. Respond to change	How well does the company respond to changes in the market or in external conditions?	Very poorly	Poorly	OK	Well	Very well
2. Minimize waste	How well does the company communicate investor and financial information?	Very poorly	Poorly	OK	Well	Very well

EXERCISE

1. Picture a prospective customer—someone you know—who could give you a 20% increase in sales. What approach would you suggest to make the 20% increase a reality and to insure retention of this customer?
2. What systems or operational steps does your company use to improve its operations? What additional steps would you suggest?
3. Assuming your company has operations in many locations producing several products, what systems or procedures does it have in place to share knowledge and design information to prevent re-inventing the wheel? What additional steps would you want to see your company introduce to improve the sharing of knowledge and information?
4. What do you consider critical in achieving a seamless exchange of knowledge and information?
5. How do you personally feel about having to make changes in your work routines or habits? Could you accept a working environment where the rules change every other day?

REFERENCES

Drucker, Peter F. 1995. *Managing in a Time of Great Change.* New York: Truman Talley Books/Dutton.

Jordan, James A. Jr., and Michel, Frederick J. 2000. *Next Generation Manufacturing: Methods and Techniques.* New York: John Wiley & Sons, Inc.

Owen, Jean V. 1999. "Have You Learned Something Today?" *Manufacturing Engineering*, April.

Pine, B. Joseph II, and Gilmore, James H. 1999. *The Experience Economy: Work is Theatre and Every Business a Stage.* Boston, MA: Harvard Business School.

Porter, Michael. 1998. *Competitive Strategy: Techniques for Analyzing Industries and Competitors.* New York: Free Press.

Senge, Peter M. 1990. *The Fifth Discipline: the Art and Practice of the Learning Organization*. New York: Currency Doubleday.

Shields, J.T. 1996. "Factory Flow Benchmarking Time." *LAI Report*. Boston, MA: MIT.

Smith, Kenwyn K. and Berg, David N. 1987. *Paradoxes of Group Life: Understanding Conflict, Paralysis, and Movement in Group Dynamics*. San Francisco, CA: Jossey-Bass.

Thurow, Lester C. 1996. *The Future of Capitalism: How Today's Economic Forces Shape Tomorrow's World*. New York: William Morrow.

Tichy, Noel M., and Sherman, Stratford. 1993. *Control Your Destiny or Someone Else Will*. New York: Doubleday.

BIBLIOGRAPHY

Capability Snapshot, Inc. http://www.capsnap.com/index.asp

Lean Aerospace Initiative. Lean.mit.edu/public/index.html

Value Stream Mapping[SM] is a registered Service Mark of the Lean Enterprise Institute. The proprietary Value Stream Mapping[SM] technique provides an analytical discipline for examining existing value streams and designing more lean ones.

Womack, James P., and Jones, Daniel T. 1996. *Lean Thinking: Banish Waste and Create Wealth in Your Corporation*. New York: Simon and Schuster.

Chapter Five

Vision, Value, and Strategic Goals

Why should a company go through the cost, the agony, of transformation? Leanness is not the prize. Profit, sustained over time, is the prize. Every business needs to go through transformation to remain competitive and be profitable under changing conditions. A company must provide value for its stakeholders. Becoming a lean company is only a means to that end, a way of winning the prize.

Any transformation of a company, any change initiative, must first pass the test of relevance to the company's strategic goals. The Lean Enterprise Model (LEM) provides an excellent guide to culture and to change initiatives that will give companies significant strategic advantages in meeting corporate goals in the early 21st Century. Nevertheless, every change initiative undertaken in the name of leanness must first promise a substantial contribution toward meeting corporate goals.

> Leanness is not the prize; profit, sustained over time, is the prize

The starting point for a company wishing to transform itself is its vision of itself in the future. Then it must delineate the value it wants to deliver to its stakeholders. The vision and value statements must be translated into strategic goals. The goals must have metrics associated with them. The metrics should be measured. The measurements should then be used for performance management so the company can demonstrate that it actually is delivering the value promised to each of its stakeholders.

VISION

Every company has a vision of itself—what it wants to be now, what it wants to be in the future. Traditional companies often have a vision by default. They want to be what they are now, however ill defined that may be, forever and forever. That is not good enough in today's competitive world.

Corporate leaders have a special responsibility for providing the vision needed in a world of change. Make no mistake. Corporate leaders always provide a vision for their companies. Even those who reject "the vision thing" project a vision by their very rejection of the need for an articulated one. It may be a vision of benign anarchy; it may be a vision of arbitrary response and control; it may be a status quo vision. Whatever the muddled message, stakeholders will respond to it, for better or worse.

Leaders of a lean company will project a vision of the company's future that is clear, concise, and understood by everyone. It will be a lively vision of striving and growth, a pulsating vision of thriving and sustained success. You and your employees will choose to work for your company because your personal visions line up with its vision. The company's investors will choose to invest because they see value in its vision.

VALUE

Chapter 3 asked, "Who is your customer?" Chapter 4 placed a great deal of emphasis on value, as customers perceive it. The people who pay for a company's products, the people thought of as "customers," are one very important class. All classes of the company's stakeholders are customers, too—customers of the value provided them.

It is appropriate for product managers to focus their attention on providing value to paying customers. That is their role in the company. Corporate executives must see a bigger picture. They must balance the flows of value to their stakeholder groups (see Figure 5-1).

Chapter 3 indicates that a company can segment the market and develop customized products, representing differentiated expressions of value for each segment. Similarly, the company can

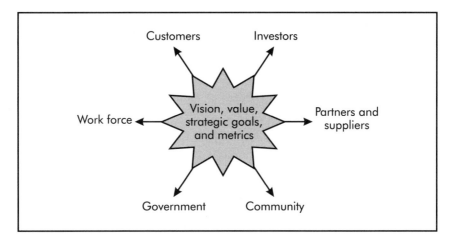

Figure 5-1. A company's flow of value to its stakeholder groups.

segment stakeholder groups and ensure that each segment receives the value it expects. It should be remembered that value is as the individual stakeholder defines it.

The vision of the future can be translated into reality when the company uses it to define a set of long-term goals. These long-term goals are called *strategic goals*. Companies express strategic goals first in financial terms, usually as return on investment (ROI) and sustained, growing profitability. Often, however, these concepts are inadequate to describe the wished-for company fully enough. Simply using financial measures may be inadequate to ensure the value stakeholders expect. Value means thinking of a company from many points of view.

STRATEGIC PERSPECTIVES

The *Balanced Scorecard®* provides one way to consider different points of view (Kaplan and Norton 1996). It gives a convenient and disciplined way to think about balanced strategic goals. Without a balance of goals, a company may focus so much on achieving quarterly financial results, market share, engineering leadership, or efficient operations, that it loses sight of what it really takes to build a strong company with a bright future. The Balanced Scorecard looks at the company from four "perspectives" (see Figure 5-2),

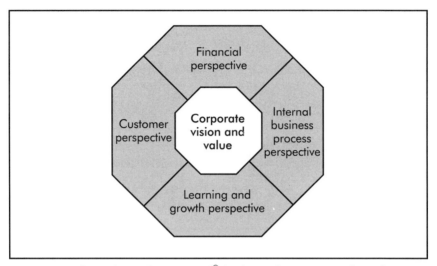

Figure 5-2. The Balanced Scorecard® *looks at the company from four perspectives.*

and uses them to focus management's attention on the goals for the business. These perspectives represent a minimum set for companies that want to thrive now and profit in the future.

Perspective I: Customary Financial Goals

The financial goals of the company are the primary concern of the financial community and the investor. They are vitally important to the person who, at the end of the day, must account for stewardship of the financial assets of pension and retirement funds, mutual funds, and individual investors. They are the responsibility of those whose risk-taking can lead to increased wealth or financial disaster.

The 21st Century company will live in turbulence, a dynamic entity, confronting and perhaps even forcing continual change. The company will have neither a stable customer base nor a fixed technology base. Even well established companies will take on the characteristics of start-up and growth companies. The 21st Century company will make investments in the face of market and technology uncertainties. Increasingly, it will operate with a preponderance of intangible assets, such as knowledge. Business cycles have shortened to the point where a company will rarely see a steady revenue stream from a cash cow. It continually will have to refresh its product families to meet evolving needs.

However, this same company also will need to show sustained profitability and shareholder value. Start-ups and growth companies must mature. They may lose money at the start. However, as many so-called "dot.coms" found in 2000, at some point there must be profit to sustain further growth and provide shareholders with a real investment return. The survivors will be companies with solid business plans that will yield profits before the next wave of change makes them anachronistic.

Perspective II: Goals Relating to Customers' Viewpoints

Profits can flow only if customers value the company and its products enough to pay the product cost plus an adequate profit. The customers' current and future needs for, and acceptance of, the company's products and services will drive the company. Customers, who have a cacophony of choices, must view a company as being so attractive that it becomes their provider of choice.

Goals based on meeting customer needs will lead to beneficial business results. These goals will create an environment resulting in satisfied customers.

Can the company make a profit, explicitly or implicitly, by serving every customer's needs? A company may choose not to serve certain customers or markets. However, it should not allow itself to be rejected by a customer or forced out of a market through customer dissatisfaction. Indeed, a decision not to serve a market should include a respectful treatment of customers the company chooses not to serve. Who knows when the company will want to re-enter the market?

Perspective III: Goals Relating to Efficient and Effective Operations

Profits come from the company's abilities to optimize time, quality, and cost factors. The concepts of leanness are most apparent in the development of products and services, in production and distribution systems, and in service support. Application of lean principles and practices, important in achieving all the goals, is most obvious in this perspective. Process reengineering should lead to less waste and the ability to respond quickly to changes in markets and technology. Every operation has to contribute directly to the realization of the company's strategic goals and profitability.

Perspective IV: Goals Relating to Preparing for the Future Through Learning and Growth

There will be no let-up in the pace of change. If anything, it is likely to accelerate. What works today will not necessarily work tomorrow. A company must stretch to see into the future, and prepare for it.

Lean principles enable a company to change in ways that minimize cost. One way to do this is to create a "learning company"— one in which the company, as an institution, and its people continually learn (Senge 1990). They learn to do today's job better by applying continuous improvement. They learn to do tomorrow's job, leapfrogging the competition. They learn so the company can stay ahead of the competition as it responds to change and becomes the leader in its field. They learn so they will not lose value as the company changes. They learn out of self-interest so their careers will not stall.

THE SUCCESSFUL 21ST CENTURY MANUFACTURING COMPANY

The authors of this book have looked specifically at the attributes of a successful 21st Century manufacturing company. In addition to the four base perspectives (Jordan and Michel 1998, 2000), such a company needs to view itself from two additional perspectives, called the *Globalization Perspective* and the *Innovation Perspective* (see Figure 5-3).

Perspective V: Goals Relating to Globalization

The economy is a global one. Communication is instantaneous. Material transport can be as fast as 600 mph, if need be, for all

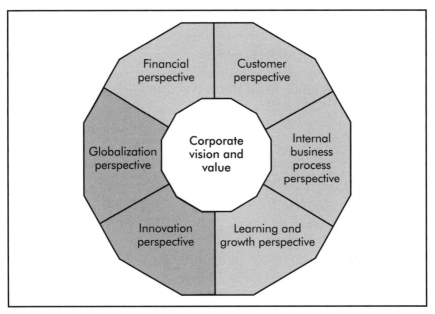

Figure 5-3. Adding the globalization perspective and the innovation perspective to the Balanced Scorecard.

but the heaviest of products. Globalization includes three important components: globalization of markets, products, and production. A company needs the ability to compete, if it chooses, in any market anywhere. It must develop products and services that, ideally, could be sold anywhere or, at least, customized for regional or country-specific markets with minimal incremental cost. For a myriad of markets and for financial reasons, a company also should have the ability to manage manufacturing operations anywhere.

Perspective VI: Goals Relating to Innovation

Many companies, like Enron, thrive today by offering products and services that did not exist five years ago, and were not even thought of ten years ago. Even companies like automobile manufacturers offer products that look only superficially like the ones they offered in past years. They are using technologies that have burst into use within the decade. They are making products using processes invented just a year or two ago, and distributing products in channels that did not exist before. Moreover, they are accomplishing this by cultivating business relationships that would have been frowned on in the 1980s.

A company will thrive if it has the ability to innovate and confront change through its timely and competitive use of the best available knowledge, employed in new and creative ways. The culture, incentives, and rewards for innovation must be put into place to realize this perspective.

A company that views itself from each of the six perspectives can set goals within each of them. Goals will differ from company to company. The balance of viewpoints will ensure that each company is asking itself: "For what should we strive?" The question should be asked in a way that ensures an optimized set of goals to enhance the company's survival—and, most importantly, its profitability.

METRICS

To sustain its competitiveness over time, a company needs to work on goals in each of the six strategic perspectives. For a manufacturing company in today's competitive world, strategic goals will have urgency about them, a sense of the value of time.

A company will want to know whether it is progressing quickly, slowly, or not at all, toward its goals. It will want an early warning if it is retrogressing. The company needs to define metrics it can use to measure progress. The measurements (see Figure 5-4) will show the company's rate of progress toward the goals. If measurements for a goal lag behind, the company has warning that it is going out of balance and that corrective action is needed.

Once the metrics are chosen, a company can use them to guide its investments in change initiatives. Transformation of the company into a lean one will require many change initiatives. The goal is to make lean investments that yield:

- the greatest value with balanced improvement in the company's metrics, and
- the least impediment to further change.

A prioritization strategy will emphasize the initiatives that will have the greatest impact on areas in which the company is weakest.

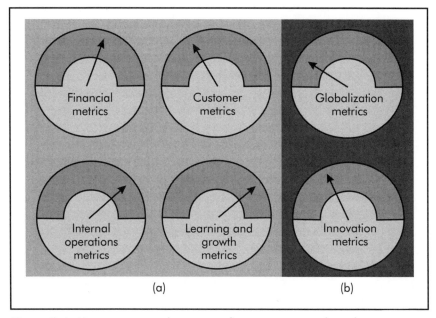

Figure 5-4. Measurements show rate of progress toward goals.

Table 5-1 gives examples of strategic metrics used to measure progress toward goals from each of the six perspectives. Most companies will choose a subset of the suggested metrics or alternatives as guideposts for management actions and investments. The important thing is that each of the six perspectives be represented in the chosen subset. Appendix B provides additional discussion of these metrics.

A company may want to reduce the subset further and display (see Figure 5-4) a set of summary measures to provide a quick overview of its position.

The assignment of metrics in the name of leanness must be tailored to the level of responsibility within an organization. The selected metrics should be meaningful tools to encourage the work force to exercise responsibility throughout the organization. The metrics should encourage lean behaviors and achievement of strategic goals. They are tools for focusing the behavior of the company, not tools that justify establishing an unnecessary bureaucratic environment. Under no circumstances should the tools be allowed to become an end unto itself.

Table 5-1. Examples of strategic metrics

1. Financial Perspective	2. Customer Perspective	3. Operations Perspective
Return on investment (ROI) Change in earnings/$ invested Turnover rate and margins % of revenues from new products and markets	Sales growth by targeted market segment and product lines Net profit by customer or segment Customer perceptions of products and fulfillment processes	Breakeven time for products and processes % of Six Sigma designs Rate of productivity improvement Accuracy and completeness of information provided to work units
Cash-to-cash cycle (from inception to first cash returns, by expenditure or investment) Revenue/full-time equivalent employee (FTE) Costs vs. competitors' costs	Total cost to the customer of product or service solutions (life-cycle cost) Elapsed time to fulfill a customer need Mean time products are out of service for repair Brand loyalty	Time to obtain product or project status Cost of scrap and rework Cost of energy and other natural resources Regulatory compliance violations

4. Learning & Growth Perspective	5. Globalization Perspective	6. Innovation Perspective
% Level of teaming qualifications Cost of training for the skills and knowledge to meet job standards Customers', partners' and suppliers' perceptions of trustworthiness	Market and major account share by geographic market Share of total market potential % of employees engaged in transnational teaming	Investment in R&D and market development as % of revenue Earnings attributable to implemented innovations % of compensation attributable to innovation
% of critical decisions made by individuals and work units Information systems literacy rate	% of systems integrated Information systems availability for all employees	Average product/process lead (lag) relative to competition Time to develop and implement next product, next process

ACHIEVING STRATEGIC GOALS

Strategic goals will best be achieved if all the company's activities are designed to help meet them. Excellent plans do not necessarily yield excellent results. Even if the plans are perfect, there may be failures of execution. Assuming the activities are well designed, there remains the need to implement them and then to track them to ensure that the expected results are achieved. A lean company will want to find failures as early as possible to minimize the cost of reworking imperfect products and faulty processes. The way a company goes about performance management can support or inhibit realization of goals.

Performance Management

A company's performance management system needs an activity view: Is the activity making the contributions it should? It should also have an enterprise view: Is the totality of the company's activities achieving the company's goals? A company needs an enterprise-wide performance management system (see Figure 5-5) for reducing cost, time, and investment while maximizing enterprise outcomes. This system should all be in alignment with the company's vision, mission, and strategic plans.

Figure 5-5 shows two kinds of performance measurement loops:

1. The *strategic loop* tracks achievement of strategic goals using the balanced set of strategic metrics. Outcomes in this loop are the inputs for revisions of strategic goals. Changes in strategic goals then drive the change process. Performance results from the strategic loops can be indicators of how well the management of the enterprise performs and may even suggest or possibly result in a re-alignment at the management level.

2. The *tactical loops* provide for measurement, analysis, and evaluation of individual activities—unit processes, tasks, and so forth. A company can compare actual measurements to established metrics, analyze deviations, and make appropriate corrective interventions. If more than simple intervention is indicated, the company can evaluate measurements and underlying processes to see if a change initiative is required.

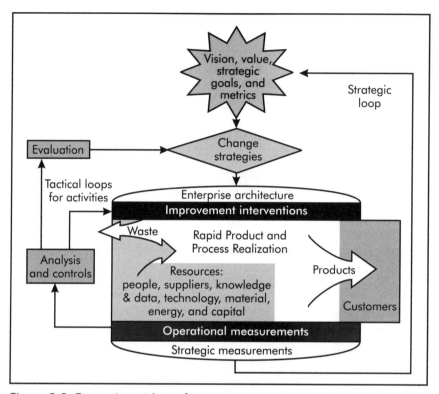

Figure 5-5. Enterprise-wide performance management system.

Performance measures for activities (the tactical loops) should be aligned with strategic goals and metrics. It may be difficult to align tactical change activities with strategic goals. The tactical change activities include routine and more ambitious change initiatives that support pervasive strategic change. Later chapters will provide a heuristic, or experiential method of dealing with tactical change initiatives. Of equal importance is prioritization of activities to build an effective investment strategy. This will be discussed in Chapter 12.

Companies' strategies for performance management will have to be accurate. Twenty-first century companies will have little margin for error (strategic loop). They will have to be lean. This means complete and comprehensive enough to achieve the strategic goals, but developed with the expenditure of as little time and effort as possible by busy people who are best used to add to product value. The strategies must also be agile, that is, designed so that they can readily adapt to unpredicted and unpredictable change.

The change process is likely to affect several parts of the enterprise. Any change must be accomplished in accordance with the enterprise architecture—through defined interfaces between teams and partners using enterprise-wide information systems.

The performance management system must:

- Identify the cost of resources required to perform significant activities of the enterprise and compare those consumed to the projected forecasts. Lean enterprises in general will want to account for costs on an activity basis to ensure each activity is contributing value. Activity-based cost data for product life cycle processes can also be used for predictive financial analyses of future product offerings. Cost-effective and timely acquisition, analysis, and presentation of financial and non-financial operations data are essential to lean operations and lean change initiatives.
- Determine the efficiency and effectiveness of activities performed and resources utilized. Process improvement requires that all resources, such as material, capital, energy, human, data, and technology, be measured so waste is minimized and outcomes are maximized. This should result in a closed-loop performance feedback process that yields accountability for every process at all levels.
- Identify and evaluate new activities that can improve the future performance of the enterprise.

EXERCISE

1. Has your company met its quarterly and annual financial goals? What have been the three most important factors in its success or failure to do so?
2. Does your company have a vision and strategic goals? Do all the employees share the vision? Please explain.
3. Has your company established and distributed metrics based on its strategic goals? Do they guide the behavior of the employees? If not, why not?

4. Based on what you have learned in this chapter on value, vision, and strategic goals, what would you recommend management do differently to help your company meet its financial goals?
5. How does your vision of your career align with the company's vision? What are your strategies for achieving this vision?

REFERENCES

Jordan, James A. Jr., and Michel, Frederick J. 1998. "Competitive Next Generation Manufacturing Enterprise: Investing in the Future." SME Technical Paper MM98-287. Dearborn, MI: Society of Manufacturing Engineers.

——. 2000. *Next Generation Manufacturing: Techniques and Methods.* New York: John Wiley & Sons, Inc.

Kaplan, Robert S., and Norton, David P. 1996. *The Balanced Scorecard: Translating Strategy into Action.* Boston, MA: Harvard Business School Press.

Senge, Peter. 1990. *The Fifth Discipline: The Art and Practice of the Learning Organization.* New York: Currency Doubleday.

Chapter Six

Operational Strategies for the Lean Company

To transform a company into a lean one requires putting in place many change initiatives. These can be ad hoc ones, chosen in response to an immediate stimulus. Alternatively, change initiatives can be identified through a systematic examination of the entire company's needs. Then the initiatives can be prioritized so the company can do the ones with the largest gains at least cost first. The authors believe the systematic approach is inherently more lean than an ad hoc one. In this way, the company will take an integrated look at all its activities.

The most recent comprehensive review of the modern manufacturing company is found in the national Next Generation Manufacturing (NGM) Project (Jordan and Michel 2000) completed in the late 1990s by nearly 500 manufacturing experts. The NGM Project developed an approach called the "NGM Framework for Action" to help systematize change initiatives.

> A lean company depends on people whose behavior is always lean

FOUR OPERATIONAL STRATEGIES

The NGM approach introduces four operational strategies (see Figure 6-1) as the basis for creating a successful 21st Century company. Three strategies relate to the people, knowledge, and the processes and equipment involved in product realization. A strategy for integration ties these three together. The NGM Framework places strong emphasis on integration, so that people, knowledge, processes, and equipment can work together efficiently and effectively when distributed geographically and over

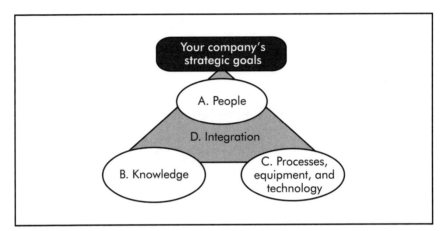

Figure 6-1. The NGM approach of four operational strategies.

time zones. Over time, all companies will need to pursue all the strategies.

Strategy A: The Right People . . . Doing the Right Things

A company cannot exist without people. A lean company depends on people whose behavior is always lean. These are productive people who can be depended upon to do the right things and make the right changes, all at the right time, and with a minimum of effort for themselves and a minimum of disruption for the company.

For most manufacturing, the lights-out factory is a wonderful dream. The reality is that people design, build, and run factories. There may be fewer people in management and on the shop floor. There may be more automation. Computers can and do many of the routine steps between design and production better than people. However, there will always need to be a balance of people and equipment. The model of the lights-out factory might have made sense, and may still be sensible, for very high-volume mass production. In today's world of mass customization, however, too many decisions have to be made, decisions with a level of complexity that just cannot be programmed.

The decisions are the key. The biggest contributions people make now are their decisions. The decisions may be very practical: how to keep a manufacturing cell running at full capacity when a machine shows signs of failure, or there's a glitch in the feedstock for one type of product. On the other hand, the decisions may be conceptual: making the compromises between initial cost and ability to be recycled, or between manufacturability and maintainability.

Decisions may be small and hidden within the enterprise's operations: when to change a drill bit, how to summarize financial data. The decisions may be larger and affect a business unit's profitability directly: what to price an offering, how to design a production line. Alternatively, decisions may be strategic and affect survival of the company: when to cancel a product platform or introduce a new technology.

Decisions made in one part of the enterprise may affect operations almost anywhere else. What one person decides deep in the supply chain may ripple through factory operations, maintenance planning, reliability, life cycle, cost analysis, and so forth. In the lean company, decisions must be timely and accurate to preclude costly rework.

This means people are unique knowledge assets, not commodities. Henry Ford's assembly lines commoditized people. Ford assumed that very nearly any unskilled person could come to the line, be taught three or four simple operations, and function mechanically. Now people are suppliers of individual pieces that fit into a jigsaw puzzle of knowledge. The puzzle is solved if we have the right individuals in the right place at the right time, and with the right shaped skills that are interlocked with those of the right other people.

People are unique knowledge assets, not commodities

Strategy B: Knowing What You Need to Know . . . Using What You Know

A company is going to win the competition by having more knowledge, and using it better, than the next company. It must know the market and the end user. It must know its business processes and those of its competitors. It must have technical knowledge about materials, technologies, and processes. It must have design, manufacturing, and support knowledge.

A company must have clear and accurate knowledge when it is needed. The value of employees lies in their ability to use knowledge to make decisions. If people do not have the right knowledge, the decisions they make are going to be faulty.

Knowledge is more than data or information. It is the stuff that people use when they are in the process of solving problems—the coupling among a database, a problem begging for a solution, and a committed act.

Knowledge is generated every day in every manufacturing company. It is stored away in people's brains. Many companies learned that the hard way when they restructured and then found that a lot of knowledge walked out in the heads of the people who were offered early retirement. They had generated that knowledge in the years they worked for their companies. However, their knowledge was not written down so it could be of future use to others. Some companies ended up having to pay big consulting fees to get the knowledge back (Kransdorff 1998).

A company needs to think about knowledge as if it were a tangible asset. The NGM Project speaks of the knowledge supply chain. It says lean concepts should be applied to managing the knowledge supply.

There is a dynamic sea of knowledge being generated out there—in R&D labs, in universities, by competitors, and by customers. It is constantly in motion and always being refreshed. The management challenge is to have processes in place so that a company's people have access to and use the right knowledge at the right time.

There is no simple mechanistic solution to a company's need to acquire, organize, and deliver knowledge. Tools from artificial intelligence (AI), can be used for specialized bodies of knowledge. However, knowledge processes require companies to take thoughtful, holistic approaches incorporating many technical and non-technical methods.

Strategy C: Using the Right Processes, Equipment, and Technology

Custom products are the ones that meet very specific customer needs different from those of the next customer. A company that is going to make the next generation of such products should use next generation processes, equipment, and technology.

While the specifics of change may be unpredictable, the company should be ready for change. It must design, build, or acquire multi-use equipment and processes. The processes and equipment should be agile. That means reconfigurable manufacturing cells, tooling that can be changed nearly instantaneously, machines that can be changed quickly from one use to the next, and programmable control systems.

Processes and equipment will become obsolete if they are not designed and selected to accommodate growth and change with the progression of customer needs. There is an obvious disconnect if it takes $5 million and 16 months to automate an assembly line specifically for a $300 product that is a specialty electronics item. This is especially true when there is a market forecast for this product of only 50,000 units in an 18-month window of opportunity. The winner in this race is the manufacturer who has flexibility to produce the product after, say, spending three months and $100,000 designing and implementing modifications required to assemble it on an existing line. The champion is the company that can reprogram its processes and equipment in a day and a half.

Strategy D: Integrating the Enterprise

The dominant word among the attributes of an NGM company is responsiveness. How can a company be responsive when it is spread across the world, and made up of dozens of teams who use a variety of systems, processes, and technologies? Rapidly responsive teaming, getting the right things done at the right time, requires high-level integration of people, knowledge, equipment, processes, and systems, using common standards.

Enterprise integration does not mean some monolithic, centralized formula imposed by the information systems department or some other headquarters group. Instead, it means all the ways a company coordinates activities and communicates information. The lean concept of enterprise integration is that it is implemented in a way that best fits the needs of specific activities of individual workgroups.

It takes a lot for a company that is spread out functionally and geographically to operate as a unified, integrated entity. It takes a culture where everyone:

- shares the company's vision, values, and goals;
- interprets verbal and nonverbal directions in a similar way;
- uses the same "language," even if it is represented in English, Persian, and Bahasa;
- feels a sense of belonging, a sense that he or she is a member of the same team;
- can trust the other person to do his or her job;
- takes pride in being trustworthy;
- adheres to a common set of standards.

In addition to a focused culture, enterprise integration requires:

- A set of business systems that binds the company together seamlessly, and that accounts for, and rewards contributions fairly.
- A robust information technology (IT) infrastructure that can acquire and deliver the right knowledge to the right people, working with the right equipment. The IT architecture needs, on a grand scale, should be similar to those of the more recent PCs with plug-and-play capabilities. If the company has to change continuously to stay on top, or ahead, of the markets, it has to be able to add functions, work units, or new equipment with little or no overhead costs. It has to be able to: change control algorithms; keep consistent, enterprise-wide versions of product and process data models; and maintain a coherent picture of finances across currencies and economic systems.
- Interfaces between machines and people that help people do their jobs better. These interfaces should be ones that do not require people to spend a lot of time translating from somebody else's jargon, or thinking about computer technology. People need interfaces that filter out information they do not need while ensuring information they do need is quickly available.
- So-called intelligent manufacturing systems built to adapt to new conditions with little outside intervention. Sometimes, the adaptation will be done automatically by the equipment. More often, it will be done by people working as members of the system.

THE NGM FRAMEWORK FOR ACTION

The four NGM operational strategies are supported by ten implementation substrategies that make up the NGM Framework for Action (see Figure 6-2). Strategy A is comprised of one substrategy, work force flexibility. Strategy B includes the three substrategies of innovation, knowledge supply, and change management. Strategy C is made up of two substrategies including pervasive modeling and simulation and agile, flexible manufacturing processes and equipment. Strategy D includes the final four substrategies of Rapid Product and Process Realization, extended enterprise collaboration, enterprise integration, and adoptive, responsive information systems (NGM Project 1997).

The NGM Framework is a strategic framework, not a tactical plan. Every company will have to choose its change initiatives.

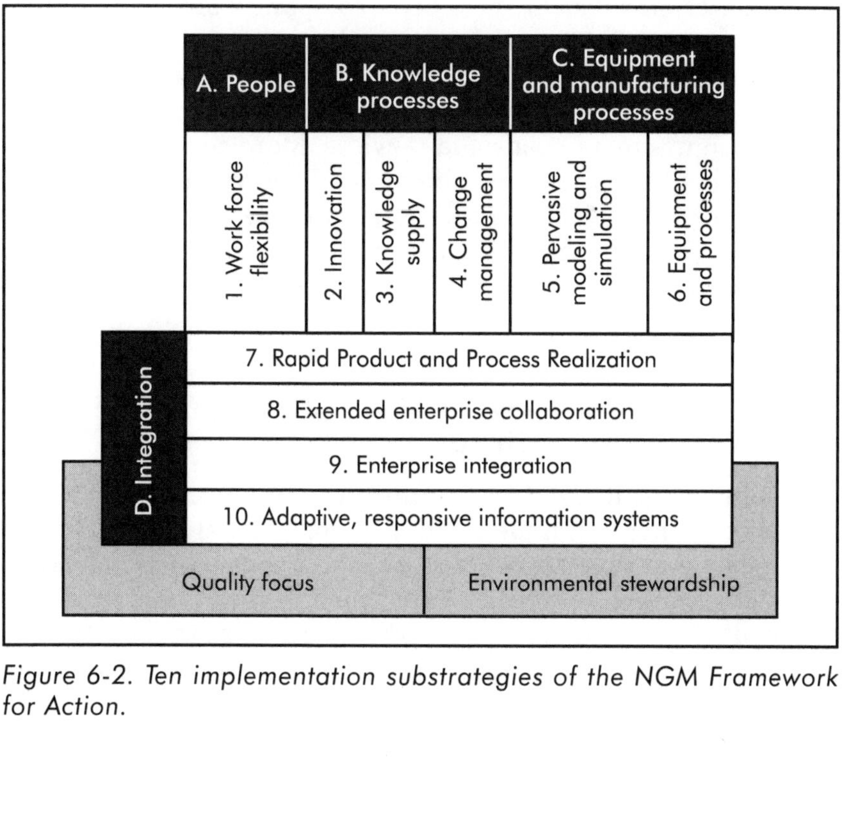

A. People	B. Knowledge processes		C. Equipment and manufacturing processes		
1. Work force flexibility	2. Innovation	3. Knowledge supply	4. Change management	5. Pervasive modeling and simulation	6. Equipment and processes

D. Integration	7. Rapid Product and Process Realization
	8. Extended enterprise collaboration
	9. Enterprise integration
	10. Adaptive, responsive information systems

| Quality focus | Environmental stewardship |

Figure 6-2. Ten implementation substrategies of the NGM Framework for Action.

There is no single best organization for all companies (Drucker 1999). So, too, there is no one prescriptive formula for transformation to a lean company. The company should use the Framework for Action to identify tactical change initiatives that will both support its strategic goals and make the company leaner.

The NGM Project chose not to address two sets of important underlying issues explicitly:

1. Quality—lean production systems teach that quality is an essential requirement for customer satisfaction and economic operations. The NGM Project took the paramount importance of quality as a given, permeating the entire Framework for Action. Some of the actions taken within the Framework improve quality explicitly. All improve the quality of some aspect of the company.

2. Environmental issues—the NGM Framework for Action weaves environmental stewardship into many of the implementation substrategies. Lean companies are going to find environmental factors increasingly important. There will be significant costs for improving and maintaining the livability of the world as its population grows, gains wealth, and consumes more goods and services. More companies are incurring the costs of reclaiming land and water resources after years of casual waste disposal. It is prudent for companies to avoid additional massive environmental clean-up costs in the future by making environmentally sound choices in the design of a product or process.

Strategy A—People: Having the Right People ... Doing the Right Things

A company is defined as a companionship of people who have melded together to pursue a common goal, namely a level of corporate business success that allows them to satisfy their individual goals. Everyone working in a company is a worker. There are differentiated roles, of course. Some workers have roles as executives or managers, others as leaders or facilitators, others as machine operators, accountants, or customer service representatives.

Substrategy 1: Work Force Flexibility

The chief NGM implementation substrategy relating to human resources is the development and maintenance of a flexible work force. As the company confronts changing markets, operating conditions, and competition, it must flex in response. Moreover, the work force must flex too. The lean company must have a set of practices, policies, and processes that support flexibility. It needs a culture that gives workers a sense of security and ownership while enabling a company to capitalize on their creativity, commitment, and discretionary efforts. The goal is to give the worker a realistic sense of belonging and stability that permits him or her to concentrate on the work at hand and not waste time and energy worrying about the future.

You can look at work force flexibility from your company's point of view or from your workers' perspectives.

The company needs to make the best decisions made in the most affordable way. It requires the worker or team who can best get the jobs done that need to be done now. Tomorrow, it will need the worker or team who can best get tomorrow's jobs done. The worker who does today's job may not have the knowledge or skills to do tomorrow's job. Today's job may require a team with 25 members. Tomorrow's job may require a team of 15, or one of 35. Today's manager may be asked to make technical contributions tomorrow. Tomorrow's job may need today's manufacturing cell operator to use his or her skills as a team leader. The company would like a work force that fits itself to the job to be done with no overhead costs. It wants a work force that is always the right size and has the right knowledge and skills, but never has inadequate or unused knowledge or skills.

Many workers, at all levels in company hierarchies, fear work force flexibility as a threat to their personal, financial and emotional comfort. When they perceive a change as having a negative impact on them, workers will not implement it efficiently. The company will have to build a culture in which the work force accepts the company's change process as one that can give them greater personal satisfaction and longer-term stability.

Workers who can flex confidently with change:

- have the ability and confidence to learn quickly to do tomorrow's job;
- can work within teams whose members frequently change roles and who come and go;
- are prepared to leave the company, if need be, with the assurance that they can find productive employment elsewhere.

Lean lifelong learning will be required if employees are to overcome rapid obsolescence of skills and be prepared to flex. The NGM report estimates that the combination of new technologies, new customer needs, and changing global economics will result in obsolescence of individual skills approaching 20% per year. Each member of the work force must be engaged in lifelong learning to cope with today's needs and to prepare for tomorrow's.

A company may need to invest as much as a month a year in education per employee just to maintain his or her employability. An employee may need the encouragement and support of their team and management to take the risks associated with such big investments in learning.

Successful lifelong learning depends on having a learning environment. A learning environment is one in which the leaders take a contagious joy in their own learning and in what their colleagues are learning. A learning environment is one:

- where questions like, "What if we did thus-and-such?", are welcomed and given respectful consideration;
- where expenditure of some discretionary effort on the hard work of learning is valued;
- where experimentation and risk-taking are encouraged;
- that is a place with few preconceptions.

Given that real-world problems are usually multidisciplinary, a learning environment encourages learning from any source or discipline that can help. A learning environment is one in which the learner pulls the knowledge for which he or she perceives the need. It is not a push environment where others' preconceived learning priorities are forced on the people.

A company will not thrive for long without a healthy extended community. Workers will not thrive for long, either, without such a community. The company and its work force will build on the resources of its local or regional community. There needs to be a community infrastructure that supports people who are willing to participate in lean companies and transitory, extended enterprises. Even a thriving region like Silicon Valley has found that individuals, even companies, cannot go it alone. Leaders from industry, education, and government in Silicon Valley have formed extended community enterprises like Silicon Valley Joint Venture to create a support infrastructure and institutionalize their community of knowledge.

The community infrastructure has the primary responsibility to prepare people to manage their careers and be lifelong learners. The company, together with other companies in the community, must integrate its resources into the community's knowledge enterprise. The community needs first to understand the needs of the work force. Then it should deliver the needed knowledge in a timely, effective, cost-efficient and readily accessible manner (see Figure 6-3).

The community will be an essential partner in the process, providing a larger integrated knowledge process for all the companies that underpin the community. The partnership is a reciprocal relationship. The community needs the companies for its economic well being. Companies need the community to provide the resources industry needs to be competitive. It is a relationship that demands

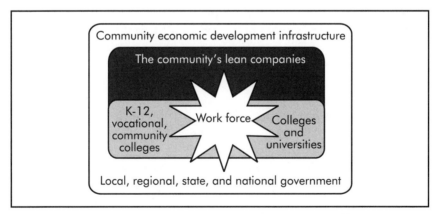

Figure 6-3. Knowledge delivered in timely, effective, cost-efficient, and accessible manners.

creative, innovative, and insightful leadership in the community, as well as in companies.

Strategy B—Knowledge Processes

In a knowledge-based competition, a company will win if it has the most usable knowledge. Knowledge is information in a form such that it can be used. Competitive advantage is a matter of knowledge arbitrage in a world where the access and flow of information is ubiquitous and the supply of knowledge is balanced. The strongest competitor at any given time is the one whose supply of knowledge and ability to use it is marginally better than anyone else's.

Data to Information to Knowledge to Wisdom

Industry has used automation for about 100 years to improve its business processes. Since the days of electromechanical punch card tabulators, there has been a continual evolution in understanding what business needs. In the 1950s and 1960s, business people talked about data acquisition, databases, and data management. In the 1970s and 1980s, they began to talk about information and information management, generally as the result of automated data analysis. Then in the past decade, business people started talking about knowledge bases, knowledge management, and knowledge delivery. The implication of the term knowledge was that information was provided in a form closer to the structures that humans use in cognitive processes—things like the rule bases of expert systems.

Recently, the term "wisdom" has been creeping into consciousness as a mature, proactive, response of a system to new conditions. Wisdom comes when skilled and knowledgeable people, acting with intuition and insight, process the company's entire experience base, all its explicit knowledge, and all its tacit knowledge.

We group three implementation substrategies together as knowledge processes (see Figure 6-4). Existing or potential markets stimulate knowledge processes by presenting challenges. "We could compete in the PC market in China if only we could sell a PC for the cost of a TV . . ." "If only we could deliver our products in two days instead of two weeks . . ." "If only we had a solution to . . ."

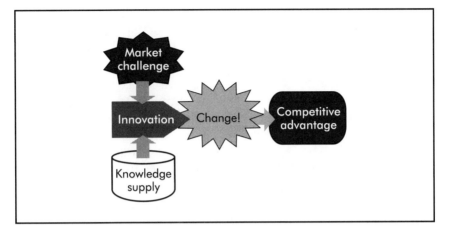

Figure 6-4. Three implementation substrategies grouped as knowledge processes.

"If only . . ." poses the challenge. The response is innovation, the process of putting together new and old knowledge to come up with a solution. Innovation depends on knowledge. "Ah ha!" does not occur in a vacuum. It occurs in a complex pattern recognition process when all the right pieces of knowledge literally jump—not fall—into place. There needs to be a supply of the right knowledge to which the innovator has easy access. Finally, any new solution will result in change, be it a product that forces the company to approach the market in a different way or a process that affects the company's internal operations. Unmanaged change can, and in many cases will, lead to destructive results.

Substrategy 2: Innovation

Innovation is the set of processes that companies use for creating solutions. Innovation includes the initial creativity that creates the solutions. It also includes the successful implementation of the solutions. Today, companies use innovation processes to improve organizational structure and business practices, technology used to develop and deliver products and services, and development of the products and services. In a lean company, continuous improvement demands a culture of continuous innovation.

Innovation is the way a company can keep ahead of, or at least differentiate itself, from competitors. Dell's use of the Internet for direct sales, beginning in 1996, shows the power of well-executed implementations of a succession of novel ideas. Dell's competitors have struggled to catch up with Dell's business model and achieve equally impressive results.

One innovation is not enough to sustain success. Dell started with a simple model that permitted individuals and small businesses to order directly using the Internet. Then, Dell expanded its model to provide direct on-line support for large customers, to link with related Internet-based businesses, and to provide customers with non-Dell branded products. Dell captured market share with one set of innovations, but its growth would have stalled out had it not followed up with additional innovations.

The lead a well-executed innovation gives a company can be squandered. IBM's introduction in 1981 of the first personal computer (PC) was a revolutionary success. It was the result of an innovative product design, an innovative outsourcing strategy, and the innovative creation of a business unit outside many of IBM's normal bureaucratic procedures. IBM's early PC organization pioneered many of the practices now associated with lean enterprises. The company's response to the PC's astounding success was to abandon the imperatives to maintain a technological advantage and build on the lean business unit. Instead, IBM delayed introduction of a more advanced successor to the PC and folded the independent business unit into a traditional divisional structure. That gave competitive clones a head start in the next round of competition. The clone manufacturers found cheaper ways to build on IBM's earlier architecture, and the market shifted to the lower price point. IBM's innovative, but higher-priced, PS/2 technology was not enough to regain market share.

Professor Clayton Christensen, has studied the difficulties that innovation can cause competitors. He suggests that a company will be most threatened by innovations it does not see coming, because they come from nontraditional competitors or incorporate radically different technologies or business models (Christensen 1997). These innovations cause the greatest disruptions in established business plans.

Managing innovation is not something to be left to serendipity. Instead, the company should structure its innovation processes to yield exploitable serendipitous results. It must look for and differentiate between incremental innovations and radically new approaches.

Substrategy 3: Knowledge Supply

Innovation cannot happen unless there is an adequate supply of knowledge of:

- market opportunity;
- product design, materials, and manufacturing processes;
- business processes;
- customers, partners, and suppliers;
- logistical support that links the enterprise and its customers.

This sea of knowledge must be filtered for the right knowledge the decision-maker needs to create a solution to a market opportunity, a technical difficulty, or a business issue.

Knowledge supply is a new concept introduced in the NGM Project. It borrows from the ideas of supply chain management and applies them to the relationships among industry, universities, schools, and associations (see Figure 6-5.) The goal is to rapidly provide the knowledge and talent needed to run businesses in a timely and cost effective manner. Knowledge supply is inherently lean, a pull process whose goal is Just-in-Time delivery of updated knowledge just before it is needed to solve problems.

One goal of knowledge supply is to generate new knowledge focused on meeting specific needs. The supply chain concept encourages continual communication—even to the point of forming knowledge partnerships. Such partnerships involve the knowledge users who identify the need for knowledge, the knowledge generators, and the knowledge deliverers. In concept, a knowledge supply chain accelerates use of the results of basic and applied research in innovative solutions needed for real tasks.

Another goal of the knowledge supply chain is to have available the educational instruments by which new and existing knowledge can be taught in a fashion that helps workers use knowledge quickly. Finally, a goal is to have in place the storage, filtering tools, and mechanisms that deliver the right knowledge from any source in

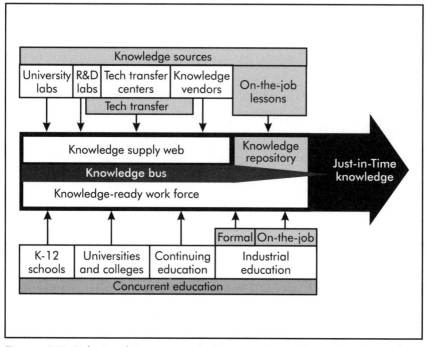

Figure 6-5. Relationships among industry, universities, schools, and associations leading to Just-in-Time knowledge supply.

the enterprise to any worker who needs it, when he needs it, and where he needs it leading to Just-in-Time knowledge supply.

Substrategy 4: Change Management

Innovation means that something new is created: a new product, a new process, or a new technology. Innovation inevitably means something is changed. Because something is changed, there is likely to be an impact that ripples across the entire enterprise. An enterprise can nurture change to minimize its costs, or mismanage change and incur very significant unnecessary costs. A wise company recognizes and manages the inevitability of change. An unwise one depends on luck to deal with change. Managing change in a lean company is so important that the authors have expanded on the concepts provided in the NGM Framework (see Chapter 7).

Strategy C: NGM Processes and Equipment— The Right Tools for the Right Jobs

The lean company will not make a commitment without optimizing chances of success. Although the company will have to take risks, it will seek to minimize them by using modeling and simulation, often coupled with agile and flexible manufacturing processes and equipment. These are two of the essentials required for competitive response to the market. They are two of the important implementation substrategies of the NGM Framework.

Substrategy 5: Pervasive Modeling and Simulation

A lean manufacturing enterprise is the sum of the large and small decisions made by people and so-called intelligent machines. A company's responsiveness ultimately depends on the speed and accuracy first of the decisions people make and then on the speed and accuracy with which they are turned into effective action. Modeling and simulation will become pervasive as an improved way of ensuring optimized decisions before costs accrue.

The vocabulary of the decision-making process in the lean company will be one of models and simulations. People in the company will ask: "Does the model say we can build the function into the product?" Alternatively, they will ask, "Have you modeled the ergonomics of customer use?" Others will ask, "Did you simulate the effects of changing the factory layout?" In the best of circumstances, someone will ask, "What is the optimum organization of the extended enterprise to produce this product?" A company will make countless decisions guided by the answers.

The goals of modeling and simulation are:

- To reduce the time to arrive at a decision. Computers can test alternative design concepts instead of having workers build physical prototypes. A computer graphics display can show flaws in processes rather than having employees find them by testing pilot implementations. Boeing's pioneering success in reducing the development time one full year by digitally prototyping the 777 demonstrates the value of this approach. So does BMW's more recent reduction of the ergonomic design of interiors for its latest vehicles by 10 months.

- To improve the quality of decisions. Modeling and simulation are in transition. They are used to translate esoteric, backroom applications of opaque mathematical and computational sciences into poorly understood descriptions of reality, yielding results that were advisory at best. Newer ones provide easily understood, dependable representations on which operational decisions can be based reliably.
- In the case of the Boeing 777, one can argue that customer satisfaction with the resultant product shows that the masses of decisions made through models were the right ones. Boeing invested greatly in developing the tools and the data to ensure that the models and simulations were accurate representations of reality. The returns have justified the investment, and have provided incentives within Boeing for even more widespread use of modeling and simulation.

As models and simulations become more accurate, their use will be extended to more and more areas of the lean company. They will make virtual production a reality, even for lower-value products. More and more production decisions will be based on modeling and simulation methods, rather than on build-and-test methods. Modeling and simulation tools will move from being the domain of technologists, to being tools for all involved in product realization, production, and business practices.

Substrategy 6: Agile and Flexible Manufacturing Processes and Equipment

Once the decision to act is made by knowledgeable people supported by accurate models and simulations, the company must take effective and responsive action quickly. That action will depend on the company having equipment and processes capable of minimizing costs and matching the needs of an ever-changing manufacturing environment.

Customers will ask the company's plants to provide simultaneously intermingled large and small lots. They will demand many standardized products at the same time they demand customized ones. A company will have to change plant layouts as workloads and product mixes change. Production lines and manufacturing cells must have built-in flexibility to accommodate processes that are changed on the fly. The ideal method is to make all changes with no overhead costs—no down time, no setup effort, and no waste of materials. The ideal is not yet reachable with today's technologies, although it may be realizable with technologies expected to become available over the next 25 years (Committee on Visionary Manufacturing Challenges 1998).

Much of the needed flexibility will come from reconfigurable, scalable, and cost-effective manufacturing processes and equipment. Companies will replace machines having static control systems designed for a limited scope of application. Instead, they will use equipment having programmable controllers that will open the scope of applications to unforeseen demands. Many companies already are retrofitting existing machines with controllers to do jobs never envisioned when the machines were first built years, even decades, ago.

Similarly, companies will employ tooling designed and built to be easily changeable and reconfigurable to quickly accommodate changes in the shapes of other manufactured parts. Computers will control the resetting, providing capability for changing the configuration in real time.

Manufacturing execution systems will support flexible, model-based, processes. In these, the controllers of a variety of machines, perhaps in several manufacturing cells, may be programmed simultaneously for specific product runs. See Figure 6-6, which shows a typical integrated factory control system with intelligent closed-loop controllers.

One lesson of the Toyota Production System and other lean manufacturing initiatives is that it costs less in time and money when a company gets it right the first time. It is less expensive to make sure each process step gives a high-quality result than it is to inspect results, and rework faulty results, during and at the end of the process.

Getting things right requires in-process measurement, analysis, and corrective action. More equipment is being built to include in-process measurement capabilities and feedback loops for continually adjusting and re-adjusting machine settings—poka-yoke, in the lean vocabulary. Analysis requires either human intervention or a control system able to make comparisons against

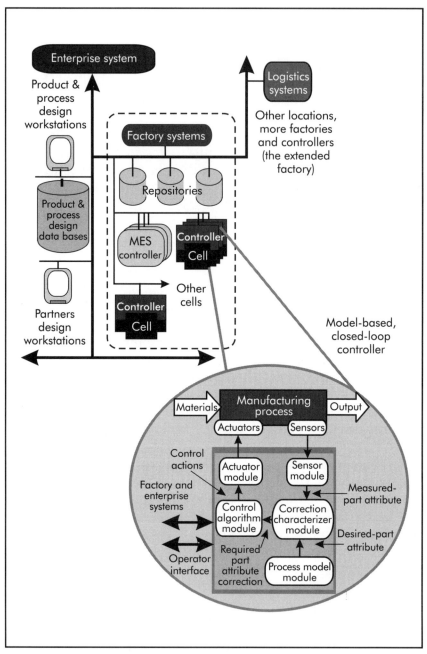

Figure 6-6. Typical integrated factory control system with intelligent closed-loop controllers.

standards predicted by models developed during the design phase. In most cases of discrete manufacturing, people take the corrective actions, but in some cases, as in continuous process manufacturing, adaptive machines make the changes needed to bring processes back into their specified tolerance band.

In time, as models and simulations become more accurate, companies will use them to guide real-time changes in processes. Data from real processes will be merged with data generated by models to simulate modified processes, ensuring that they meet the desired quality standard before they are implemented. Once implemented, the models and simulations will form the standard for control actions.

Strategy D: Integrating the Extended Enterprise

The CASA/SME New Manufacturing Enterprise Wheel (see Figure 6-7) is a response to the need to view the manufacturing company as an integrated enterprise. The current Wheel is a graphical representation of the third generation of integration models. Successive versions have moved from a systems approach to computer-aided manufacturing (CAM) to the factory automation of computer-integrated manufacturing (CIM). The latest version provides an integrated view of the entire enterprise (Computer and Automated Systems Association of SME 1993).

Older versions of the manufacturing enterprise wheel looked primarily at automation and integration inside the company. The newest version looks outside as well and describes six fundamental elements for competitive manufacturing:

1. The central role of the customer and evolving customer need.
2. The role of people and teamwork in the organization.
3. The revolutionary impact of a shared knowledge and systems to support people and processes.
4. Key processes from product definition through manufacturing and customer support.
5. Enterprise resources (inputs) and responsibilities (outputs).
6. The manufacturing infrastructure, which includes customers and their needs, suppliers, competitors, prospective workers, distributors, natural resources, financial markets, governments, and educational and research institutions.

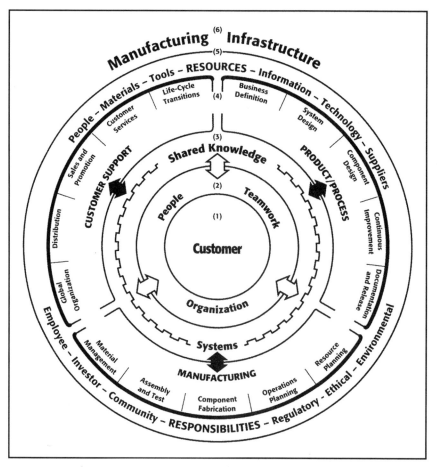

Figure 6-7. The CASA/SME New Manufacturing Enterprise Wheel.

The NGM Framework for Action amplifies the systematic view of integration. In the Framework, four implementation substrategies, numbered 7 through 10, tie people, knowledge, and equipment and processes together. Substrategy 7 is the mega-process that spans the product life cycle. Given that few companies can or would want to support every aspect of the product life cyle, RPPR is a mega-process spread over an extended enterprise and requires extended enterprise collaboration. The collaboration of teams or work units in the extended enterprise requires enterprise integration (see Figure 6-8).

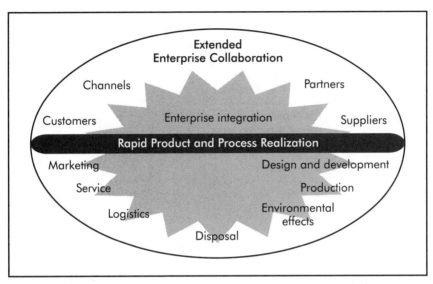

Figure 6-8. The collaboration of teams or work units in the extended enterprise.

The information systems and technologies that make modern enterprise integration possible are described in the implementation substrategy for adaptive, responsive information systems.

Substrategy 7: Rapid Product and Process Realization

The way a company makes a profit is by supplying goods, or combinations of goods and services, to customers who want their value so strongly that they are willing to pay prices high enough to include a satisfactory profit margin. Rapid Product and Process Realization is the collective name for processes that result from:

- integration of customer needs and wants;
- a systematic Integrated Product and Process Development (IPPD) methodology;
- cross-functional integrated product teams;
- and a computer-integrated environment.

The key to the success of a lean company is getting RPPR right. IPPD is so important that it is one of the Lean Enterprise Model's overarching lean practices—see Chapter 4. RPPR (see Figure 6-9) is a superset of IPPD. RPPR begins with market conceptualization

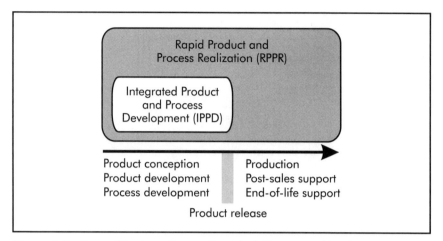

Figure 6-9. One of the Lean Enterprise Model's overarching lean practices.

of a product and extends to delivery of the product to the market, and beyond that through ownership, use, and final disposal. IPPD deals specifically with product and process development, including life cycle considerations. RPPR goes further by incorporating post-sales processes within the company's integrated systems. There is an emerging understanding that the delivery of the product does not end the manufacturing company's involvement. The company has responsibilities, potential liabilities, costs, and opportunities for profit that extend through final disposal of the product at the end of its useful life.

RPPR is accomplished by including, in a highly concurrent manner, all stakeholders in design, development, manufacturing processes, maintenance, and customer support. The stakeholders should be involved from concept development through planning for product disposition. The stakeholders may include investors interested in maximizing returns on their investments and financial organizations that may finance the customers' purchases.

Integrated Product and Process Development (IPPD) provides a structure for cross-functional communications and knowledge-filled decision-making. IPPD facilitates parallel product and process development. IPPD is intended to minimize the time and effort needed to bring a product to market. It is intended to create an overall product solution faster than would be achieved with the use of the traditional "design it and then figure out how to build it" approach. The goal is to find the best solutions, make the best decisions, and take the best actions, in the timeliest way throughout the development cycle. These decisions must take into consideration all the functions performed throughout the product life cycle.

There are many ways to structure IPPD. The key is to make the best decisions in a timely way, with transparency so that all can understand why the decisions were made, and with accountability. Accountability is needed for many reasons including:

- for the commitment implied by decisions made within a group;
- to reward the decisions and actions contributing to product success;
- to create an audit trail to facilitate learning from failure.

The structure should include defined prerequisites for commitment on product development, major product and process design decisions, and for entry into production. The structure should capture the design experience in ways that can be translated into useful knowledge repositories. The design knowledge will be used as the basis not only for the production processes, but also for maintenance and user documentation.

A key for the lean company will be accurate and timely communication that translates user wants into valued products. One way to structure communication for effective IPPD is to use Quality Function Deployment (QFD), see Figure 6-10, a popular technique to force the customer's view of quality into product and process design (Shapiro 1994). QFD uses a sequence of matrices to learn what the customer thinks is important and to translate that into design and manufacturing processes. The rows of the matrix are the "whats"—the intended results. The columns are the "hows"—the ways to achieve the intended results. At the intersections of the rows and columns is an assessment of the degree of influence a "how" has in achieving a specific "what."

For example, the first matrix in the QFD sequence shown in Figure 6-10 relates the customer's requirements of the product, usually stated in qualitative, user-oriented terms, then translated to quantitative technical characteristics. A qualitative statement, "I want good, maybe not great, performance in my next car," is

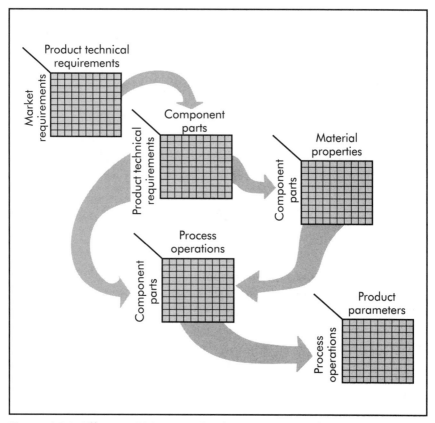

Figure 6-10. Effective IPPD using Quality Function Deployment (QFD).

translated into "0 to 60 mph in 9.5 seconds." "I do a lot of passing on two lane roads" becomes "45 to 65 mph in 4 seconds."

Auxiliary information can be important. If the customer thinks the fit and finish of the car's door handle is important, then the designer may choose a cast and coated handle rather than a cheaper stamped one. Information on preferences like this can be carried in rows and used as inputs to prioritization of the customers' wishes, technologies and materials to be used, and production processes to be employed.

It is important to listen to the voice of the customer, especially on matters dealing with functionality trade-off, ergonomics, and economics of acquisition and operation. Boeing found that including customers on the design teams of the 777 greatly reduced rework.

It is just as important to hear the voice of another set of customers—the tool designers, operators, assemblers, and others who have the responsibility to make the processes work. It makes no sense to design a spiffy new product if the processes are so clumsy that workers cannot produce the product efficiently, reliably, and with high quality. As the successive QFD matrices are used to translate customer needs into the specifics of how the product will be made, the inputs from the production work force may force iteration. The costs of meeting the specific needs may be greatly reduced if they are slightly modified so they can use less costly processes.

Essential elements of IPPD. Within the structure of IPPD (see Figure 6-11) the first essential element is an accurate understanding of the customers' needs and requirements, validated with the customers' key operating units and staff, and with the customers' financial backers. Complementing this knowledge is an understanding of competitors' offerings to meet these needs.

The first step in delivering a profitable product is to understand customer requirements so the company can build a product that gives the customers more value than the competition does. The product must give enough value to justify customers paying

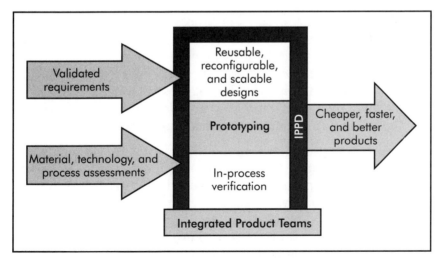

Figure 6-11. All of the essential elements of IPPD are required for sustained success.

its cost and a good profit margin. This requires an up-to-date knowledge of relevant technologies—their state of readiness, their costs, and their special requirements. A hundred years ago, an individual mechanic could understand and use the technologies needed to build an automobile, or even an airplane. The repertoire of materials was equally limited. For decades, new technologies and materials crept slowly into products and processes. However, today the waves of change in technology and materials can sweep products on or off the market in weeks.

Companies need to make two kinds of assessments. First, the company needs to assess the technologies, materials, and processes that it uses now or can predict will become important. These are part of the company's technology portfolio, and should be the subject of continuous assessment within a tracking function in the company's research and development organizations. It is especially insightful to understand the processes the competition is using. Second, other technologies and materials may emerge unexpectedly and require ad hoc assessments. At these times, immediate access to expert knowledge sources becomes important.

IPPD includes re-use of successful designs that are easily reconfigurable for new applications. The goal is to develop families of designs that can be quickly modified for customizing needs. The economics of design dictate the use of designs that are:

- reusable in many product or process applications;
- parameterized and scalable so their technical attributes can be sized appropriately to the need;
- adaptable to differing materials and technologies so the designs do not inhibit use of less expensive or better processes;
- modular and reconfigurable, with defined interfaces, to provide flexibility in production and encourage interchangeability.

Today, innovation is at a premium, but not for its own sake. Innovation is important to differentiate products. It is important for profitable new products and less costly processes. It is wasteful of time and creative talent to design a part specifically for each product variation if its function is found in most of a company's product variations. Better to use the designer's time and creativity on parts that will be unique, or that are subject to more than normal wear, or which otherwise give an important, differentiating value for the customer. Accomplishing this requires prototyping of products, processes, and systems, with emphasis on so-called virtual prototypes constructed through computer modeling and simulation, augmented by rapid prototyping technology.

A goal of the lean company should be to first freeze the design as soon as it has reached the established benchmark of maturity and then minimize engineering changes after initial design release. Every engineering change order incurs extra costs that get larger the closer the product is to release for manufacture. Better to get the design right the first time using models and simulations for digital prototyping.

Over time, the lean company will create virtual factories (see Figure 6-12). A myriad of design decisions will be made, integrated, and shown to work before any physical process is put in place on the floor or before a new physical factory is built.

In-process verification, both of IPPD and of the developed processes, should be completed to detect quality defects before incurring costly and time-consuming fixes. Lean demands first-time quality. It requires that no time is wasted between production start-up, production, and delivery, and that no costs are incurred by allowing the process to create scrap or rework. Much of quality can be designed in, but tools wear, materials have flaws, processes can drift, and data is corrupted. Even the best-designed processes can fail in many ways.

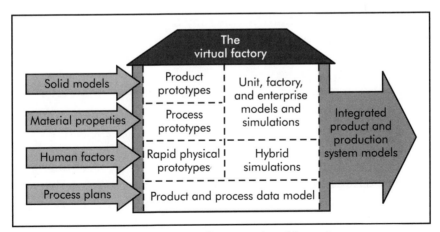

Figure 6-12. The lean company will create virtual factories.

Instrumentation designed into critical manufacturing processes can make measurements that can drive adjustments in real-time. Measurements of real processes also can be used:

- as inputs to simulations that can validate, or invalidate, the utility of a planned process that is to be integrated with the real ones;
- to provide realistic inputs for operator-training simulators;
- as inputs to model-based control systems used to diagnose problems and initiate corrective actions.

Another aspect of in-process verification is in-use monitoring. Smart products that have built-in diagnostics are becoming common. For many years, railroads have monitored bearings on rail cars and over-the-road transport companies have monitored the on-road performance of their tractors. General Motors is advertising its On-Star™ product in which the car automatically notifies a GM service center if it has suffered a catastrophic event. Another example is the instrumentation in an aircraft that enables the cockpit crew to signal ahead what part needs to be replaced to minimize delays at that stop.

Integrated Product Teams (IPTs) include all the relevant stakeholders, including, possibly, customers, operations personnel, and financial stakeholders so that at any point in RPPR the right knowledge and skills are available and used.

The QFD model provides a guide for staffing the IPTs. Who are the right people to contribute to the solutions of issues posed in any given matrix? Unless the company is a small one, the chances are that different sets of people would participate in each exercise. A core team would consist of:

- the project manager,
- the chief product designer,
- the chief process designer,
- the production manager,
- the chief tool designer,
- the quality manager,
- and the individual responsible for customer support.

These may be the only people to participate in all the QFD-mediated discussions. Experts may be brought in when the discussions require knowledge that is more detailed.

The IPT needs continuity. The core team should have responsibility and accountability for the product until launch, and even after launch until service personnel can maintain the product unaided.

Often financial stakeholders are not heard until late in the development process. Since an essential aspect of the modern manufacturing company's success is the confidence that the financial stakeholders have in the company's business plan, it is best to involve them in IPTs early in the process. Financial trade-offs may be needed for the development of products that represent a major departure from existing product lines, or introduction of "you-bet-your-company" processes. When trade-offs must be made, the financial community can provide guidance to minimize financial risks and convey confidence to the investors.

Substrategy 8: Extended Enterprise Collaboration

Modern commerce is a complex endeavor. Many different kinds of knowledge and skill must be combined in the RPPR process. Few companies can afford the cost or time to build and maintain all the knowledge and all the skills they need. To produce, distribute, and service even a moderately complicated product to serve global markets—say, cellular phones that include advanced materials, micro-electronics, and mechanical actuators in rugged packaging—may be beyond the competencies of any one company. Instead, companies seek alliances of one form or another to collaborate with or to procure from companies that have specialized expertise. The result is a formal or informal collaborative extended enterprise. The progression toward extended enterprises is shown in Figure 6-13.

A common form of the extended enterprise is the managed supply chain. This form has gained prominence through the efforts of major manufacturers to establish dependable relationships with groups of companies who can be relied upon to contribute expertise and deliver high-quality products and services.

The responsiveness of the extended enterprise depends on the quality of the collaboration among the partners. Extended enterprise collaboration is the seamless integration of a group of stakeholders who create and support a timely and cost-effective service

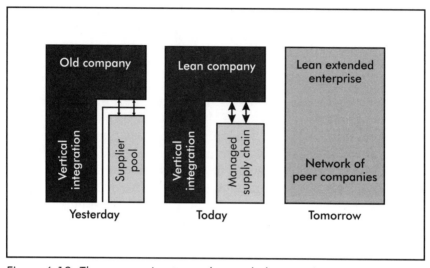

Figure 6-13. The progression toward extended enterprises.

or product. The stakeholders typically include customers, both as buyers and as the end-users and the first line of maintenance. They also include suppliers, service providers, and the internal and external investors who finance the development and purchase of the product. The stakeholders may include the education community as a resource for applied research and as a medium of knowledge delivery. Stakeholders may also include government agencies that provide new technology or impose regulatory constraints.

In the extended enterprise, one company's systems must integrate with those of the partnering companies. The extended enterprise may include shared production tasks, say basic assembly processes in a factory in China and a finishing process in Belgium. In such cases, there must be compatibility of manufacturing systems. A company's systems are inevitably a reflection of the company's culture. Each company in an extended enterprise must have a rudimentary understanding of the other company's cultures. Just as inevitably, the extended enterprise will develop its own unique culture. That culture may reflect for good or ill, back into the partners.

The partnerships of collaborative extended enterprise collaboration should exhibit the following qualities (Block 1993):

- Purpose—each partner has a clear understanding of its own purpose and then engages in sufficient dialogue with the other partners to gain a clear understanding of their common objective.
- The right to say no—each partner feels free to disagree with prevailing ideas, but also feels the obligation to offer better ones.
- Joint accountability—each partner assumes responsibility for the enterprise's outcomes and for the current situation. The outcomes and quality of cooperation within a unit are everyone's responsibility.
- Honesty and openness—each partner is honest. Each is willing to share all the information needed to achieve the common purpose with the others. Similarly, each partner is willing to accept the information and suggestions the others provide.
- Common standards—partners should adhere to a common set of standards used in all of the extended enterprise's business and manufacturing systems.
- Ethics—to respond competitively, partners in modern extended enterprises must trust one another. The basis for trust is ethics. Every company has a set of ethics: expressed, implicit, or both. The company uses its ethics to guide its behavior and relationships with others. The ethics are part of a shared corporate culture. Companies expect workers to behave in a way consistent with those ethics. An employee's personal ethics may not be the same as the company's, even if he or she is comfortable with them. Moreover, a company's ethics are likely not the same, in detail, as those of the company down the street. The behavior of a company, derived from its ethics, almost surely will differ from what its European, Asian, or African partners regard as ethical behaviors. To the extent that ethics are shared, though, they provide an axiomatic basis for trust and for lean behaviors within the extended enterprise.

The world's dominant ethical systems have a minimal set of common rules which, when applied to business, say:

- Each company is to avoid doing things that are harmful to others;

- Each company is to be accorded the respect due an autonomous peer;
- If an autonomous company freely enters an agreement, the company is ethically bound to honor it;
- Lying is unacceptable and no company is ethically permitted to lie.

These principles are the minimum to govern the ethical behavior of companies that are operating within free market economies (Quinn and Jones 1995). Some companies add these additional principles:

- A company should promote the well-being of others.
- A company should treat others fairly and equitably.

Obviously, it is easier to build trust relationships among partners who subscribe to all six principles.

You need to be able to establish trust quickly if you and your partners are going to address market opportunities in a timely manner. You need to create a vision for your company's role in the collaborative extended enterprise. You need to agree with your partners on a common set of goals and metrics of success. You need a shared risk/reward agreement.

Ideally, when you give partners in an extended enterprise your trust, you do so because they adhere to a common set of ethical business practices. Such a set of practices, even if arrived at by different culturally affected reasoning mechanisms, can define an ethic for the extended enterprise's corporate culture. When, because of differing societal cultures or other reasons, the partners do not share a common ethic, each of the partners' sets of ethics needs to be articulated so each knows what it can expect from the others.

An understood set of ethics is just a starting point for trust. Trust is iterative. It is built through experience. A company builds the trust of its partners depending on its performance across seven dimensions (NGM Project 1997):

1. Accountability—each partner has a specific role in the extended enterprise, a role that is well defined, understandable, and measurable for all to see.

2. Currency—each partner makes the current state of its activities relative to the extended enterprise visible for the other partners and has the current state of the extended enterprise available to it. Each partner bases its commitments and efforts on a truthful rendering of the current state.
3. Accessibility—each partner is accessible quickly, at the convenience of the other partners.
4. Accuracy—each partner's data, information, and knowledge are factually correct.
5. Completeness—each partner's input to the extended enterprise includes all the necessary information, including context, assumptions, and qualifiers to allow the other partners to understand the input in the context of their own activities.
6. Integrity—each partner's input is uncorrupted with irrelevant matter or by information motivated by hidden purposes.
7. Security—each partner respects the property and interests of the other partners.

If, as measured by these dimensions of trust, a company meets its commitments fully and reliably, then others will consider it trustworthy.

Substrategies 9 and 10: Enterprise Integration Using Adaptive, Responsive Information Systems

Enterprise integration is defined as connecting and combining the people, processes, systems, and technologies of the extended enterprise to assure that the right information is available at the right location, with the right resources, at the right time. It comprises all the activities necessary to ensure that, whether operating as an independent unit or as a part of an extended enterprise, a company can execute RPPR as a coordinated whole.

There are two important aspects of enterprise integration including integrated information systems and integration of people into systems.

Integrated information systems focus on bits and bytes, the technological issues of information acquisition, transport, storage, and delivery. The lean company needs adaptive, responsive, and transparent information systems modeled on the existing technologies that support the Internet and other networked systems. These systems can be reshaped dynamically to meet new needs. New functions can be added, and others replaced, without interrupting the system. In the best of circumstances, data flows are automatically redirected as functions are added.

Nirvana is interoperability, with no costs (other than the cost of the added functionality) and no down time. Nirvana has not been achieved, yet. Web-based, modular enterprise resource planning (ERP) functionality and application service providers (ASPs) model the future of the needed systems.

Information systems that are adaptive, responsive, seamless, and transparent are achieved by:

- establishing high-speed communication links, with bandwidth that can scale for future needs, using standard protocols;
- establishing company-wide systems architecture, and countrywide, uniform standards for data interfaces;
- creating software function modules that can reside on servers anywhere on a global network and that can be readily configured or reconfigured into new systems using standardized data interfaces. The system architecture should be such that every user has access to the needed data almost immediately after the need has been articulated;
- incorporating data management tools to ensure the compatibility of data, so that the entire enterprise is working with consistent descriptions of products, processes, and operations results;
- facilitating access by customers, on the one hand, and by suppliers, on the other, as much as is consistent with the company's security and integrity requirements;
- developing a framework or infrastructure that allows individual users—through a security shield of authorizations—to easily create, modify, store, access, and execute individual modules and configured systems.

Integration of people into systems is the second important aspect of enterprise integration within the company's systems. This effort is deeper than digital systems integration. It is the integration that requires people to understand common purposes and goals, have behavior toward one another that is tacitly understood and accepted as trustworthy, and use all their intellectual powers to achieve the enterprise's objectives. This integration recognizes that individuals are complicated, idiosyncratic mixes of cognitive processes and muscles.

A lean company will take into account risks created by people who are not well integrated into its systems. The effects of what a worker does in Dacca may ripple across oceans and result in the failure of a crucial decision made by a plant manager in Milan. A decision made in Terre Haute, couched in terms of a U.S. company's culture, may lead to disaster if it is misinterpreted by a peer manager in the Ukrainian culture of a plant in Kharkov. Enterprise integration is the tricky business of getting people to trust one another, understand one another, and work together under the stresses of modern life and the pressures of a common competitive goal.

SUMMARY

Transformation to a lean, 21st Century company requires two things. First, it requires a lean culture in which people make decisions in accordance with lean principles and practices. The Lean Enterprise Model is one checklist that can focus people's attention on building a lean culture.

Second, transformation requires action. Transformation is a slow process that happens as people make their decisions. The decisions should lead to actions that are lean. However, that is not good enough. The actions should be specifically directed toward meeting corporate goals. The NGM Framework for Action, with its four essential operational strategies—people, knowledge, processes and equipment, and integration—provides an integrated representation of actions that might be taken.

EXERCISES

1. Consider the technological changes you have encountered since you started thinking about your career. What changes do you anticipate before you retire? How will you keep abreast of and use those changes?

2. Your company faces the same technological challenges. How well prepared is it to meet them? What strategies should it implement to stay competitive?

3. How would you go about finding the right people with the right knowledge and the right skills to fill the job openings in your company? Recognizing that you will be introducing new materials and processes all the time, what would you do to keep your employees up to date?

4. Assume your company is a manufacturer with a line of products that has been very profitable. Suddenly you find your market share dropping in favor of a previously unknown competitor. What might have prompted the competitor to enter the market?

REFERENCES

Block, Peter. 1993. *Stewardship: Choosing Service over Self-Interest*. San Francisco, CA: Berrett-Koehler.

Christensen, Clayton M. 1997. *The Innovator's Dilemma: When New Technologies Cause Great Firms to Fail*. Boston, MA: Harvard Business School Press.

Committee on Visionary Manufacturing Challenges for 2020. 1998. Washington, D.C.: National Academy Press.

Computer and Automated Systems Association of the Society of Manufacturing Engineers 1993. CASA/SME New Manufacturing Enterprise Wheel. Dearborn, MI: Society of Manufacturing Engineers.

Drucker, Peter. 1999. *Management Challenges for the 21st Century*. New York: HarperCollins Publishers, Inc.

Jordan, James A. Jr., and Michel, Frederick J. 2000. *Next Generation Manufacturing: Techniques and Methods*. New York: John Wiley & Sons, Inc.

Kransdorff, Arnold. 1998. *Corporate Amnesia: Keeping Know-how in the Company*. Boston, MA: Butterworth-Heineman.

NGM Project. 1997. "Next Generation Manufacturing: Framework for Action." Bethlehem, PA: Agility Forum.

Quinn, Denis P., and Jones, Thomas M. 1995. "An Agent Morality View of Business Policy." *Academy of Management Review*, vol. 20. January.

Shapiro, Larry M. 1994. *Advanced QFD: Linking Technology to Market and Company Needs*. New York: John Wiley & Sons, Inc.

Chapter Seven

Transformation by Change Initiatives

Lean companies are not wished or willed into existence. Transformation to a lean company occurs through a series of systematic actions called *change initiatives*. Some are massive, involving every person in the enterprise. Others are smaller, involving only people in individual work units. Every change initiative takes time and carries costs. Some of the costs are monetary. There may be need for investments in equipment, in education, or in hiring people. Some of the costs are people's time and attention—implementing change takes time and may divert attention from other opportunities. Some of the costs are psychological. The change may force employees to think of themselves, their customers, and their co-workers in unfamiliar ways.

When a company enters transformation, people will suggest many change initiatives based on their particular responsibilities and points of view. A strong, innovative, work force will suggest many more initiatives than the company can absorb, unless the initiatives are shaped into a coherent enterprise-wide plan and then prioritized. The authors' purpose in this book is to help with the process of transformation into a lean company and with prioritization of investments in change initiatives.

Change happens

In this chapter, the authors discuss change in general, not necessarily limiting it to changes directly targeted on transformation to a lean company. Ultimately any lean initiative will compete for resources with change initiatives motivated by other strategies.

Change initiatives are often the foreseeable results of innovations. Change can be structured as an orderly process when an innovation is an informed and knowledgeable response to a defined cultural imperative—as with lean. It can be an orderly response to changing market conditions, to a changing global environment, or to the introduction of new technology.

However, change often happens in another, less orderly, way. When things are going badly—say product designs do not meet functional requirements, customers are unhappy with product quality, or costs are unexpectedly high—people may say, "Something's got to change!" So a company targets what it thinks is the problem, usually something obvious, and changes it. It fires the product designer and hires another. Or the company institutes a high-visibility quality program. Or it orders an across the board 10% reduction in expenditures. It acts quickly to make a change.

The change process can be viewed as one more process that should be lean. One mark of a lean company is its ability to make changes quickly with minimum costs. The lean company needs a lean "change culture." A systematic methodology to introduce and accept change into the organization should be embedded in this culture. A company gains competitive advantage if it can incorporate lean principles and practices as it manages change proactively, at the same time minimizing negative effects on existing operations.

Change happens. Managers can stand back and hope they can muddle through to a successful end. However, this is less and less likely in an age of growing complexity. Companies need to view change as something to understand, shape, and manage intentionally. Managing change means:

- prioritizing changes the company will undertake—always with an emphasis on meeting the company's strategic vision and goals;
- recognizing that a change may affect other planned changes, coordinating changes so the effect of one change on another is constructive;
- minimizing destabilizing effects on internal operations and external relationships.

This chapter looks at two aspects of the way change happens in companies. In the next section, the authors will consider many different ways to look at change. The following section describes a corporate change process for lean companies. The authors close with a look at the special case of change via merger or acquisition.

WHAT IS CHANGE?

There are many ways in which to think about change. The NGM Project described the dimensions of change from various points of view (Jordan and Michel 2000). In this book, the authors limit discussion to a review of some experiential characteristics of change.

Many people dislike change. Change is a very common, very human phenomenon—and most humans do not like it. Some children approach change with a joyful sense of adventure. Most adults are more cautious; they have scar tissue from uninvited changes for which they were unprepared. Some people do choose to live in an environment of change; they have a sense of ownership, even control, over the unknown. However, most people view change—especially if it is imposed on them—as a burden to be avoided. It is a disruption. It causes extra work. People usually see it as unsettling, risky, and unrewarding. People on the factory floor are particularly sensitive to changes, since changes often affect shipping schedules, something that is anathema to operations people.

People need to become comfortable with change—both with specifics of particular changes that affect them and with the idea that they live in a constantly changing world. This is an educational process. The more people know, the more comfortable they can be —unless, of course, they feel threatened by change and are unable to find a way to accommodate to it.

Continuous education is a powerful way to reinforce understanding of change as continuous, inevitable, and perhaps, as children know, even fun. There is a practical need for employees to expand their personal knowledge of the new technologies and business processes a company uses. The more employees know, the better able they will be to maintain and grow their long-term employability.

Change management should focus on:

- the problems to be solved and need for solutions;
- the need for creativity and collaboration to find the best solutions;
- the personal rewards and opportunities that can come from change.

Most employees want to contribute to their company's success and will participate proactively in the change process when they understand it to be in the company's, and their own, best interests.

A change is a process, not an event, or a product. Each change is a process—a transformation from the present state to the future one. Every change requires planning, preparation, development, implementation, acceptance, and evaluation. Each change should be accompanied by a process plan crafted to ensure that the change achieves its goal with minimum organizational disruption and costs, and maximum effectiveness.

Change always takes time. In the 21st Century, time is likely to be more valuable than money. A major risk in today's fast moving, competitive environment is that a change will not be in place in time to be effective. A timely change may provide strong competitive advantage; a delayed change may result in a window of opportunity lost forever.

Often change takes more time than first estimated. There are many reasons for this. Any change is a move into the unknown, maybe just a small step, but often a leap. Sometimes development of the components of change and their integration into a system takes additional time. Often, initiators of change underestimate the psychological impact and the time it takes employees to internalize change.

Any change, large or small, has costs

Any change, large or small, has costs. At the end of the day, the decision to make a change should be based on achieving reasonable and foreseeable benefits that outweigh costs, factoring in risks. Chapter 10 describes the many categories of cost and risk.

Not all change is good! Those critics of a change initiative may be right! There is always some risk that a change will prove ineffective, or worse. It is important to identify failure as quickly as possible in the change process and adjust to it. It makes no sense to make further investments of time and resources if a change initiative cannot succeed. Implementation of an unproductive change may result in disastrous effects on the organization, no matter how much a company has invested in the change. However, change initiators can learn from a failed initiative if they understand the reasons why it failed.

Most of the change initiatives companies undertake are so complicated that they involve many steps. The design of a change initiative should be similar to a good product design, modular with well-specified interfaces between modules. We call those modules *chunks*. The change project should be viewed as one more project to be managed, with timelines, milestones, resource allocation, tracking, and periodic reviews.

Where possible, the change project should lead to generation of early and intermediate results. Early results:

- if positive, demonstrate that the project is on schedule, delivering on commitments made to the company, which leads to confidence on the part of the change project team, the organization, and its executive leadership that the change is on track;
- can illuminate the need for additional refinement, either in the completed module or in work yet to be completed;
- in rare cases, may demonstrate that the change was a bad idea—a change that seemed so promising may prove to be the wrong solution—killing the effort early on saves the company money and people a demoralizing experience.

Each chunk should be measurable and be measured so that its effectiveness is validated before it is integrated into the rest of the change initiative. The project plan for the change initiative should include checkpoints at significant milestones in development or implementation of each chunk. When the initiative has intermediate results—for example, when implementation of a chunk leads to a different way employees work—effects should be noted, measured, and evaluated. Even when intermediate results are not part of the plan, there should be measurements to permit in-process verification against the project plan.

Change has side effects. Even when change mimics the best practices of other companies, a change initiative made in any given company is likely to have idiosyncratic results. Some unpredicted effects may prove beneficial, others less so.

Change has side effects

For example, in the 1970s IBM developed VNET, its internal network analogous in many respects to the Internet, so that product developers could share design data. The motivation was a straightforward engineering solution to a product development need. The capabilities of the network, however, led to profound, but unforeseen, changes in business processes and systems that provided IBM with unpredicted competitive advantages. Side effects can be less benign. For example, Federal Express implemented new (to FedEx) schedule-optimization software. The change was very successful in optimizing aircraft utilization, but had such an adverse impact on FedEx's pilots that they threatened to strike. FedEx abandoned use of the scheduling program until more reasonable—from the point of view of the crews—constraints were imposed.

THE UPS AND DOWNS OF A CHANGE

Transformation to a lean 21st Century company will be the cumulative result of many, many tactical changes. Tactical changes may be planned, systematically, to achieve strategic transformation. Alternatively, people may autonomously respond to strategic vision and initiate tactical changes. Either way, tactical changes should be undertaken deliberately with an understanding of the time line of a change initiative. Change initiatives have life cycles analogous in many ways to product life cycles (see Figure 7-1).

Suppose the company perceives an opportunity, or a challenge, or a threat, or some other problem. Someone comes up with a good idea: "If we change such-and-such, we'll profit from the opportunity, or meet the challenge, or blunt the threat, or solve the problem. We'll win." In the enthusiasm of the moment, people focus on the positives. They tend to build optimistic expectations into change.

The creative burst of energy should lead to a proposal, one that presents the expected value of the change. It should describe how to implement the change. It should consider costs and risks associated with the change. The proposal should be thorough enough to build sufficient confidence in the change process to result in a commitment.

People are inclined to exaggerate and follow fads. Often what starts as a realistic set of expectations is inflated beyond credibility. Sometimes, the group with the idea claims more for it than is

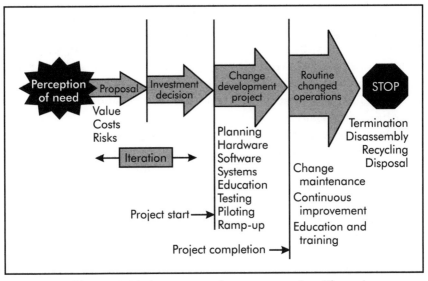

Figure 7-1. Change initiatives are analogous to product life cycles.

warranted. That is a natural response. They are so focused on the problem at hand that they do not realize all the complexities that lie between a company and its goals. Sometimes uncritical adherents grab hold of the idea and trumpet it. The rush to hard automation in the 1970s, to artificial intelligence solutions for knowledge delivery in the '80s, to robotics in the '70s and early '90s, and the recent rush to e-commerce all set high expectations. When expectations are not met, great disappointment sets in and the mood turns pessimistic.

Even when a company manages expectations realistically, negatives emerge as the change is developed and implemented. Some people always see the glass half-empty rather than half-full. They start pointing out both perceived flaws in the change vision and possible negative side effects. Attitudes toward the change become more pessimistic.

Inevitably, some flaws appear in the development and implementation of a change initiative. Technologies do not work quite the way the book, or the salesman, says. The work probably takes longer than hoped. Fine-tuning is needed in the implementation. If people tend to be overly optimistic when they plunge into a change, they also tend to be overly pessimistic when they run into problems. A good change leader listens to negative concerns and evaluates their validity and possible impact on the project. He or she then responds to them firmly and moves ahead with courage. Strong and consistent leadership is needed to keep the change team stable and focused. This is a time for the leadership team to be confidently visible.

Finally, a change is implemented. It is fully implemented when a company has gone through the learning curve, and the pain of doing things differently has faded into comfort with new routine modes of operation. It is well worth the effort then to look back and celebrate successful results. Moreover, it is worth reminding all in the company that they will be called on repeatedly to accomplish more changes. There will come a time, inevitably, when a particular change becomes irrelevant to the newest realities of business. Then, it is time to let go of that creative idea and move to the next change.

THE CHANGE PROCESS FOR THE LEAN COMPANY

Change happens all the time, and so does the need to manage the change process. One change initiative is hardly implemented before the next begins. The rate of change is accelerating. To respond effectively, the lean company must have a robust change process—one that itself is lean and yields quick results. (See Figure 7-2.) The process should give the company the ability to sustain continuous change and to respond to calls for both dramatic and small changes. The change management process should be an extension of ideas of proactive continuous improvement.

1. Recognize the Need to Change

A company needs to anticipate actively or at least detect quickly the need to make changes in its business. A company must watch for threats to its business plans from all quarters (Grove 1999). Company executives can see the need for change clearly if there is a sudden negative trend in strategic measurements. Companies that are in financial trouble quickly understand the need for change. Nevertheless, even if a company is enjoying success, it

Figure 7-2. A lean company must have a robust change process.

should be wary. Successful companies often are blind to innovations that undermine the market, technology, and business factors that generated their success in the first place. Today's model for success may be obsolete tonight—and certainly will be obsolete before its creators retire.

Innovations that drive changes are divided into two types (Christensen 1997). There are *sustaining innovations*—the stream of improvements in existing technologies, processes, and techniques that can sustain a company's leadership in pursuing its established business model. There also are *disruptive innovations*—often not apparent until they disrupt the status quo. These innovations create entirely different business models. Disruptive innovations are those likely to threaten a company, and therefore they must be identified and observed.

The way a company views its world—its set of business models—provides the basis for assigning importance and priority to selective types of information. A company often ignores information that lies outside this framework. The challenge is to think outside a company's worldview, to recognize and identify the disruptions coming from innovative technologies or innovative competitors. Note that these disruptions often come from areas outside a company's immediate market segment, from totally unexpected directions.

2. Create and Articulate a Vision for the Lean Company

A lean company must have a vision before creating an effective response to the need for change. The vision should convey an image of a company that is ready to meet the challenges of the future. Since nobody can predict what the world will look like in 10 years, the company must be prepared to re-tune its business processes continuously. The vision must be articulated by corporate leaders and communicated to all stakeholders—employees, partners, customers, and equity holders. Stakeholders need to see the vision as a constant point of stability, although the company is changing continuously.

In today's turbulent competition, the lean company will change from day to day. A company's management must lead the company's transformation from a static image of itself to one in which change is viewed as routine, from the picture of a traditional company to that of one continually becoming leaner and leaner.

Change requires that many people, in many separate actions each day in their work, perform in a manner different from what they have come to believe is normal. These actions rarely are defined in specific detail in procedures or manuals. The guiding force for people is their understanding of the company's goals and objectives and the picture of the future they carry in their minds. If they do not have a consistent, clear picture of the future state toward which the company is driving, their daily decisions will not help move the company toward that vision.

Further, the company's leaders must help all stakeholders in the extended enterprise understand that there is no end to the total business change process, although changes in a specific task will have a point of completion, with metrics defining success.

Failure in Projecting a Vision

It is the job of the executive leadership to project a clear vision if it expects the work force to respond with initiative and autonomous decision-making. There are several ways executives fail to sustain vision and achieve change (Kotter 1997):

- Complacency—assuming change will happen without additional executive effort just because the executive has approved the change. Although the executive may have a sense of urgency, he or she cannot assume the rest of the organization shares it.
- Weak guidance—providing little ongoing guidance to shape change so it is in good alignment with the vision and strategic directions of the company.
- Under-communicating the vision—visions are learned through repetition, communicated in many different ways to a work force embodying many different learning styles.
- Allowing obstacles to go unchallenged—the reality is that there always will be obstacles. If leaders do not challenge the obstacles—finding solutions to the real ones and deflating the imagined ones—obstacles can destroy the change effort.
- Not anchoring changes in company culture—even if the change is in the culture itself, the executive must understand and use the existing culture to direct transition to a new one.

Change Champions

Systemic changes, like the transformation to leanness, will not happen unless senior leaders champion them. These leaders must articulate the vision of corporate goals and the expected contribution of change to those goals. Then these leaders must actively support and fill in the vision with a vigorous, visible, role in making changes and taking associated risks.

> Systematic changes will not happen unless senior leaders champion them

Often, there needs to be one visible symbol of change—the *change champion*. The champion leads the change process and fights the battles encountered in implementing the desired action. In general, the higher the champion is in the organization, the greater are chances of success in fully deploying change. Change championship is a skill that requires stamina and fortitude. It also requires willingness to disrupt the status quo, but to do so sensitively and always for the long-term good of the company.

Change-comfortable Culture

The greatest obstacles to transformation to leanness are human nature and human limitations. People resist change because they are uncomfortable, perhaps even fearful, of risking the costs of doing things differently from the way they have learned. People are like that, and so are companies. Change initiators must create a vision and culture in which the overhead human costs of change are minimized and in which people are comfortable even as work changes. A change-comfortable culture is one that:

- minimizes the waste that results from inertia. Managers in older, established companies, who work within familiar bounds, often are unaware of need for change. Their employees, also unaware, will resist changes from which they perceive no benefits. The resulting inertia will strongly inhibit and may even sabotage change initiatives. Effects can be costly to overcome. A company's leaders must probe and listen to customers, operations personnel, and first-line management to identify the most-needed changes. Then, they should act with confidence and alacrity. Employees need to know that their personal success will come from contributions they make to the success of the company, not from always continuing to do the particular tasks that are familiar and comfortable;
- encourages trust. Company leaders must trust employees and vice versa. Every change entails some risk. Each individual must be able to take risks with a sense that everyone in the company will work to transform those risks into positive results;
- has change competencies built into the work force. The work force must understand that work changes constantly. It also needs to know that the company is focused on meeting strategic goals and respects their interests. Each person in the work force needs to understand his or her role in the change process. Each person should have learning skills and be able to learn and apply new procedures quickly and actively, without undue emotional cost. The change process itself should be designed, not only to capture the best change experiences within the company, but also the best change practices outside the company, even outside the industry;

- builds decision-making skills. Decision-making should be done where it can be most effective. In the lean company, the practice is to place decision-making as close to the action as possible. Even workers on the plant floor need confidence in their problem-solving and decision-making skills. The decision-support structure must require long-term strategic decisions to be made at a corporate level, tactical decisions at the point of engagement, and operational decisions on the factory floor.

3. Assess the Current State to Identify Required Changes

If you do not know where you are, it is hard to set a direction toward your vision. The change initiatives that you undertake should define transition from a state that is objectively defined to one that is defined as objectively as you can define something in the future.

Chapter 5 describes one way to establish the current state. In principle, the current state is defined by all measurements that a company can make right now. In practice, executives control a company using an approximate description—the metrics and measurements that correspond to a company's strategic goals. The current state, then, is defined by those measurements—made now.

Strategic metrics provide a minimum description of the current state. In Chapter 6, the authors give a more detailed picture of a 21st Century manufacturing company, a picture that looks in depth at the company's people; knowledge resources; technologies, equipment, and processes; and integration. It may be necessary to examine each of these dimensions to get a complete enough assessment of a company's current state.

The survey questions in Appendix A can provide additional evidence on the current state of the lean culture in a company. In the lean company, there should be no dearth of ideas on how to improve on the current state, especially in those areas that have been identified to require improvement. The work force should challenge existing processes and continually work to improve processes and products. If the work force has a factual description of the current state and a vision of the future state, it will generate many suggestions for change initiatives. The challenge then is to prioritize initiatives that survive scrutiny.

In Chapters 9-12, the authors will give an example that shows the use of objective metrics for change initiatives. These metrics should be linked with the strategic metrics so that progress toward a specific tactical change results in progress toward strategic goals. The authors also discuss the need for baseline measurements, so that progress is measured as the change initiative is implemented and results begin to flow.

4. Build an Integrated Plan for Lean Change Initiatives

You have a good assessment of the current state of your company. You have a vision of its desired future state. How do you get from here to there?

Change initiators use a compass and a roadmap. Strategic goals and metrics provide the compass, the statement of direction. Tactical change initiatives provide segments of roadway. Each goes a little of the way. The challenge is to meld these segments into an integrated highway system to take you from now to the future. The goal is to incorporate segments that do indeed move the company toward its vision, rejecting those that go off on tangents or lead to dead ends.

Develop Plans for Change Initiatives

Having identified the needed changes, the change initiators and the work force will propose initiatives. A change initiative is a process, consisting of a set of steps, each of which is essential. Pursued methodically, the steps lead to changes that are well planned, well developed, well executed, and well measured. Change initiatives that include these steps yield sure knowledge. It will be clear why the change initiative succeeded, or why it failed. The steps are shown in Table 7-1. In Chapters 9-12, the authors examine a detailed example of a change initiative using this discipline. Readers should note, however, the centrality of the project plan. The plan spells out benefits—including furthering strategic goals and achieving greater leanness—and outlines costs and risks. It should also provide schedule information.

Table 7-1. A discipline for change and change measurement

Project Phase	Step	Metrics and Measurements
Planning	1. Align change goals with strategic goals	Change metrics and targets
	2. Develop project plan	Progress metrics
———————	*Commitment*	———————
Implementation	3. Develop change components and system	Progress measurements
	4. Implement change components and system	Progress measurements
		Interim change measurements
Assessment	5. Analyze results	Change measurements
	6. Evaluate strategic effects	Corporate strategic measurements
Completion	7. Integrate into continuous improvement process	Change metrics

5. Focus and Sustain Commitment to Change Initiatives

Transformation to leanness will not happen unless the vision is backed up by commitments of time and resources. There is no such thing as instant gratification. There is, as the saying goes, no free lunch. The project plans for change initiatives should provide realistic work breakdowns, schedules, and cost estimates. If the company is unwilling to commit fully to making people—with the right skills—available for the time they are needed, or to providing the required budgets for people and equipment, then the company should not attempt a change.

Leaders and employees must have time to develop and learn new skills and new methods required by the change initiative.

They need time to recognize the impacts of change and to plan and develop mitigating efforts for the most disruptive impacts. Everyone must recognize that there is a time lag between implementation of changes and realization of the benefits. Companies need to be prepared for the offset between costs and savings. A company that is unprepared may not provide an adequate commitment of cost and time. Lack of commitment may result in a shortage of funding, lack of time to plan and implement the change efforts, or an unwillingness to invest sufficient resources (people, tools, equipment, and systems) to implement the change successfully.

6. Learn from Change Experiences

Every change creates a learning opportunity. You can learn from the change process and responses of stakeholders. You can learn what you should do next. You can learn what not to do. Lip service often is paid to the idea of a post-change audit. It seems like a good idea, but there always seem to be more pressing issues. A lean company will recognize that it will not get full value out of a change initiative unless it does an assessment. Otherwise, the company may lose the opportunity to build its corporate knowledge base and end up reinventing wheels months, or years, in the future.

7. Continuously Challenge Progress

It is not possible just to put a change in effect and walk away. A lean company must always have measurements or assessments of progress. It cannot afford to invest in transformation without seeing expected results—or without quickly learning that expected results will not be forthcoming.

Is the vision being achieved? Stakeholders need to be satisfied that the vision is becoming reality by reassessment of the current state—in whatever detail is required. Such a reassessment almost inevitably identifies the need for additional change initiatives.

One lean enterprise principle is continuous improvement. An assumption of the change process is that each employee and each work group is empowered to make what improvements they can to the changed processes. So, although a change initiative may be planned with care and implemented according to plan, there is always the expectation of further improvement.

A Special Case: Change by Merger or Acquisition

The rationale for many mergers or acquisitions, which should be thought of as enterprise-wide change initiatives, is that synergies will permit the combined company to operate more efficiently. The motivation for the merger is for the combined entity to be leaner.

There is evidence that more than half of all mergers ultimately fail. Usually, they fail because the difficulties of post-merger integration have not been identified or have been underestimated. Often they fail because it is not enough for the combined company to be leaner. Being lean is a means to the successful achievement of vision, value, and goals. Merged companies regularly exhibit a lack of (Habeck et al. 2000):

- A clearly articulated vision for the growth and long-term future of the merged company, for example, in late 2000, the vaunted DaimlerChrysler merger was in danger of collapse because of controversy over the vision of its chairman.
- Visible leadership—a merged company that is slow to put leadership in place, or that puts in place leaders whose actions are not visible and congruent with the company's vision runs the risk of losing the dedication of its work force. Although joint or co-leadership may help consummate a merger, it hardly ever works out as the merged company begins operations because of differences in personalities that are reflected in differences in vision. Eventually, one individual will emerge as the leader.
- A sense of purpose—just as lean is a means to an end, savings from synergies are means to an end. In both cases, the focus should be on growing a thriving, profitable company.
- Early wins—quick, tangible, results provide demonstrations that help persuade the company's stakeholders of the efficacy of the merger.
- Steps to recognize and overcome cultural barriers—here again the DaimlerChrysler case appears to provide an example

where difficulties in assimilating Chrysler's culture into the dominant Daimler Benz culture appear to have been under-estimated.

- Communication—the best forms of communication come from leaders: who visibly lead; whose actions correspond with the articulated vision; who specifically address uncertainties and frustrations of the work force; and who actively participate in the merger communication plan.
- Risk management—unless risks are assessed realistically, it will be hard—if not impossible—to minimize their potential damages and keep them from becoming disasters.

EXERCISE

Suppose your company has about 75% of the world market for the product that accounts for 90% of its profit. On a trip to a trade show in Hong Kong, you see a product from a new Taiwanese company. The product can do the same job as yours, but is being sold at half your price. You have been caught by a disruptive innovation. How prepared is your company to prevent the competition from stealing your customers? What suggestions do you have to better prepare it to withstand shocks like this?

Continuing the example, suppose you immediately notified the people back home and asked them to e-mail you a recovery plan within the next two days. What would you expect in the plan? What will you propose if the plan is not aggressive enough to protect your competitive position without having a fundamentally detrimental effect?

Finally, suppose the actions you feel to be necessary will have a major effect on your employees. Survival may demand a major cut in personnel and retraining of the majority of the remaining work force. How would your company deal with this issue and at the same time act to avoid loss of morale?

REFERENCES

Christensen, Clayton M. 1997. *The Innovator's Dilemma: When New Technologies Cause Great Firms to Fail*. Boston, MA: Harvard Business School Press.

Grove, Andrew S. 1999. *Only the Paranoid Survive: How to Exploit the Crisis Points that Challenge Every Company*. New York: Bantam Books.

Habeck, Max M., Kroger, Fritz, and Tram, Michael R. 2000. *After the Merger: Seven Rules for Successful Post-merger Integration*. Harlow, UK: Pearson Education Limited.

Jordan, James A. Jr., and Michel, Frederick J. 2000. *Next Generation Manufacturing: Methods and Techniques*. New York: John Wiley & Sons, Inc.

Kotter, John 1997. *Leading Change*. Boston, MA: Harvard Business School Press.

Chapter Eight

Lean Initiatives

There are three major ways by which a company can convert from a traditional company to a lean enterprise (see Figure 8-1), from the mass production paradigm to the lean one.

First, the company should make an enterprise-wide commitment to transform itself. It bases the transformation on the vision it has for itself and on its understanding of its current culture and behavioral norms. The company then undergoes a coordinated, integrated set of change initiatives to achieve transformation of its culture, behaviors, and operations.

From the mass-production paradigm to the lean one

An important part of an enterprise-wide transformation may be the adoption of the lean principles and practices embodied in

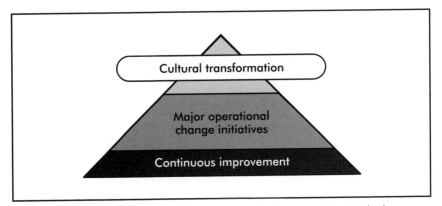

Figure 8-1. Transformation from the mass-production paradigm to the lean one.

the Lean Enterprise Model (LEM). Alternatively, the company can adopt a similar set of principles and practices based, for example, on observation of the Toyota Production System model. As the principles and practices are developed and adopted by the company, consistent decisions should be made—consciously or unconsciously—that drive the company toward leanness.

Second, the company begins specific initiatives—investments in particular projects that transform the company with the specific objective of making it leaner. These are major projects the company undertakes to become more competitive and achieve its corporate goals. The decisions to invest or not invest in these projects will define how the company "walks the talk." The next-generation operational strategies and implementation substrategies described in Chapter 6 provide a comprehensive framework for possible initiatives to which a company might commit. The focus of the next chapters is on decision-making for projects at this level.

Third, individuals take actions as they go about their daily work. Few individuals are called on to make major investment decisions. Yet, every individual makes decisions on his or her use of time—on his or her discretionary efforts—within his or her area of responsibility.

In a lean enterprise, individuals are given wide latitude in their discretionary efforts. When every member of the work force puts the lean principles and practices into effect in all of the daily decisions they must make, they feed the continuous improvement process. A company's leadership can set a clear vision of a lean culture by making investment decisions that reinforce lean principles and practices. If the work force sees the leadership's example, they will make continuous improvement a priority.

Transformation can occur through various strategies. One strategy is to let transformation bubble up from within the organization. Spontaneous transformation can happen, for example, when adoption of new technology forces systemic changes throughout an organization. However, it is much more likely that transformation will start with decisions and commitments made by senior executives and the board of directors, based on a newly developed vision for the company.

Then, the issue is one of whether to undergo transformation in incremental steps or press forward in all areas of the business. In theory, a quick transition from the present state to the envisioned one is best, since it brings immediate realization of benefits. In practice, for reasons discussed in Chapter 7, any change is difficult and time-consuming. Furthermore, any significant change has costs and entails major risks that could increase costs in unforeseeable ways. Unless a company has excess cash on hand, or investors with deep pockets, changing all of its activities at once may prove too costly in the short term.

The most likely way a company transforms itself is through a combination of enterprise-wide initiatives that set cultural expectations and project-by-project investment decisions that demonstrate meaningful commitment. In the language of Chapter 5, transformation happens through successive, and successful, chunks.

Transformation happens through successive, and successful, chunks

CORPORATE TRANSFORMATIONS

There you are—part of a management team faced with customers who want better functionality, higher quality, and lower cost products, all delivered in a timely way. You know you are in a tough, global competition. You buy into the lean concept. But how do you transform your company?

The three principal components of transformation to leanness are:

- the cultural transformation;
- transformation of cross-functional infrastructure and processes;
- a roadmap for a succession of change initiatives that transform operations throughout the company.

The Cultural Transformation

The culture of an enterprise is defined by people's perception of their relationships with it and with each other. The strongest corporate influence on a company's people comes in their observations of and relationships with company leaders.

In the absence of leadership, corporate culture is defined by, "We've always done it that way," and by the camaraderie, or lack of it, among the work force. Without leadership, "We've always done it that way," is subject to individual interpretation. Information theorists say that data becomes corrupted unless there is active maintenance of the database. Culture is that way, too, as each individual puts his or her bias on cultural messages. Each individual is biased by his or her lifetime of experiences and by his or her worldview. Over time, without the continuing renewal of corporate vision, the result is a sloppy, ill-defined culture in which well-intentioned people behave in ways that can be wasteful and counterproductive as they adhere to fuzzy perceptions of cultural norms.

Vision

"If you don't know where you are going, you are not likely to get there . . . no matter where 'there' is." One of the themes in this book is that, without a vision of where the company is going, its work force will not understand why it is undergoing transformation. Simply saying a company is going to adopt lean principles and practices accomplishes very little.

The projected vision of leanness need not be complicated. It just needs to set the context and introduce standards by which people can measure themselves. Indeed, the best vision is a lean one—say, "We will use lean principles and practices to provide our customers with the best available products to meet their needs now and in the future. We will do so at costs that will allow us to prosper and grow shareholder value."

Such a vision provides people with a simple rationale for the choices they make in their daily work. Leanness is internalized in the corporate culture as they make those choices. Of course, the vision needs elaboration. In this example, all the stakeholders most likely will need education. They will have to know what are lean principles and practices. They will need to understand their customers' immediate needs and have a picture of how those needs will evolve in time. Workers will require some mastery over the economic situation that frames their work. They will have to be taught how to go about implementing leanness.

Executive Leadership of the Lean Enterprise

In a lean enterprise, leadership and decision-making are delegated to the lowest possible level. However, the executive leadership always bears special responsibility to set the company's vision, guide its strategies, and shape its progress. How a company's executive leadership carries out these responsibilities provides a strong imprint on company culture. Whether leadership style is out-front flamboyant or behind-the-scenes quiet, the choices leaders make and the ways in which they act establish the tone of the corporate culture.

Because of the visibility of a company's executive leadership, the entire work force consciously or unconsciously responds to its behavior patterns. Leadership's modeling of lean behavior is crucial for lean transformation. If leadership does not, "walk the talk," the talk will crash like waves on a seawall of impenetrable indifference.

Kim Clark, dean of the Harvard Business School, has written of six essential attributes of executive leadership (McClenahen 1999). There is a component of leanness in each of the following attributes.

Global perspective. Global perspective includes an appreciation of differences—and similarities—in the world's cultures. Integration of global enterprises requires respecting important cultural differences, while using commonalties as the basis for enterprise-wide systems.

The authors believe this principle also applies to the executive's need to understand cultural differences within the company's diverse work force and functions. Lean culture has to be woven carefully across ethnic, national, and functional cultures. The executive's challenge is to weave lean concepts into the company's cultural bases in the most effective and least costly ways. This usually implies balancing a drive for quick results against the emotional toll that change extracts.

For example, in the United States there is enough scarcity of labor that the culture has a generally positive view of automation and labor-saving machinery. A lean change initiative based on using automation to free people to do higher-value work would be viewed favorably. In contrast, in a country with high unemployment, eliminating any job at all may be greeted with anger. A lean change initiative designed for the U.S. might not work in India, where a different approach might achieve greater productivity without threatening jobs.

There also is a subtle interplay of the ways in which national cultures define and protect themselves through their currencies, regulations, trade restrictions, and specific national interests. These interactions play out in global, regional, and national politics, themselves a part of the work force's culture.

Entrepreneurial spirit. Clark is quoted as saying an entrepreneurial spirit is, "The ability to see value where others can't," and then to put into place the resources—from inside and outside the company—to realize the value. Leanness asks the work force to assume the spirit of entrepreneurship. Seeing that spirit in executives makes it easier for them to take risks—"Hey, I thought that was a crazy idea, but it gained us a real advantage ... maybe I should try out my idea for doing my job better."

> The work force must assume the spirit of entrepreneurship

Technical literacy. Leaders must know and understand the work of their group or company. They need not be experts in all the technical details. They do need to know essential concepts, essential attributes, and essential issues so that they can ask the key questions and make key judgments, quickly and efficiently, that drive their companies ahead.

Generally, a system of staff support to general managers is not lean enough. It wastes the efforts of the manager and the staff. It responds slowly. In the lean enterprise, reliance on staffing alternatives and seemingly endless contention over the perfect solution must give way to crisp decisions. Those decisions must be made by informed judgment when, in the press of time, they are needed. They may have to be made in the face of some uncertainty, knowing that a timely decision is often more important than one that is theoretically correct but made after the window of opportunity has closed.

Again, if individual members of the work force see executives prepared to make timely, knowledgeable decisions, they are more likely to emulate both the preparation and techniques of lean decision-making.

Enterprise design capability. Executives have to design and redesign entire enterprises. They design not just their companies, but also the extended enterprises of customers, partners, alliances, and suppliers in which they work. Then they have to put together the new teams that can manage and execute the new design.

This, of course, lies at the core of lean leadership. Executive leaders have to be sure-footed in enterprise design, because the effects of executing a new design quickly affect everyone in the enterprise. A sloppy design, unwieldy and costly to implement, saps the work force's motivation. A design that requires constant fixing, as opposed to one designed to flex as conditions change, costs time, money, and work force commitment. A design perceived as nothing more than a faddist, "emphasis program of the month," inspires contempt. In contrast, an enterprise design that adheres to lean principles and practices inspires lean process design and, at the individual level, lean continuous improvement.

Leader as teacher. In the press of continual transformation, leaders cannot just set an action in motion and then expect their people to follow. They have to teach their employees today's reality and at the same time prepare them for tomorrow.

The authors' emphasis is on leadership by example. It is painfully obvious if there is no integrity in words and actions. However, words do matter. Part of the leader's job is to ensure the whole organization is operating in reality, even if reality is changing very quickly. Another part of the job is explaining decisions, especially if those decisions disrupt the work that people do today, or the way they do it. A third part of the job is providing knowledge the work force needs to minimize effort in accepting a new approach and making required changes.

Leadership by example

Fundamental values. The lean practices assume the company adheres to a set of fundamental values: a code of ethical behavior, integrity and trustworthiness; respect for the value and dignity of other people; and a sense of personal responsibility. If executives do not exude these fundamentals, or if their actions are not consistent with these values, leaders do not command respect from the work force.

Applying values when making hard decisions may pose a difficult challenge. The decisions must be made within the framework of fundamental values and reflect lean principles and practices. There is often the temptation to subvert values to gain tactical advantage vis-à-vis customers or suppliers, or to reduce costs, especially labor costs, or to speed decisions. Some companies, Cisco Systems for example, have found it useful to hire corporate ethicists, spiritual advisers, or other experts to help decision-making in ethically ambiguous situations.

Transformation of Cross-functional Infrastructure and Processes

One effect of the transformation to lean and agile is for the company to become much more project-oriented. It recognizes its customer's need. It forms an Integrated Product Team, or some similarly named cross-functional group. It builds a project to meet the need. Once the need is met, the project is finished. The team disbands, with its members moving to other projects. Employees come to think of the company as a collection of loosely bound, episodic projects.

The project-based approach to commerce is a good one. It provides focus on the paying customer and his or her need. The team is measured by how well it meets that need with minimum expenditure of resources. This approach works well when coupled with activity-based costing. Individual activities can be measured by their direct contribution to the value of a product or service. From the lean perspective, activities with negligible contributions can be eliminated. Remedial effort can be focused on those activities the contributions of which do not seem commensurate with costs.

It is undeniably right to focus a great deal of attention on lean projects that lead to profitable solutions for specific customer requests. However, as Toyota has found as a multi-project enterprise, it is unusual for projects to be so self-contained that they do not share some activities, functions, and facilities with other projects (Cusumano 1998). A specific product or a transient project team may not be able to justify building the infrastructure a company needs to sustain multiple projects. Simple, project-oriented, accounting systems do not adequately encourage activities and investments that support cross-project infrastructure (Kaplan and Norton 1996).

Some companies, in a rush to adopt lean principles and practices, have neglected infrastructure operations and investments in advanced technology research and development (R&D), robust information systems, or strong human resource systems. Consequently, their specific projects may be lean, but the infrastructure issues, having been overlooked, may eventually impose untenable cost and waste. Companies may have superb quarterly returns as long as results of one or two lean projects carry them. However, they then may exhibit great difficulty at the end of product life cycles, or when competitive conditions change. The production system may have been lean, but the enterprises were not.

In a rush to eliminate the costs of activities that cannot be shown to contribute value, and to reduce those of under-performing functions, companies may decimate what in time will prove to have been the necessary underpinnings of their sustained success. The loss may be devastating. Many companies in the 1980s and 1990s went through downsizing exercises that eliminated functions and skilled people perceived not to be worth their costs. Many of the companies had to rebuild those functions and develop new sets of skilled people when it turned out that survival of the companies depended on those functions and skills.

Outsourcing: the Make/Buy Decision

One simplistic way to deal with infrastructure is to make a utility out of it, charging utilization costs to individual projects. For example, in the days of centralized information systems, companies chose to make the information systems (I/S) organization a cost center, requiring the organization to recover its costs from users. In well-run organizations, the effect was to control I/S costs. Users in less-well-run organizations looked for alternative, less costly solutions to their I/S requirements.

Once a company has made the intellectual leap to considering infrastructure services as utilities, it is easy to consider obtaining those services from a low-cost bidder, a separate company. This approach, of course, is now well known as *outsourcing*. Because the company is paying only for services it uses, it need not make capital investments in obtaining the services. This improves Return-on-Assets (ROA), an important measure of financial performance.

A company can outsource nearly anything these days, including facilities management, information systems, and financial accounting. It also can outsource engineering design, production, supply-chain management, customer-relations management, and post-sales service. It even can outsource its work force—an attractive option for small companies that do not want to deal with the arcane policies and regulations that govern employment.

There is a strong argument that management should outsource all competencies except for the company's core competencies. That is, it should outsource all functions except those that constitute the company's unique value. This argument has gained strength with growth of successful virtual enterprises, alliances of companies that come together quickly to offer a product or service.

The lean enterprise inevitably will turn to outsourcing to offer specific products and services. It will seek alliances with groups whose core competencies will contribute competitive advantage to the offering. This project-by-project view of the company is consistent with lean principles and practice.

The lean enterprise also should consider outsourcing infrastructure functions, but the issues are subtler.

Is the infrastructure in itself a core competence? Is it so fundamental to the company's image of itself that to outsource would wound the company? It may be that the company's ability to direct the right people, prepared appropriately, to the right project at the right time is key to its success. Such a company's human resource infrastructure is too fundamental to be placed outside the company's control. On the other hand, some of the record-keeping elements of human resource management might be outsourced cost-effectively.

Will outsourcing break the systems by which the company operates? For example, when functions started managing or outsourcing I/S facilities outside the centralized I/S organization, they often achieved short-term efficiencies and cost reductions. However, as companies moved toward operations that are more integrated and several functions with autonomous information systems had to collaborate closely, the costs of sharing data and information grew. What had seemed to be a lean solution turned costly.

Some companies that outsourced their I/S organizations, selling them off to I/S services vendors, find it necessary to bring some of the I/S functions—especially the important ones relating to systems architecture, design, and operating policies—back into the company.

The I/S issue remains, made more complex by proliferation of networks of personal computers, workstations, and servers. The balance, though, has shifted toward partial outsourcing with the emergence of open systems standards that reduce barriers to and costs of integration. In this instance, the benefits realized from outsourcing specific functions may outweigh transaction costs— the overhead costs of transacting with partners in an alliance.

Will outsourcing leave the company without the capability to respond to change? A company cannot outsource all its capabilities to offer goods and services. At the very least, it must be able to plug its core capabilities into profitable ventures. The outsourced capability must be well integrated if it is expected to respond in near real time to changes in the company's vision and operational procedures.

At times, it is difficult to achieve an appropriate balance in lean infrastructures between cost reduction and change capability. Sometimes, outsourcing results in loss of response time and quality of service. One example is outsourcing human resource functions, such as payroll and insurance services. Where in the past employees could make personal contacts to resolve problems or obtain answers to questions, they now have to deal with a for-profit organization. In many instances, they have to interface with automated answering systems that are cumbersome, unresponsive to the issue in question, and lead to frustration (Brady 2000).

Infrastructure Systems

The operational strategies of Chapter 6 are supported by four major infrastructure systems. Each of the systems, outsourced or not, is required for an enterprise to function in a timely fashion, efficiently, and with transparency. Each of the systems must be lean, but now emphasis should be on quick, low-cost adaptation to change. This issue indicates clearly that leanness must be viewed, not only in terms of near-term benefits, but also in its effectiveness and usefulness over the long haul. This is a time when thinking lean means preparing for the future.

Human resource systems. Who embodies a company's core competencies? The lean company thrives if it has the right people— doing the right things, using the right knowledge, and making the right decisions at the right time. That is not going to happen serendipitously. Having the right people in place happens when systems are in place to:

- recruit the people needed for the work force;
- prepare people for their work now and in the future;
- reward their immediate individual and team contributions;
- track and reward their growth as more valuable company assets;
- provide the support all people need as they are buffeted by stresses of modern life;
- enforce disciplines of a lean, productive work place.

A company may choose a highly centralized system that closely controls assignments, tracks performance, and rewards contributions. The dangers of a centralized system are:

- It may place a costly overhead burden on managers and supervisors.
- It may lack enough knowledge of actual work to be done that it makes poor assignment decisions.
- It may lack credible knowledge for assessing and rewarding contributions.
- Ultimately, it may lack flexibility to respond to rapidly changing customer demands or technology changes.

Alternatively, a company may choose a decentralized system, dependent for the most part on teams or work groups to operate the system as well as do their work. Now the danger is lack of uniformity and equity in personnel practices. The team may operate with equity within its bounds, but there may be inequities from team to team.

The need is for a culturally defined, human resource system with as much low-level decision-making as possible, but within the bounds of accepted practices. The practices should themselves be lean, with as little disruption of productive work as possible, and as flexible as they need to be given changing conditions.

Information systems. The authors have already written (see Chapter 6) about the lean company's need for a strong information systems architecture because it:

- minimizes the financial, time, and human interface costs for development, transmission, and application of data, information, and knowledge;
- permits rapid adaptation to changing conditions;
- enables any group or organization to participate in specific projects with little or no transaction cost;
- is user-friendly;
- is reliable and transparent.

In addition, the information systems must be capable of supporting present and future globalization.

Physical facilities. A company's physical facilities can be important assets or crushing liabilities. The company needs to have the right facilities available when and where it needs them to support project activities. It needs them at the right time and with minimum cost.

This is a classic case where the make/buy, or own/lease, decision can be quite complex. Large organizations with slowly changing needs for facilities often find it advantageous to own their facilities, assuming that nearly all the capacity will be used productively nearly all the time. Other companies find their needs for facilities fluctuate greatly, so they can justify the transaction costs of shorter-term leases and fit-up. Some companies speculate in facilities as a business. Some companies invest in land in anticipation of future needs. Unless great care is taken in separating the motivations for investments in facilities, results can be unsatisfying.

Physical co-location of a company's facilities often seems desirable, reducing communications and logistics overheads such as transportation. On the other hand, physical co-location with customers may be important, for example, for suppliers to automobile plants that require Just-in-Time deliveries. In the latter case, the company must have assurances of a long-term relationship with the customers or flexibility to move its equipment easily and quickly to other locations.

Facilities with fixed lines and tooling may be lean if looked at in the narrow context of volume production of standard commodities. Nevertheless, in most 21st Century enterprises, facilities need to be as agile as the customer's mind, with the flexibility to produce quantity-of-one products as efficiently as they can produce volume quantities. One only has to look at the change in philosophy that has taken place in design of automobile assembly lines. While the guiding principle used to be hard automation, today's lines, like Toyota's, depend more on the knowledge of the work force populating the line.

Management systems. Management infrastructures that support corporate control systems, including financial controls, often chew up resources that could be better spent on value-producing activities. Lean principles require that management systems also be lean.

Management systems must also be lean

Reporting requirements can place excessive burdens on personnel. In one classic case, IBM reduced the number of reports from its field service units by about 85% with no loss in effective management control, but with the release of valuable human resources for revenue-generating activities.

One of the revolutionary results of 1990s' reengineering of management was restructuring corporations to eliminate costs and delays associated with middle-management structures. Cost-effective information systems allow near-real-time operating information to flow electronically. This means that performance of work units can be monitored automatically. Higher management can intervene directly when the performance falls outside accepted bounds. Corporate executives depend less on the filters middle managers and support staff place on data from operating units. More decision-making can take place in the work units. Consequently, its effects are more visible across the whole company. Corporate executives can make better and much timelier decisions, given the information available to them. Above all, for systems to be lean, they must be user-friendly and present information so that it can be understood readily and quickly. The information is meaningless if the reader has first to study and then interpret it before he or she can apply it.

This coupling of enterprise-wide information systems with management control and decision making make possible many advances by a lean company.

The Roadmap to the Lean Company

Becoming a lean company entails much more than a lean culture. What makes a company lean is not its culture, but the results of its actions, the activities it chooses to do and how it does them. Transformation to lean comes through an accumulation of planning, decisions, actions, and results, each of which exhibits lean principles and practices.

So what should a company do? Unless it is truly a startup—which provides the great opportunity to start lean—it cannot begin with a blank sheet and create leanness overnight. Establishing the vision is the starting point. Then the company will have to sequence the actions it plans to take. At each stage of its planning and investment cycle, it can pick its next steps based on important external changes it foresees. However, the company needs to put these steps together in an orderly fashion. It is better, more efficient and lean, to have a lean roadmap.

The roadmap is a broad-based, high-level sketch of how a company will move into the future. It guides the company's choices. The roadmap reflects specific corporate strategic goals, important trends in its industry, and is based on lean principles and practices. Such a road map sets direction. Within the roadmap, there still is room for opportunistic choices. With the roadmap, there is greater assurance that the opportunistic choices will further lean transformation.

Readers should peruse the paragraph above a second time to understand what the authors mean by roadmap in the context of lean transformation. The term *roadmap* is used in many different ways. An industry roadmap is a consensus vision of an industry's structure and future trends. For example, the Next Generation Manufacturing (NGM) Project developed a composite roadmap based on examination of more than 150 published industry-sector roadmaps grouped into 13 industry sectors: agricultural products, aerospace, automotive, biotechnology, chemical, construction, electronics, information systems, machine tools, materials processing, transportation, general manufacturing, textiles and apparel. The structure of the NGM composite and industry sector roadmaps include (NGM Project 1997):

- vision of the industry in the near-, mid-, and long-term;
- goals for the industry as a whole re-examined in time;
- external economic, technological, political, and social drivers such as those outlined in Chapter 2;
- needs that describe the essential behaviors or attributes that will lead to success in the industry;
- barriers that confront the industry as it seeks to meet its needs;
- enablers that can help the industry overcome barriers. The enablers include technology enablers for products, processes, and infrastructure, business practice enablers, cultural enablers, and environmental enablers.

The NGM Project estimated the significance of various drivers, needs, barriers, and enablers over time.

A second common use of the term roadmap is in technology. Technology roadmaps are projections of the development of a technology or family of technologies over time. An example is the Integrated Manufacturing Technology Roadmap (IMTR) developed at the Oak Ridge Centers for Manufacturing Technology. This roadmap looks at several families of technology in which development will affect manufacturing in the future.

The lean roadmap uses these other kinds of roadmaps as inputs. They provide background information that helps set a company on the path to its unique transformation.

The company's lean roadmap provides a guide to the scope and timing of the major infrastructure developments the company must undertake to sustain leanness over time. The roadmap also may provide guides for driving lean concepts into major operational initiatives. That is, it may set checkpoints for the kinds of lean attributes a company targets for various functional areas and kinds of activities.

Benchmarking as an Input to the Lean Roadmap

A lean roadmap may use other guides. Say you are confronted with the task of making your company leaner. You may even have identified the biggest barriers to transformation. Now is it easier to invent your own solution or is it better to copy someone else's? The answer is a qualified "yes" to the second option. Why reinvent the wheel? When you do reinvent a solution, it may not be as lean as your competitors' solutions. Better to be sure that your solution is at least as good as theirs. Better yet, use their best solutions as benchmarks and ensure that yours are even better.

Lean is a journey, not a destination. A company that wants to be world-class, or compete with companies recognized to be excellent, needs to compare its processes with those of the world's best, through individual and cooperative benchmarking. Internal information is not sufficient for setting targets for lean transformation.

It is best to know the leanest solution currently available. Maybe the company can copy it. More likely, the company can learn from it, so that it implements as good a solution, but one better suited to it.

A company should use benchmarking to bring knowledge of applications of lean principles and practices to the entire work force. The term "work force" includes corporate executives, functional and project managers, manufacturing engineers, process planners, and even machine operators. Benchmarking should stimulate the continuous improvement process. In this usage, benchmarking is not part of an audit or management control process, but rather it is part of the knowledge supply process. It is key that the work force understand and accept the difference.

A company should be careful though to recognize that what works well for a competitor, or even in the company's plant on the other coast or in another country, may not be right for a plant in a different location. A best practice in Honda's Marysville plant might not work in DaimlerChrysler's Windsor plant. The blind use of best practices without first analyzing their applicability can lead to problems. What are the underlying assumptions of documented best practices? Does a particular plant fit those assumptions? What was the culture in which the best practices were employed? Does that culture match? Rather than adopt a best practice out of the box, modifications should be made to adapt it to a company's operation to ensure success. Is a company's understanding of best practices deep enough to stimulate innovative juices, so that its process becomes the new best practice?

Resources for benchmarking. Many industry associations and R&D consortia, such as the Consortium for Advanced Manufacturing-International (CAM-I) and the National Center for the Manufacturing Sciences (NCMS), conduct cooperative benchmarking efforts. The results are shared among members of the association or consortium and reduce the cost of benchmarking for member companies. The Best Manufacturing Practices Center of Excellence (BMPCOE) is a U.S. Navy-sponsored center that identifies, researches, and promotes exceptional manufacturing practices, methods, and procedures in design, test, production, facilities, logistics, and management.

For smaller companies in the U.S., the NIST-supported Manufacturing Extension Partnership (MEP) has established a nationwide network of technology transfer centers that can provide best practices information in their areas of expertise. Similar centers exist in most developed and developing countries. One example of such an activity is the Fraunhofer Institute, which has a number of centers throughout Germany. These centers work in close cooperation with the industry in their region, even to the point where they exchange personnel with the companies with whom they participate.

Rapidly growing smaller companies often exhibit a few essential best practices, the practices that are carrying the company through its growth phase and which provide competitive advantage (Strozniak 2000).

MAJOR OPERATIONAL LEAN CHANGE INITIATIVES

The most visible and productive aspects of a company's transformation to leanness are the major operational change initiatives it undertakes. These are substantial projects, requiring major financial and intellectual investments and resulting in new infrastructure, new products, and new processes, and facilities. The projects result in important shifts in the way significant parts of the company operate.

Operational change initiatives often are cross-functional projects. They may be projects that are related solely to infrastructure development—for example, development of a new information systems architecture to be used throughout a multidivisional company. They may be projects that come from a company's line operations— say, those directed toward using integrated product teams to develop and produce new products. Line operations depend on infrastructure. Usually, change initiatives contain components that affect both line operations and infrastructure.

The lean roadmap provides a guide to major operational change initiatives showing how they fit within the roadmap and how they support the journey to leanness.

Major operational changes are not made with the purpose of making a company lean. That is not an end goal. Being lean is an excellent tool to achieve the real purposes of achieving sustained profit and other strategic goals. Applying lean principles and practices focuses the company on meeting strategic goals.

The lean roadmap helps a company make the right changes at the right times by helping it understand precedence, interaction, and priority. Some change initiatives build on others. For example, an initiative to move to computer-mediated, integrated, platform teams does not make sense if basic information systems architecture is not in place. Company survival may dictate that a small, revenue-generating initiative has priority over one that will provide an important incremental improvement in business processes.

The roadmap helps identify "quick hitters" that will yield early results. Especially when a company is undergoing a deep process like transformation to lean concepts, some quick positive results are helpful. Early successes will raise the level of confidence in the entire plan. They can be used to validate that the transformation is well planned, underway, and making progress. They also serve as learning experiences. The lessons learned from the application of lean principles and practices in projects yielding quick results can provide models for application in longer-term projects. Some projects, often at the core of a transformation, may have to be longer term because of their size and complexity. There must be a balance of quick hitters and longer-term efforts.

CONTINUOUS IMPROVEMENT

Lean transformation is never complete. A company is fully engaged in the transformation not only when major operational initiatives are lean, but when the entire work force undertakes its own personal lean initiatives every day. Companies generally speak of this process in terms of continuous improvement programs. These have to do with each individual being observant about his or her work, knowledgeable about the work and related activities, curious about potentially better ways to do it, and entrepreneurial enough to try those ways. To make sensible improvements, a worker must know what goes on upstream and downstream from him.

Continuous improvement can occur throughout the company. For example, a mailroom clerk may organize the sorting area so left-handed or right-handed clerks can do sorting efficiently. A machine operator may find a way to stage work-in-process better so less time is lost in fixturing each piece. A financial analyst may find a way to automate data reporting, eliminating manual reports. A manager may find a combination of personal and electronic communications that results in better work unit dynamics. A corporate executive may find a way to reduce the number of steps in a process for routine decisions.

EXERCISE

Suppose your company—in the business of building bicycles—has been stagnant for a decade, with revenues and profit margins slowly eroding. The board has decided radical change is needed. It sets a target of annual 20% earnings growth.

You are the leader of a "swat team" given responsibility to start from scratch and develop a plan to achieve the target in three years. Identify what you think to be the problems and from those develop an outline of your plan for presentation to the board for approval. Then:

- define the steps that need to be taken to flesh out the outline;
- identify the resources needed for implementing the plan;
- develop a time line and identify the metrics for measuring progress.

REFERENCES

Brady, Diane. 2000. "Why Service Stinks." *Business Week*, 23 October.

Cusumano, Michael A. 1998. *Thinking Beyond Lean: How Multiproject Management is Transforming Product Development at Toyota and Other Companies*. New York: The Free Press.

Kaplan, Robert S., and Norton, David P. 1996. *The Balanced Scorecard: Translating Strategy into Action*. Boston, MA: Harvard Business School Press.

McClenahen, John S. 1999. "The Successful Executive." *Industry Week*, 7 June.

NGM Project. 1997. *Next Generation Manufacturing: Framework for Action*. Bethlehem, PA: Agility Forum.

Strozniak, Peter. 2000. "Good Things Come in Growing Packages." *Industry Week*, 27 November.

BIBLIOGRAPHY

Best Manufacturing Practices (BMP). http://www.bmpcoe.org

Consortium for Advanced Manufacturing International. http://www.cam-i.org

Fraunhofer-Gesellschaft. http://www.fraunhofer.de

National Center for Manufacturing Sciences. http://www.ncms.org

National Institute for Standards and Technology (NIST) Manufacturing Extension Partnership. http://www.mep.nist.gov

Chapter Nine

Benefits of
Lean Change Initiatives

In this chapter, the authors discuss ways to assess benefits of lean change initiatives—how to know if the initiative will give value. Chapter 10 discusses costs and risks of lean change initiatives. After a discussion of the conduct of lean change initiatives in Chapter 11, the authors provide a discipline in Chapter 12 for choosing among the many lean change initiatives in which a company might invest. The authors recommend reading all four chapters before attempting to design a lean change initiative.

Lean is a way of thinking that reaches into every aspect of a company. The process of becoming lean may transform a company from its existing style of operations to an entirely different one. A company, a division, even a department, must identify and prioritize the initiatives and projects it will undertake to become lean. Some projects involve process reengineering; others involve new technologies and different equipment. Others may require significant changes in policies and practices for human resources, education, and training. Most require better utilization of a company's knowledge assets.

Lean change initiatives—initiatives that involve many of the company's people and require a significant commitment of resources—are the centerpiece of lean transformation. Lean change initiatives demonstrate a company's commitment to lean, provide stakeholders with examples to follow as they internalize lean thinking, and—most importantly—lead to higher sustained profits and better competitiveness.

Make the right changes at the right times

Lean change initiatives should help a company to achieve its strategic goals and become leaner. The first priority in designing change initiatives should be to focus on strategic goals. That itself is an example of lean thinking. Change initiators should not let things that do not fit their goals distract them. If the strategic goals truly represent what initiators want their company to achieve, then doing things that do not fit the goals wastes its resources. Doing nonstrategic initiatives leaves a company without resources to pursue strategic ones.

The second priority in designing lean change initiatives is to shape their contribution to meeting a company's lean objectives. Once change initiators have aligned initiatives with corporate goals, they can focus on the leanness of the initiatives themselves—using, for example, the Lean Enterprise Model to develop a checklist of lean attributes.

A company's strategic planning process will suggest a bewildering assortment of change initiatives. In Chapter 6, the authors presented an approach to systematizing them based on the NGM Framework for Action. Few companies can invest immediately in every project implied by transformation to leanness. The challenge is to pick the initiatives that best contribute to strategic goals, while moving the company toward leanness. Then, initiatives are prioritized within limits of company resources.

The framework for lean manufacturing implementation is:

- Make changes consistent with strategic goals and with lean principles and practices. This chapter provides a discipline for identifying the benefits of lean change initiatives, including selection of metrics by which to evaluate and track results. It offers a methodology for linking the goals and metrics of a project or initiative to a company's strategic goals and metrics. It also provides the basis for tracking the effectiveness of implementation of the selected initiatives.
- Make the right changes at the right times, get precedence and priorities right, and balancing quick hitters versus long-term projects. In the last chapter, the authors wrote of the need for a roadmap for lean transformation. They return to this in Chapter 12 when they consider investment decisions a company must make.
- Measure progress and evaluate results to ensure that expectations are met. No change should be made without a well-defined purpose. If a change does not achieve its purpose, the

resources spent on the change are wasted, except perhaps as a learning experience.

ALIGNING CHANGE GOALS WITH STRATEGIC GOALS

The value of a change initiative is measured not so much by a raw financial cost/benefit analysis as by the capability to help a company achieve its strategic goals. A company has to act from a position of balance if it is to respond to sudden changes in markets, technologies, and competitors. The lean company's corporate strategies must be multidimensional for the company to retain its balance. In addition to traditional financial measures, corporate strategy must focus on:

- The baseline health of the company—today's returns, today's operations. These must be sustainable and structured for growth.
- The future health of the company for continuing success—having the right people, processes, technologies, and culture to respond to changes. Changes will flow from a combination of known trends and unpredictable events.
- Actions satisfying market requirements—building and retaining a satisfied customer base for the company's core competencies while at the same time recognizing that market requirements are dynamic and the core competencies needed to meet them have to change.
- Operations that are lean enough to be profitable and agile enough to respond to change.
- Skillful and knowledgeable employees, working in a culture that promotes continued success. At the same time, knowledge assets, global competition, and technology become increasingly complex and important.
- Satisfaction of the interests of all the stakeholders, including shareholders, customers, employees, suppliers, communities, and even the nations in which the company operates.

The Balanced Scorecard[SM], discussed in Chapter 5, provides four ways to look at corporate goals: the financial perspective, the customer perspective, the operations perspective, and the learning and growth perspective (Kaplan and Norton 1996). The authors of this book have added two more views—the global perspective and the innovation perspective—that they believe are especially important for a modern competitive enterprise (Jordan and Michel 2000).

For balance, a company should define goals within each of the perspectives and should associate metrics to measure progress toward the goals. Once it has chosen the metrics, the company can use them to guide investments in change initiatives. A specific prioritization strategy, for instance, might give precedence to initiatives that provide improvement in several perspectives. In Table 5-1, the authors suggested metrics that corresponded to a set of generic strategic goals in each perspective.

The first step is to align the goals of an initiative with the company's strategic goals. A fictitious example can illustrate the process.

Whiz-Bang Consumer Electronics Company

Put yourself into the role as the Chief Operations Officer (COO) of the Whiz-Bang Consumer Electronics Company. Known throughout the industry as Whiz-Bang, the company is a mid-sized manufacturer of consumer entertainment equipment, personal computers, home automation, and security products (see Figure 9-1).

Whiz-Bang started as a radio manufacturer, the Worldwide Radio Co., during the Depression of the 1930s. It has managed to stay independent, while many of its competitors have merged or gone out of business. The Worldwide Radio Co. enjoyed success for several decades, despite being a little late in making the transition from vacuum tubes to transistors.

The Worldwide Radio Co. did not live up to its ambitious name. It concentrated on conservative, brand-focused, markets in the United States. In the 1970s, it began to diversify with additional consumer entertainment products—stereos and other components that could be used in "entertainment walls."

In the early 1990s, Worldwide Radio bought a small personal computer manufacturer, Whiz-Bang Computing. Since then it has continued to market PCs, developed by a small group of the company's systems people, manufactured by contractors, and sold mostly to its loyal cadre of consumer electronics customers. In the late 1990s, Worldwide Radio adopted the Whiz-Bang name. It was

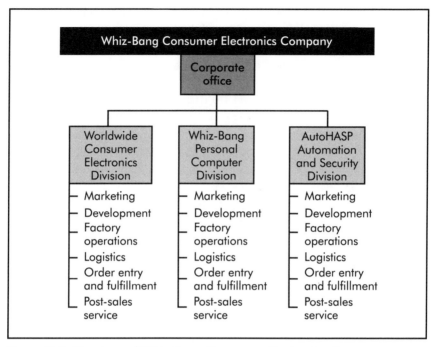

Figure 9-1. Structure of Whiz-Bang Consumer Electronics Company.

more in keeping with the onset of the new millennium and in recognition of the need to appeal to younger customers.

In early 1998, Whiz-Bang bought AutoHASP, a company that made home automation and security products. The argument for buying AutoHASP was that there could be synergy across the three product lines. Whiz-Bang could use the synergy to grow its markets and develop higher-value, multifunction products. That synergy has not paid off yet, but will continue to be pursued as one of the drivers of corporate vision.

Today, Whiz-Bang has a traditional, hierarchical organization with separate divisions for its three distinct product lines: consumer entertainment products, personal computers, and home automation and security products. There is little cross-fertilization of people and products, or commonality of technologies or processes across divisional lines. Whiz-Bang's products are solid, functional, and still command enough brand loyalty to justify a small price premium. However, they are not innovative, nor do they generate excitement among younger customers. The company's financial performance (see Table 9-1) has been mediocre for the past five years.

Profit margins are under pressure—lower than the industry average and getting lower each year. Whiz-Bang's annual revenue of about $175 million comes from products averaging $500/unit. In 2000, Whiz-Bang sold 350,000 units with an average profit of $10/unit. Inventory costs seem significantly higher than the industry average. Whiz-Bang sells through one channel, an established group of distributors. To be competitive, the company needs to reach beyond its traditional markets. It especially needs to reach growing markets outside the U.S.

You spent your first years at Whiz-Bang fighting fires, helping make sure that the three existing divisions remained profitable. Whiz-Bang has decided that to be competitive it needs to transform itself into a lean company. You have brought in advanced manufacturing technology, introduced a quality program, and installed integrated product teams. Things seem to have stabilized to a point where you believe Whiz-Bang is ready for the next phase—making it leaner, stronger, and more profitable. Although Whiz-Bang's financial performance has been slipping, it has budgeted $3 million for change initiatives. The company has an additional $17 million in retained earnings that it might draw on.

Strategic Goals and Metrics for Whiz-Bang

Whiz-Bang recently established a balanced set of corporate goals. The leadership team looked at each of the six perspectives and determined that, out of the possible set of goals, it would adopt the ones shown in Table 9-2.

The strategies behind adopting these goals are:

- The leadership team believes that focusing on improving profit margins is the quickest way to improve Whiz-Bang's bottom line.
- The team needs to augment Whiz-Bang's customer base. It wants first-time buyers to be so delighted that they will return frequently as satisfied customers.
- The team believes that the biggest improvement in internal operations would be to build processes resulting in greater production flexibility and reduced inventory.

Table 9-1. Whiz-Bang's financial performance ($K)

		1996	1997	1998	1999	2000
Consumer Electronics	Revenue	105,000	110,000	105,000	95,000	100,000
	Margin	7%	6%	5%	4%	2%
	Earnings	7,350	6,600	5,250	3,800	2,000
Personal Computers	Revenue	70,000	65,000	55,000	60,000	50,000
	Margin	10%	8%	6%	5%	2%
	Earnings	7,000	5,200	3,300	3,000	1,000
Automation & Security	Revenue			15,000	20,000	25,000
	Margin			10%	6%	2%
	Earnings			1,500	1,200	500
Total revenue		175,000	175,000	175,000	175,000	175,000
Total earnings		14,350	11,800	10,050	8,000	3,500

Table 9-2. Whiz-Bang's strategic goals

Strategic Perspective	Balanced Strategic Goals
Financial	Improve profit margins
Customer	Improve retention of first-time customers
Internal operations	Reduce inventory costs
Globalization	Increase revenues from offshore
Innovation	Grow revenues with innovative offerings and processes
Learning and growth	Increase distribution options

- Since Whiz-Bang's offshore revenues are miniscule—less than 2% of gross revenue—it is natural to explore revenue growth from offshore sales.
- Whiz-Bang needs to become more innovative for a hard headed business reason: improved revenues.
- To grow revenues, Whiz-Bang needs to discover and explore alternative ways to distribute its products.

Now that the strategic goals are selected, the question is how to measure progress. The leadership team chose the strategic metrics shown in Table 9-3. The metrics are straightforward. The only metric that might be difficult to put into practice is the one for the innovation perspective. That would cause the financial analysts some pain. It would require careful tracking of revenues before and after introduction of a new process. Even then, it might be difficult to isolate the effects of innovation from other factors. Nevertheless, the team thought it a good way to drive more innovation into Whiz-Bang, thereby making its products more attractive to customers and its processes more competitive.

The team constructed a display (see Figure 9-2) of corporate strategic metrics. It was posted in public areas of the company and distributed as an automatically updated screen saver for Whiz-Bang's workstations. This helped the work force focus on corporate strategies and reduce effort that did not contribute to meeting them.

Once the leadership team had determined the strategic metrics Whiz-Bang would use, it commissioned a data-gathering effort to ensure that it had solid baseline data against which to measure

Table 9-3. Metrics that correspond to Whiz-Bang's strategic goals

Strategic Perspective	Balanced Strategic Goals	Balanced Strategic Metrics
Financial	Improve profit margins	Gross-profit margin
Customer	Improve retention of first-time customers	First-time customer satisfaction index
Internal operations	Reduce inventory costs	Costs attributable to inventory
Globalization	Increase revenues from offshore	Offshore revenues
Innovation	Grow earnings with innovative offerings and processes	Earnings attributable to innovation
Learning and growth	Increase distribution options	Number of viable options available

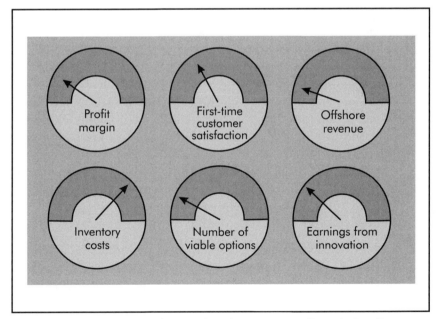

Figure 9-2. The company's financial performance: mediocre in last five years.

progress. Whiz-Bang's team developed a good baseline for all but the innovation perspective. That required going back to reconstruct measurements implied by past data, none of which were directed at the innovation question. This meant that, although the team could make anecdotal comparisons, any dependable comparisons would have to be based on new measurements.

Whiz-Bang then challenged its operations personnel to propose change initiatives that would help it achieve the goals and make the company leaner. A number of good ideas were submitted. Because Whiz-Bang had only a limited amount of cash on reserve and available on credit, the proposals had to compete for investment of time, effort, and money. Each initiative carried with it a unique combination of benefits, costs, and risks. Three initiatives were selected for consideration by the corporate team that had to decide to invest in one, all, or none of the initiatives. The decision process is covered in this and the next chapters.

Lean change initiative #1: on-line distribution channel. You had heard a great deal of hype about e-commerce from one of your assistants who was rebuilding a 1931 Model A coupe using parts found on the Internet. He suggested it was time for Whiz-Bang to go digital. Sure, some "dot.coms" have failed spectacularly. However, on-line capabilities had become an important reason for sustained success at many companies where the World Wide Web was routinely used to support product distribution. The fall of Dell's stock had to do with "how do they sustain their growth rate?"—not with any failure of the company's on-line distribution model. A business model that included an on-line distribution channel seemed natural for Whiz-Bang. The company assembled a team to put a proposal together for the initiative.

The team began with this concept: "I'll bet we'd make more profit if we had an on-line distribution channel." Using the idea as a starting point, its first challenge was to align the goals of the distribution channel with Whiz-Bang's corporate strategic goals.

- If, using the distribution channel could reduce sales costs, there would be an immediate improvement in profit margins.
- On-line ordering would reduce somewhat the time for delivery and, given the highly competitive nature of the consumer electronics business, should improve customer satisfaction.

- An on-line capability would reach wherever the World Wide Web reaches. That would be a low-cost way to test global markets.
- Creating a cadre of people who could develop and operate an on-line distribution channel would give Whiz-Bang skills and knowledge to develop and operate other channels and on-line facilities.
- Having a successful departure from long-established processes would encourage further innovation.

As the team considered the strategic perspectives and goals, it realized that obtaining orders on-line would provide accurate information on which Whiz-Bang's plants could base their build plans and inventory control. That would give the team the possibility of a change initiative that would reduce both time-to-delivery and inventory costs. So the initiative the team proposed defined the need for a two-stage computer system. The front end would allow customers to enter, pay for, and track their orders. The back end would use order information to trigger production and control inventories of materials, parts, and finished goods.

The change goals the team came up with are summarized in Table 9-4.

Table 9-4. Change goals for the on-line distribution initiative

Strategic Perspective	Balanced Strategic Goals	Change Goals
Financial	Improve profit margins	Reduce sales costs
Customer	Improve retention of first-time customers	Reduce time for delivery
Internal operations	Reduce inventory costs	Tailor inventory to real-time demand
Globalization	Increase revenues from offshore	Test global markets
Innovation	Grow earnings with innovative offerings and processes	
Learning and growth	Increase distribution options	Train a cadre of on-line distribution experts

The next step: the team needed to define metrics that would correspond to the change goals. These are summarized in Table 9-5.

The way to see whether Whiz-Bang was reducing sales costs would be to measure per-unit sales cost, tracking it on a weekly, monthly, or quarterly basis. Tracking the elapsed time for order fulfillment would measure how well the company was reducing time to delivery. A prerequisite for tailoring inventory to real-time demand would be how quickly the new system would update inventory. The number of orders from outside the United States would show whether or not the Internet would yield offshore customers and how many. Showing that the new system resulted in higher earnings would reinforce the value of innovation. The number of people trained to develop and operate on-line systems would be a measure of Whiz-Bang's capability to build and implement other on-line systems. The skills gained first in building this system and then in operating it would be transferable if Whiz-Bang wanted to build and implement other, similar systems.

How much of a change is enough? The team proposing the initiative then had to set targets for the change initiative. The difference in measurements needed to be large enough to justify the change effort. On the other hand, the targets had to be realistic and consider risks. Benefits of the change initiative had to outweigh Whiz-Bang's costs—its use of time and other resources. The team looked at current operations, established baseline measurements, and then set credible targets (see Table 9-6). It also summarized benefits to be achieved with implementation of the initiative.

Aligning the On-line Distribution Initiative with Lean Objectives

After working through the goals, metrics, and targets for the on-line distribution initiative, the change team was able to articulate benefits of the initiative and relate them directly to Whiz-Bang's strategic goals. However, there was another alignment it needed to consider. This was the alignment with the objective of transforming Whiz-Bang into a lean enterprise. Whiz-Bang used the Lean Enterprise Model (LEM) as a ready-made checklist for lean alignment.

Table 9-5. Metrics for the on-line distribution initiative

Strategic Perspective	Strategic Goals	Strategic Metrics	Change Goals	Change Metrics
Financial	Improve profit margins	Gross profit margin	Reduce sales costs	Per-unit sales cost
Customer	Improve retention of first-time customers	First-time customer satisfaction index	Reduce time to delivery	Elapsed time for order fulfillment
Internal operations	Reduce inventory costs	Costs attributable to inventory	Tailor inventory to real-time demand	Elapsed time to update inventory data
Globalization	Increase revenues from offshore	Offshore revenues	Test global markets	Percent increase in revenue
Innovation	Grow revenues with innovative offerings and processes	Revenue attributable to innovation	Increase earnings	Percent increase in earnings due to new system
Learning and growth	Increase distribution options	Number of viable options available	Train cadre of on-line distribution experts	Number of employees trained in on-line systems

Table 9-6. Benefits for the on-line distribution initiative

Strategic Perspective	Change Goals	Change Metrics	Baseline Measurements	Target Measurements	Benefits
Financial	Reduce sales costs	Per-unit sales cost	$150/unit	$125/unit	5-point increase in profit margin
Customer	Reduce time for delivery	Elapsed time for order fulfillment	12 days	8 days	4 days reduced float
Internal operations	Tailor inventory to real-time demand	Elapsed time to update inventory	24 hours	30 seconds	Inventory reduced by 1 day
Globalization	Test global markets	Revenue from offshore sales	$1,000/ week	$10,000/ week	$4.7 million/yr in added revenue
Innovation	Increase earnings	Percent increase in earnings due to new system	0	250%	$8.75 million/yr in increased earnings
Learning and growth	Train a cadre of on-line distribution experts	Number of employees trained in on-line systems	0	10 developers 20 operations	Cadre can be used to teach others

Alignment with the LEM serves two purposes. First, it ensures that the initiative will result in a leaner enterprise. An initiative that cannot be shown to have at least potential to result in a leaner company should be regarded as suspect. Second, aligning the initiative with the LEM reminds the planning team of the need to design leanness into functions of the initiative. It will guide Whiz-Bang's implementation. Tables 9-7 and 9-8 present the on-line order entry initiative's alignment with the LEM's lean principles and practices. The tables include a qualitative judgment on the degree to which the initiative supports lean practices and principles. The arbitrary rankings are:

- High—the initiative will significantly advance the principle or practice.
- Medium—the initiative will visibly advance the principle or practice.
- Sustaining—the initiative will support company efforts for adoption of the principle or practice.
- Negligible—the initiative will have little effect on company efforts for adoption of the principle or practice.
- Nonsupportive—the initiative is counter to the adoption of the principle or practice.

SUMMARY

The design of a lean change initiative is often a challenge for which the solution is compromise. Best practices are often practices that are best compromises among design considerations. Design for the sake of leanness alone is empty. What is needed is the design of initiatives that are lean themselves and promote leanness in the company, but that contribute directly to meeting corporate strategic goals.

EXERCISES

1. Think about the company for which you work or a company with which you are familiar. Build a balanced set of corporate strategic goals to attain an annual earnings growth rate of 25%.

Table 9-7. Alignment of on-line distribution initiative with lean principles

Lean Principle	Support of Principle	Alignment with the Initiative
Minimize waste	High	Makes order entry transparent and reduces the efforts of customers and of Whiz-Bang. Reduces cycle times and makes the inventory process more accurate.
Respond to change	Sustaining	Increases Whiz-Bang's distribution flexibility. Proper implementation will help Whiz-Bang incorporate further changes in Web-based distribution systems.
Right thing, right place, right time, right quantity	Medium	Fewer opportunities for errors in orders. More accurate order entry data will help inventory control ensure that the right materials, parts, and supplies are there when needed to fulfill the customer's order.
Effective relationships within the value stream	Sustaining	Improved relationships with customers/end users and among the sales, production, and inventory functions.
Continuous improvement	Medium	Proper design and implementation will accommodate further improvements.
Optimal first delivered unit quantity	Sustaining	The improved quality of the order entry process will better ensure that delivered product meets customer needs.

Table 9-8. Alignment of on-line distribution initiative with lean practices

Lean Practice	Degree of Support	Alignment with the Initiative
Focus on the customer . . . continuously	High	Reduces time to deliver and improves communications with customers
Implement IPPD	Sustaining	Application of IPPD brings together the right people for improving internal operations
Identify and optimize enterprise flow	Medium	Helps identify opportunities for improving flow between plant and shipping
Assure seamless information flow	Medium	Supports seamless information flow within the distribution system and across interfaces with other operating systems
Ensure process capability, maturity, and yield	Sustaining	Assures that each order is filled accurately and that inventory control has accurate inputs
Challenge existing processes for continuous improvement	Sustaining	The initiative represents a departure from Whiz-Bang's existing processes
Promote lean leadership at all levels	Sustaining	Challenges employee participation and input to innovation process
Make decisions at the lowest level possible	Negligible	Challenges employee participation
Optimize the capabilities and use of human resources	Medium	Reduces effort expended in routine order entry and fulfillment, and frees personnel for other needs
Develop relationships based on trust and commitment	Sustaining	Initiative will require a cross-functional team from all three operating divisions
Nurture a learning environment	Medium	A major departure requiring significant learning at Whiz-Bang
Maximize stability in a changing environment	Negligible	The system will interface with Whiz-Bang's existing distribution system and operate in parallel with it

2. Think of three change initiatives that the company might implement. Choose one and develop goals and metrics for the initiative that are aligned with strategic goals and metrics.
3. Assess the benefits of the initiative you have chosen.

REFERENCES

Jordan, James A. Jr., and Michel, Frederick J. 2000. *Next Generation Manufacturing: Methods and Techniques*. New York: John Wiley & Sons, Inc.

Kaplan, Robert S., and Norton, David P. 1996. *The Balanced Scorecard: Translating Strategy into Action*. Boston, MA: Harvard Business School Press.

Chapter Ten

Costs and Risks
of Lean Change Initiatives

At this point in the design process, Whiz-Bang knew the potential benefits of the on-line distribution channel initiative. Whiz-Bang also had assurance that the initiative would contribute to its lean transformation. However, that was only part of the information Whiz-Bang needed to prioritize this initiative in a universe of attractive initiatives. In addition, the company needed to understand costs and risks. Only with this additional information could Whiz-Bang compare the initiatives, prioritize them, and make investment decisions.

COSTS

There is always a window of opportunity

Most cost factors can be measured directly in financial terms, except for time costs. See Figure 10-1. Timing must be viewed differently. The authors assert that timing can be as important for 21st Century companies as financial stability. It is appropriate, therefore, to think explicitly about the amount of time an initiative will take, the opportunity, and the possible missed revenue if the product does not reach the market in a timely manner. The following are typical financial costs:

- development expenses,
- operations expenses,
- education and training costs, and
- capital costs.

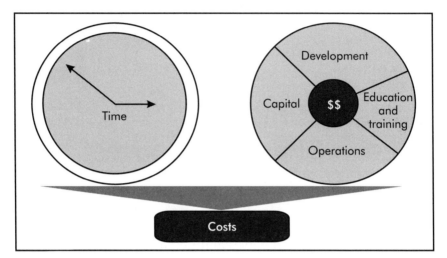

Figure 10-1. Change leaders often must balance time costs against financial costs.

Time Costs

There is always a window of opportunity—that period when a change initiative can be most effective. This is most obvious when the initiative has to do with product offerings. Can a company respond fast enough to profit from a customer's needs, before the needs change? You are in competition to get to market early and often. If a company gets to market first, it can grab market share before others saturate the market. If a company is late, although it has a superior product, it may be shut out of significant participation in the market. Of course, if a company is in the market, it has to refresh its product continually, and probably lower its price in successive steps, so that it continues to lead the competition.

The window of opportunity for a new technology or process may seem subtler. Will a company lose profit or market share if it deploys new technology or a new process after competitors do? If deployment is late, a company may not be able to amortize costs of a new process before a still newer one replaces it.

If a company is early in the window of opportunity, it may be able to set industry standards. If it is late, it may have to retrofit its processes to meet industry standards set by competitors that are more aggressive.

Time cost is cost resulting from opportunities lost when a change initiative is made operational after the opening of the window of opportunity. Generally, these costs should be minimized. However, even if a company has a well-designed initiative, it may not have the initiative operational when the window opens. The company may have to discount potential benefits.

Are there ways to reduce the time cost? This cost may be irreducible if company leaders think of the company as a self-sufficient box. If workers need to learn how to use a new technology, it is going to take time—and there are few shortcuts to learning once the company lays out a well-prepared course of instruction. If new machines or new tooling are required, some minimum amount of time is required to order, build, and install them. Of course, the company might think outside the box:

- It could reduce learning time by hiring someone who already knows how to use the technology.
- It could buy time on existing machines owned by some other company.
- It might forego some profit by collaborating with another company that uses technology as a core competence.
- It might incur premium costs for additional knowledge or other resources it obtains by going outside the company. If those premiums reduce the time cost and the company gains a significant competitive advantage, they are well worth it.

Development Expenses

The lean change initiative is a project that has familiar categories of expense. However, there may be special development costs to be considered as well. They are:

- Initiative definition—it takes resources to ensure that a company's effort is the right one for its market. The market may be a customer who pays for products, or the market may be work units just down the value stream. Thinking lean means doing the initiative right the first time. It also means that the company knows what it wants to achieve.

Thinking lean means doing the initiative right the first time

- Intellectual resources—the costs for intellectual property and assets are likely to grow in a knowledge-based economy. Company leaders need to assess the value of needed knowledge when developing cost figures. They need access to knowledge and to people with skills to turn that knowledge into practical processes. The company should have an inventory of the knowledge needs of the initiative and a catalog of sources.
- Personnel—the people needed to develop the initiative often are among the most in demand in the company. They are likely to have unique and valuable knowledge and skills.
- Hardware and software—expenses for developing or buying any additional hardware and software components needed to support the initiative.
- Systems integration—nearly every initiative undertaken involves a system with many components. Integration is still as much an art as a science and it often requires specialized knowledge and significant resource expenditures. It is a common failing to underestimate the time and financial resources needed for systems integration.
- Pilot implementation—change initiatives likely to affect a company's bottom line or other strategic goals are often ambitious and risky. It may be prudent to run a pilot implementation first, say, for a subset of products from one of the company's operating divisions.
- Operations roll-out—bringing an initiative to the point where it is accepted as part of a company's routine operations may require a ramp-up in productivity, a period of redundancy with displaced systems, and other start-up expenses.

Operations Expenses

Once the initiative has entered routine operations, there are continuing expenses. A lean design seeks to balance one-time development costs against continuing expenses of operations. Except for initiatives with short lifetimes, operations costs over the lifetime of an initiative most likely will substantially exceed the development costs. In this case, careful attention needs to be paid to making operation of the process as lean as possible. However, a company should guard against sacrificing reliability of the system for the sake of reducing development and operating costs. Unexpected and unscheduled shutdowns can undo the benefits of the initiative. Continuing expenses can include the costs of:

- Personnel—the people required to run the new system will either be diverted from other company activities or be hired specifically for the initiative. Personnel costs depend on the availability of people with the required skills. Opting for an initiative design that requires high skill levels may mean that the company will have to incur additional education and training costs. In the worst case, an initiative that requires specialized skills where demand exceeds supply may be delayed and cause significant time cost.
- Quality—there is substantial evidence that expenditures for quality are more than compensated for by gains in revenue and reduction in rework, scrap, or warranty costs. Nevertheless, costs are incurred in quality assurance. The application of the Six-Sigma concept in design and on the factory floor, so that quality is designed and built into the product and processes and not inspected into it, will minimize the cost of the product.
- Hardware and software—the acquisition cost of hardware and software and their upgrades may be a continuing expense, whether hardware and software are leased or purchased outright.
- Systems—the integration of systems will be a continuing expense if, for example, hardware and software are upgraded or if the systems' capacity is ramped up over time.
- Incremental improvement—in the lean enterprise, there is expectation of continuous improvement. A reserve for investment in continuous improvement may result in funding of small changes that enhance benefit flow.
- Maintenance—every system requires maintenance. Most people are familiar with regular preventive and emergency maintenance programs for hardware and software. As important, and often more difficult, is regular maintenance of data, information, and knowledge bases. The skills of personnel and the rigor with which they conduct operations also require a maintenance effort. Finally, the system needs to be

maintained as an integrated entity. The use of predictive maintenance may further contribute to leanness. Using statistical data to anticipate and schedule maintenance intervals can minimize maintenance cost. Placing sensors at strategic locations can further enhance this approach by providing information on impending failures. This permits maintenance scheduling at more opportune times in the process. The goal is to maximize uptime or availability and lengthen the intervals between shutdowns.

- Documentation and tracking—documentation and tracking of operations is valuable for four reasons. First, documentation provides a factual and objective basis for communications. Second, inexperienced people gain benefit from those who have greater experience. Third, if problems arise there is adequate data on which to base corrective action. And fourth, documentation provides a model for future similar activities.

Education and Training Costs

Education and training costs during development and implementation of a change initiative are important to a lean company. The lean company will always be trying something new as its work force challenges the company's existing processes. Education and training provide confidence for stakeholders as the company attempts new approaches.

Education and training are important components in the following instances:

- Initiative development, or just developing the initiative, may require new skills. For example, Whiz-Bang's first web-based customer interface would require some skill with the ergonomics of windowing system design.
- Operations pilot and ramp-up, the successful introduction of an initiative into routine operations, requires people who should be able to do things right the first time. These should be people who know enough to take corrective action fast when operators do things incorrectly. The skill level of the existing work force may need upgrading if the implementation is to be lean.

- The rest of the enterprise—a major change initiative is likely to have ripple effects across the entire enterprise. Acceptance of a major initiative may require active support by company stakeholders, whether or not they are directly involved. The level of education may be quite general, limited to intent, context, and visible attributes of the initiative.

Development costs, operations costs, and capital expenses are typical for a development project. Recall, however, that education and training costs cover more than the special education needs of the project team. They also cover education of others in Whiz-Bang who will interface with the new distribution system, presumably seamlessly. They also cover the education of customers. Recurring educational costs for operations personnel should be part of the operations budget.

The required level of education should be well thought out and accommodate future needs. The education the work force receives may prepare them for lean change initiatives that would involve them directly. Similarly, the education for customers and suppliers may prepare them for further change initiatives that result from the continuous improvement program—especially changes in the way the company relates to them.

Whiz-Bang's on-line distribution channel is an appropriate example. The company will find that an education campaign for distributors in the current channel is important. It will help them understand what will appear at first to be a threat to them.

Regulators will need education on the way the change initiative is likely to affect compliance with regulations. Finally, stockholders and investors will need education on the way the initiative is going to affect short- and long-term financial performance.

An important part of maintenance of capabilities of the work force will be refresher training and training for upgrades or changed conditions. This type of training cost should be included in the operations budget.

Capital Costs

There are likely to be capital costs incurred, first in development of the initiative, then in its implementation. Costs will be for facilities, hardware, and perhaps software and systems.

Risk Management Costs

There are often other indirect costs hard to define in financial terms. Examples are customer reaction to change, psychological factors, and cultural issues especially when offering a new product in other countries. Some of these risk factors are considered in the next section. Managing these risks results in costs to the company. The company may want to establish a separate account for collecting the costs associated with and resulting from risk management.

Costs in the On-line Distribution Channel

The costs of Whiz-Bang's proposed on-line distribution channel initiative are summarized in Table 10-1.

Of course, Table 10-1 presents a fictitious case, intended to give a concrete example of factors that go into the decision process. Cost metrics and targets are those from the budget that Whiz-Bang's proposal team should have developed as part of the project plan.

In this case, the benefits described in Chapter 9 are predicated based on completing the initiative's first chunk in four months. After this chunk is completed, customers use the Web-based front end to order and track Whiz-Bang's products. The benefits as-

Table 10-1. Costs for on-line distribution channel

Cost Category	Metrics	Budgeted Targets
Time	Time to routine operations	Customer front-end: 4 months; inventory control back-end: 6 months
Development	Development budget	+$1.50 million
Operations	Operations budget	+$750K/yr
Education & training	Budget	+$125K
Capital	Capital	$300K

sume that the second chunk, which provides interface between the front end and Whiz-Bang's inventory control system, take an additional two months to complete. A rigorous analysis might show the revenue loss for every month the schedule missed. The analytical process should also be used to predict when the window of opportunity to gain competitive advantages closes, precluding Whiz-Bang from realizing any significant benefits.

RISKS

Every initiative carries some risks that need to be considered in evaluating potential initiatives. Often, of course, the greater potential benefits the higher the risk. Usually, the more an initiative is a challenge to existing operations, culture, and practices, the more risk.

Each company has its own threshold for risk. For example, one company on the brink of financial disaster may opt for low-risk initiatives that give smaller returns, but have high probabilities of success. Another company in similar circumstances may play "you bet your company" with a higher-risk initiative that, if successful, will ensure financial stability for several years. Some instances of high-risk initiatives have been very successful—IBM's 360 series of computers and Boeing's first jet airliner, the 707. However, the "you bet your company" approach often is used as a rescue operation for a company in serious trouble. The methodology presented in this book will not help company leaders choose which of these strategies is better for their company. It will help them develop information they need to make an informed decision.

There are many types of risks to consider:

- acceptance risks,
- alienation risks,
- partner, supplier, and distributor risks,
- development risks,
- operational risks, and
- organizational risks.

See Figure 10-2.

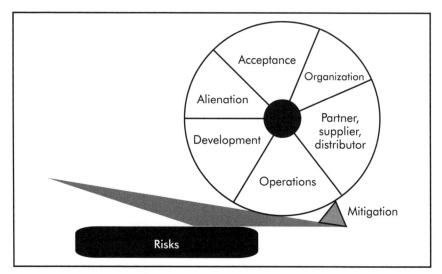

Figure 10-2. The many types of risks to consider.

Acceptance Risks

When an initiative enters routine operations, it delivers products or services. It may deliver them to paying customers or users of internal processes and systems. Either way, there is risk that the people for whom results are intended will reject the initiative. If the initiative results in a product or service offering, rejection takes the form of mediocre sales. If its results are intended for internal use, rejection means that the users grumble and seek alternatives.

Several factors help determine acceptance risk:

- Timing—the initiative may give results that are too late. The user may already have adopted an alternative solution. On the other hand, if results come before the user needs them, they may be unnoticed or may not be appreciated. Often companies with solutions to problems that are not yet visible will put solutions on high, dusty, shelves where they are soon forgotten—only to reinvent them when need emerges. However, even when users' needs do develop, changed circumstances may dictate a different solution. A lean company tries to match need and solution. In any event, it encourages use or reuse of solutions that are on the shelf.

- Cost—if the results cost more than the user values the initiative's results, he or she will reject them. There is an acceptance risk if a company overestimates the value the user will perceive, or if it underestimates the costs the user will incur.
- Quality—poor quality is almost a guarantee for rejection at a time when Six-Sigma is considered the standard for quality programs.
- Features—the features presented by the initiative's results must match the user's perceptions of his or her needs. If the necessary and sufficient features are present, and obvious to the user, then minimum criteria for acceptance are met. Additional features that the user sees as clearly having value may further tip the scales toward enthusiastic acceptance.
- Design—the features may be there, but if they are presented in a poorly designed package, the user may opt for a better-designed alternative. Poor design may be a physical package that is clumsy to carry or that places controls in ergonomically unfriendly positions. It may be a computer interface that requires extra effort to learn and operate. In addition, it may be a process with an unnatural ordering of steps, or any number of other factors.

In each case, the user will seek the design that requires the least amount of extra effort and, especially if the user is a paying customer, is aesthetically pleasing. For example:

- Fit with other systems—rarely does a result of an initiative stand alone. Usually it must fit with the user's other systems. If the result disrupts those systems, or makes them difficult to use, the user is likely to reject the initiative. In lean terms, the change should not disrupt flows or upset stability in the user's organization. Alternatively, acceptance is much more likely if results fit seamlessly and improve the users' enterprise flow.
- Cultural fit—a product that is accepted in one culture may not be accepted in another. There can be many subtleties that range from product name, and other language and images used to describe the product, to possible violation of cultural taboos implied by functions of the product.

Alienation Risks

Acceptance risks are neutral—the user simply rejects the offering and chooses a different solution. Alienation risks are more sinister. They are risks that occur in pursuit of the initiative. A company offends the user, and as a result, he or she rejects the initiative no matter what the company proposes. Examples of alienation risks are:

- A common source of alienation is forced obsolescence of an existing investment. For example, many have felt alienated by the computer industry, especially the software industry, because of frequent releases of new versions of standard software not completely compatible with the existing software, or even the hardware, that they are running. This forced obsolescence can lead to a kind of guerilla warfare against the initiative, similar to that which initially fueled development of the Linux computer operating system.
- Users, especially customers, who have grown comfortable with ways a company communicates with them, may be alienated if the company changes communications channels. For example, when a company replaces its local service force that provided face-to-face contact with a toll-free number, users frequently rebel. They rebel even if the toll-free number leads to more knowledgeable people and better service solutions. In the Whiz-Bang example, some customers who are uncomfortable with Internet transactions may be alienated if they think Whiz-Bang is forcing the Internet upon them.
- If the user is forced to adopt the results of a company's initiative, but then must revamp other processes, he or she may turn ugly. The user may accept the results because there is no viable alternative, but will surely work against adopting anything further.

Partner, Supplier, and Distributor Risks

An initiative may threaten a company's relationship with its partners in its formal or informal extended enterprise. A frayed relationship may affect a partner's trust and continued involvement in activities unrelated to the initiative. The risks may be viewed in two ways:

- Implied commitments to existing suppliers and distributors, or partners depend on one another. Formally, dependence and mutual obligations are spelled out in contractual agreements. Informally, though, partners depend on each other to behave in established patterns. They may view those patterns as implied commitments. If a company's change initiative abrogates those commitments, its relationships may be soured.
- Partners' revenue losses and capital obligations—the partners may, in fact, lose revenue. For example, Whiz-Bang's on-line distribution channel is likely to drain some orders away from existing distributors. If Whiz-Bang does not do anything to compensate those distributors, they may retaliate by placing less emphasis on Whiz-Bang's products.

In some cases, partners may incur capital obligations—say, for example, to position a parts factory close to a partner's assembly line. If the second partner's initiative makes that investment obsolete, the first partner likely will seek compensation.

Development Risks

Development of a lean change initiative is a project that carries familiar categories of risk:

- Availability of people—access to people with needed skills may be problematic when knowledgeable people are in short supply.
- Availability of knowledge—a company needs access to knowledge, in addition to access to knowledgeable people. Ultimately, the success or failure of an initiative rests on having accurate knowledge. Without such knowledge, a company operates in uncertainty and depends on luck as much as skill.
- Requirements definition—if company leaders really don't understand the requirements well enough to document them accurately, they run the risk of turning out a solution when there is no need.

- Timing—given time pressure in today's competition, a missed development schedule puts an initiative at risk.
- Components and system integration—the integration of complicated systems often poses more challenges than were initially understood and estimated. This is the case whether those systems are information technology (IT) systems or, more typically, a mix of people, equipment, technology, and IT.
- Quality—the quality of the development process affects the quality of the initiative's results.
- Regulations—while there are increasing efforts to make regulatory processes less arbitrary, new or changed regulations can significantly impact initiatives, especially those that represent major departures from the company's usual operations.

Operations Risks

Even when the development of the change initiative proceeds without a major glitch, risks remain when the initiative is in operation.

- Human resource requirements—there is always concern that the people who are needed when an initiative enters routine operation will not be available. The people available may not have requisite skills. Education and training programs may fail to bring them to an acceptable skill level.
- Process yield failures—processes, whether they are manufacturing processes or business processes, break down for any number of reasons. In these cases, the initiative yields faulty results, fewer results, or requires more time to fix than expected. If processes cannot be fixed quickly and inexpensively, both actual effectiveness of the initiative, and stakeholders' perceptions of it, are jeopardized.
- High maintenance costs—if the cost for routine maintenance is low, held within budget, it does not present a challenge to the initiative. On the other hand, higher-than-expected maintenance costs, and especially high emergency maintenance expenses, can scuttle the initiative.
- Infrastructure breakdown—if the initiative depends on, say, for instance, an efficient transport system, or a high-bandwidth communications system, and those systems prove un-

reliable then the initiative may fail even if it is otherwise perfectly suited to the need.

- Recycle/disposal costs—increasingly, manufacturing companies must think about recycling or disposal of products, manufacturing equipment, and processes when they are at the end of their service lives or are replaced by newer ones. Recycling and disposal is often governed by increasingly restrictive regulations. An initiative that does not clearly demonstrate cost-effective recycling or disposal well within the envelope for regulations runs risk of incurring uncertain, possibly high, end-of-life costs and financial liabilities.
- Product and process liability—does the initiative make the company's offerings more or less liable to dangerous misuse? Can the initiative inadvertently damage others, members of the work force, or customers? A lean enterprise will avoid the excess overhead costs of litigation by limiting foreseeable causes for incurring liability. Endangering and subsequent loss of life cannot be traded off with cost.

Organizational Risks

There are risks relating to the ongoing health of the organization:

- Employee morale—some like the excitement of fresh ideas and new ventures. Others prefer the familiar, especially if they associate their economic and emotional well being with it. An initiative that is perceived as threatening will depress morale of the affected group. Of course, if the initiative threatens people with loss of employment, the result is likely to be significant work force disruption. Depending on their influence within the enterprise, the group's response may depress the morale and productivity of others in the work force.
- Process "fit" and disruption—an initiative that works easily with the company's existing systems has little impact on risk since little disruption may be necessary. Introducing lean manufacturing processes that make possible consolidation of manufacturing sites will prove to be disruptive. So will reorganizing a company's marketing functions along product lines

rather than by geographically determined territories. Such initiatives may be more disruptive than predicted.

- Stockholder understanding—investors view the company through the narrow lens of financial value. If an initiative's potential impact on present and future value of the company is not well understood, financial analysts and investors can cause significant disruption in public perception of the company, and hence of its operations.

Risks in On-line Distribution Channel

Table 10-2 summarizes the risk categories for Whiz-Bang's proposed on-line distribution channel. A metric is assigned to each risk factor. Observing and analyzing deviations from the plan in the corresponding measurements during the initiative's development and implementation is one way to identify whether the risk factors were properly assessed and are being realized.

Although there is a whole science of risk analysis, the evaluation of risk is fundamentally subjective when an initiative is presented for funding. Results of a formal risk evaluation are rolled into a qualitative judgment of high, medium, or low. Because risk is perceived subjectively, the authors indicate ways to reduce or mitigate risk. One factor that enters into the evaluation is the judgment of how well risk-reduction activities minimize risk.

Much of risk reduction or mitigation comes in setting peoples' expectations correctly, so that they do not view the change initiative with fear. People can help overcome risks when they are "on board"—when they understand their roles and the benefits that accrue to them. In the example initiative, Whiz-Bang continues to use the existing channel as it promotes the alternative. Then, the highest risk for the on-line distribution initiative is that it may damage relationships with the existing distribution channel to the point that it breaks down. Risk mitigation may require helping the distributors through a transition period, even providing them with additional compensation.

Otherwise, in the example, evidence is that there is little risk for the customers not willing to accept a reasonably well-designed Web interface. There is a risk, however, that once customers begin to use the interface, any fault in the system will irritate them or,

Table 10-2. Risks for on-line distribution system

Risk Category	Metrics	Degree of Risk	Risk Reduction Activities
Product acceptance	Product revenue	Customers—low Inventory control—medium	Awareness, education, and training programs
Customer satisfaction	Customer satisfaction index	Medium	Early involvement of customers in the design, quality assurance
External partner satisfaction	Partner satisfaction index	High	Communications plan, special compensation
Project development	Time/cost to completion	Medium	Project management
Operation of new system	Operations costs	Medium	Operating cost containment, continuous improvement
Organizational disruption	Employee satisfaction index	Medium	Awareness, education, communications, training, retraining, and reassignment programs

worse yet, discourage them from using it. The suggested mitigation is to involve customers early in design, as one might expect when an IPPD methodology is used, and then to focus on quality assurance to preclude the end users from experiencing frustrations. Part of risk mitigation is a well-thought-out plan for gracefully transitioning customers from the old system to the new one.

Some risk mitigation is just good project management—keeping track of progress and costs, and intervening as soon as deviations from schedule or budget become obvious. Such mitigation applies both in reality and in analyzing projections. The continuous improvement process should provide adequate action based on the size of the problem.

SUMMARY

The previous chapter and this chapter characterize the benefits, costs, and risks of competing initiatives, taking into account lean concepts. Figure 10-3 shows a quick graphical summary for an initiative. It is an example of Whiz-Bang's on-line distribution channel initiative. If the competing initiatives are characterized in a similar way, a company can systematically prioritize them. This is discussed in Chapter 12.

EXERCISES

1. Think of the way your company handles risk. In your judgment, how acceptable is it? Does your company have established procedures for managing risk?
2. If you were responsible for assessing the risks of a major change initiative, how would you do so? What criteria would you use to determine whether the risks are reasonable?
3. Consider the initiative you chose to analyze in Chapter 9. Using the categories of this chapter, outline the costs and risks of the initiative.

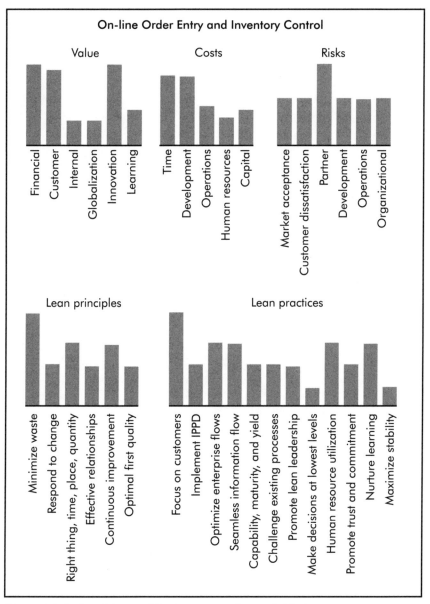

Figure 10-3. A quick graphical summary for an initiative.

Chapter Eleven

Conduct of Lean Change Initiatives

This chapter moves beyond the issue of choosing between lean initiatives. The focus is on ensuring that lean change initiatives are themselves lean. The way change initiatives are conducted can affect the way you analyze their benefits, costs, and risks. They should be designed so the initiatives can respond to the dynamics of the environment while being accomplished with the least wasted effort.

A change initiative begins when a compelling need is perceived. The need for change could emerge because of an urgent competitive threat or an obvious technology advance. Alternatively, the need for change may come from a subtle frustration that there must be a better way to achieve corporate goals. The company must validate the need for change, then create and analyze its planned response. It should develop a change initiative that can be presented in the practical form of a project plan. The company must evaluate the costs and risks of the proposed initiative as well as the benefits.

Lean change initiatives need to be themselves lean

Usually the evaluation of an initiative will be iterative (see Figure 11-1). Beneficial results need to be evaluated for ways that will increase them. Costs and risks may need to be reduced. The first cut at a plan may prove too costly or too risky. The benefits may prove elusive. Iteration will refine the plan until it converges on an acceptable compromise that can be presented for the investment decision. In the best of circumstances, the acceptable compromise is close to an optimal solution.

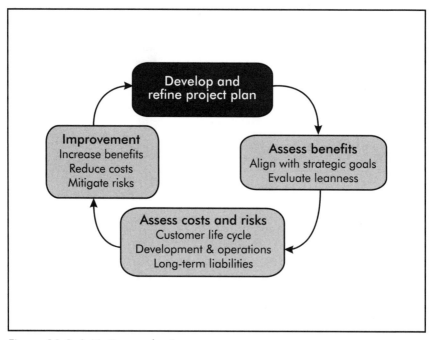

Figure 11-1. Initiative evaluation.

Once the investment decision is made, the company can manage the initiative like any other development project. At some point the change will be accepted as part of the way the company routinely operates. Even then, the change will live on through continuous improvement and maintenance efforts. Finally, the change will have lived out its usefulness. All that will be left will be the effort to tie up loose ends and to dispose of equipment and intellectual baggage that is no longer needed.

Table 11-1 summarizes the steps of a change initiative. Metrics and measurements are important aspects of a lean change initiative. The company undertakes an initiative to achieve specific goals. The metrics are designed to tell whether it is making progress toward the goals. With this information, daily decisions affecting the conduct of the initiative can be made quickly, with certainty, and without wasted effort. Upon completion of the initiative, the company will begin to evaluate the results to determine whether it is meeting its targets.

THE PROJECT PLAN

The project plan has three purposes:

1. It is the source document for the investment decision and commitment of resources to the project.
2. It is the plan for the work needed to develop and implement the initiative. You will use it to organize, monitor, and manage the effort.
3. It is the starting point for the communications required to establish the trust relationships among the stakeholders whose support will be crucial for the change initiative's success.

Chapters 5 and 9 provide the model for Steps 1 and 2 (see Table 11-1), in which the goals and quantitative objectives of the proposed project are established within the context of a company's corporate strategic goals. The basic cost estimate will come from the resources required to accomplish each stage of the project plan. The checklists given in Chapter 10 can be used to determine the cost and risk considerations.

A part of the project planning process should be a continuing examination of the degree a project conforms to the two lean meta-principles, including:

- There should be a minimization of the waste that the change will generate. Not all efforts and resources will contribute constructively to meeting the change goals. The change may render some of the company's existing resources and asset base redundant, obsolete, or unusable.
- An ability of the initiative to accept further market, technology, and regulatory changes as it is developed and implemented is needed. The initiative must be designed with a flexibility that allows the changes encountered in a dynamic world.

Elements

The project plan should be as lean as the initiative and as elaborate as it needs to be, but no more so. The change initiators should put enough effort into it that it is right, but no more than needed. Typically, whether the plan is elaborate and formal or simple and informal, it should include:

Table 11-1. A discipline for change and change measurement

Project Phase	Step	Metrics and Measurements
Planning	1. Establish corporate strategic goals	Corporate strategic metrics
	2. Align change goals	Change metrics and targets
	3. Develop project plan	Costs, risks, progress metrics
	Commitment decision	Adjust cost, risk, and progress metrics
Implementation	4. Develop change components and system	Progress measurements
	5. Implement change components and system	Progress measurements Interim change measurements
Assessment	6. Analyze results	Change measurements
	7. Evaluate strategic effects	Corporate strategic measurements
Completion	8. Integrate into continuous improvement process	Change metrics

- a project overview,
- a project vision and goals,
- an activity plan,
- a schedule,
- a communications plan, and
- a project management plan.

Project Overview

The overview should provide a synopsis, an executive summary of the change project, describing the chief goals, targets, and benefits. It should identify costs, project timing, and resource requirements. Since any change involves moving into the unknown, the overview should also summarize the risks. Not making the change carries risks, too. The overview also should discuss the risks of not making the change.

The overview should define the roles of all stakeholders affected by the change. It is especially important to have a clear understanding of the roles of executives and other change leaders, the change team, and the employees who will have to accommodate to the change. It is equally important that the customers, suppliers, and investors understand their changed roles to the extent to which they are involved in the change.

The overview is the single most important document of a change initiative, since many people will not have the need to review the details of the project plan. They will however, want to review a short, succinct, and complete explanation of the initiative. Assume that a wide range of both technically proficient and nontechnical readers will read the overview. As little specialized language or detailed technical jargon as possible should be used. When specialized language has to be used, provide short, simple, and clear explanations. Spend time to make the overview clear and concise—lean enough to convey all the essentials without wasting the readers' time.

Project Vision and Goals

If the change is an organizational one, the plan should describe the vision for the changed organization. Clearly, a vision is needed if the initiative encompasses the whole company. A vision is also needed if a group of people in only a small part of the company is affected in a major way. The vision should be fleshed out appropriately to specify:

- the new organizational structure;
- the way the new structure will interface with the remaining structure;
- personnel policies;
- authority and task-responsibility distributions;
- managerial values and practices;
- performance review systems;
- reward systems;
- relationships with external groups, and expected performance outcomes.

A test of this future state is: can it be supported with a credible schedule, an activity plan, and a realistic budget estimate? At a minimum, this section should include:

- the analysis of change goals as developed in Step 1 of Table 11-1;
- a statement of the targets defined in Step 2;
- a presentation of the benefits to the company upon achieving the targets.

The discussion of benefits should consider time. If the change is being made to meet a window of opportunity, then it is especially important to assess the value of an early completion of the change, or the cost of a delayed completion.

Activity Plan

The activity plan for the initiative will build on the company's present situation and systems. It is important to set priorities for change, identify relevant subsystems, and assess their readiness and capability for the contemplated change. How will the change affect existing systems? How will the change affect flows of value, materials and parts, and information and knowledge across the company and the extended enterprise?

The activity plan should incorporate a scenario of the transition to the changed state that is comprehensive of the adjustments that have to be made in existing systems. It should specify the critical activities and events of the transition period, including:

- what must be done in preparation for the change;
- how the change will be done;
- what has to happen as the change is implemented;
- what resources, especially people, are required.

The plan should provide an appropriately detailed work breakdown plan.

Development and implementation of a significant change initiative usually will involve several functional groups. Somebody does the design. Someone else does the development. Others serve as suppliers—of materials, parts, equipment, knowledge, or information. Somebody has to operate and maintain the initiative. Others will be the users or customers, just like in product development and production. Moreover, just like product development and production, the initiative should be developed by an integrated cross-functional team, using an appropriate adaptation of the company's methodology for Integrated Product and Process Development (IPPD).

If separate work groups, or even customers or suppliers, are involved in the change initiative, the activity plan should clearly show how the work-in-progress, parts, materials, information, and knowledge would flow from group to group. The activity plan should indicate how those flows fit within the flows of the rest of the extended enterprise.

The plan should have a logical sequence of events designed to achieve the change within the window of opportunity. If the change has been broken into chunks, each should be described separately, with the subplans rolled up into the project plan. As mentioned earlier, the interfaces of the chunks must fit functionally and rationally like the pieces in a picture puzzle.

The plan should include contingency planning and fallback positions if, for example, resources prove not to be available. It should also identify high-risk areas and list actions to be taken to reduce them.

Considerable thoughtfulness has to be exercised in project planning for the lean company. In a lean company, each work group takes responsibility—and earns rewards—for meeting its assigned tasks. In return, the work group is given the freedom—within the bounds of the vision for the organization—on how it will accomplish its tasks. The project plan should tell the work group what outcomes are expected of it and what resources are allocated to it. However, the project plan should not preempt operational and organizational decisions better left to the work group.

Schedule

The schedule should start with the time at which the initiative must be completed to be effective in helping the company achieve its strategic goals—perhaps the time when you expect the window of opportunity to open. Remember, the company is not doing the project for its own sake. It is doing the project to improve the company's profitability. The goal is to reduce costs and provide the company with a better product, service, or process that results in its customers valuing its offerings more than those of competitors.

The schedule should show the logical sequence of activities and events and include important milestones. The milestones should identify critical precedence and other constraints so that each activity provides the right thing when and where it should, and in the right quantity. There should be quality targets in addition to timing and quantity targets. Each chunk of the change should be described by its own subschedule. PERT scheduling and critical path analysis are two invaluable tools for creating a practical and effective scheduling system. The schedule should reflect alternative paths, especially in the areas of highest risk.

Keep initiatives within windows of opportunity

The schedule should be tuned to ensure that when the change is made operational it has matured to the point where you and the downstream users can have confidence in both the throughput and the quality of its yield. If, for example, you are introducing a new process, you may want to test it in successive stages. Models can be used to simulate the process as it is designed. Chunks can be tested off-line as each is completed and subsequently integrated with the others.

Real inputs can be used to test the resultant system in simulation. If the development was right the first time, the simulations will help train the work force to operate under the changed conditions. If the development was not quite right, the simulations offer an opportunity to make changes before the system's general release, thereby minimizing possible errors and the total project cost.

Rapid prototyping can cut development time and costs. The idea is to quickly put together a working prototype, implement it in a pilot application, and then use it as a model for the full application. Rapid prototyping can validate both product and process designs. In many instances, rapid prototyping does save time—enough time to keep initiatives within swiftly changing windows of opportunity.

Some rapid prototyping technologies—laser sintering or metallic printing—provide parts robust enough for production use. There is a danger, however, when the prototype appears robust enough for use as a working part for the full application. Later it may prove not to be. The users' immediate needs are met, but the solution is not reliable in the longer term. In this instance, to be lean means using the time and cost advantages of rapid prototyping in the initial development, but then separately ensuring that the many demands for quality and reliability are also met. The software industry has also used rapid prototyping. Here it is often more difficult to assess the danger of assuming a working prototype is robust enough for routine operations.

Because of the complexity of modern products and processes, the manufacturing industry has adopted the reuse of designs and families of designs of parts and products. This approach is illustrated by the vehicle platform concept in the automotive industry, where 80% of the design effort for several distinct models is done only once in the platform design. Design reuse is an important element of lean practice for creating a new process or product, avoiding the cost of redundant development. It is a model that is valuable in operations, too, reducing the learning or relearning that operators and service personnel otherwise would have to undergo.

The complexity of some products and systems is such that few test procedures can test all of the possible ways in which a user might use, or abuse, them. In the software industry, many companies release so-called Beta versions of their new programs to volunteer users. Beta testing by a few friendly customers has gone on for many decades, but the advent of the personal computer and then of openly available software has led to Beta testing on a large scale. The users provide a response—hopefully a positive one that helps marketing—to the program designer, in essence helping the designer to debug the program and thus improve its quality. This method appears to be acceptable in the computer industry, although quality issues sometimes lead to intense criticism.

Other industries where products are mission critical, such as automobile tires in the first and each subsequent use, do not have the luxury of letting users find problems. A close relationship with a trusted customer may permit you to conduct controlled pilot tests, arranged to be fail-safe.

The Communications Plan

The Project Plan should include a communications plan. Much of the waste associated with change occurs because people do not fully understand what needs to be done—and why and when.

Communications prepare the organization for change, reduce the uncertainties and anxieties employees may have about change, provide employees with reasonable expectations, help with education and training, and reduce the learning curve. The plan should cover both the internal communications for the company and its work force, and the external communications with outsiders who will perceive differences in their relationship with the company because of the project.

Communications, starting with communications from the executive management, will lubricate the process and help ensure success. Depending on the magnitude of the change, the sectors of the enterprise targeted for communications can be extensive. Communications should get enough understandable knowledge to each sector so that it can play its role in ensuring the enterprise's success as it undergoes change. Communications should continue throughout the development and the initial implementation of the project.

Project Management Plan

There are three aspects of project management: The first is administrative—tracking the progress, or lack thereof, of the development and implementation, and tracking the availability and use of resources. There is no substitute for the use of appropriate automated project management tools that can be updated quickly with near-real-time data. Such tools provide the manager—and everyone else responsible for the initiative—with a quick and accurate status picture.

The second aspect is cost tracking and control. This is a natural extension of the administrative functions. In the lean enterprise, deviations from expected costs should trigger problem-solving and decision-making, not hand wringing or simple dictums of cost cutting. A higher than expected cost in achieving a milestone may indicate that you underestimated the effort, possibly because you really did not fully understand it. The higher cost may indicate that your team pursued a wasteful solution and they will be penalized when the time comes to hand out rewards. Finally, the higher cost may indicate that the initiative is just too costly to pursue and that the company should cut its losses sooner rather than later.

The hardest aspect of project management, especially in a lean company, is in leading work groups back into compliance with the project plan when they deviate from it. In the lean company, the project manager is not so much the problem-solver as the facilitator who ensures that others comply with the plan and solve the problem. The project manager needs the information and skills to focus quickly on the problem or the changed condition. Then he or she must lead the work groups to an acceptable solution that will cause minimum disruption in their efforts to complete the tasks and the initiative on time.

Implementation Phase

Once the commitment is made to begin a change project, the implementation phase begins. There are two principal parts to the implementation phase: development of the hardware, software, and systems needed for the change, and then implementation of the changed operations.

Leadership is essential during the implementation phase. This is the time when the company will be most doubtful about the change, the time when investments are made but before results are seen. Leadership must be coupled with a continuous assessment of the change process to ensure that it stays on track toward the overall vision. If the initiative does not go according to plan, leadership is required to determine the corrections required to bring it back on course.

> Leadership is essential during the implementation phase

Progress Against the Project Plan

Measurement is important during a change project to ensure that it does not go off track. There are two aspects of measuring progress:

- Some measurements show the progress made in implementing the change initiative.

- Other measurements tell whether expected operational results are achieved after specific chunks of the initiative are implemented.

A change project is like any other project. All the familiar tools of project management should be used to keep the project on target. The project plan for any but the simplest changes should include milestones, namely definable results mapped against time and cost. The simplest measures then are binary: did the project reach the milestone on time and within budget? There are often other important measures contained within the project plan, for example, percentage of resources consumed and availability of resources for completion.

A change initiative moves from a promise made to a promise partially fulfilled

Measuring progress can lead to confidence that the project will be completed as planned. The company can anticipate using results of the initiative and begin planning ways to extend its expected benefits. The reality of a change initiative moves from a promise made to a promise partially fulfilled.

The measurements can also flag problems. Is the change more difficult to achieve than thought? Will it be completed in time to make a difference? What should be done to aid success of the change?

Intermediate Results

For many change projects, the implementation of a chunk—say a new subsystem—means that some new function is brought into operation and its effectiveness can be measured. These intermediate results also provide early validation of the change, demonstrating that the change is beginning to yield the promised results.

It is important, however, to be cautious about intermediate results achieved until the change is fully put into operation. Intermediate results can be indicators of eventual results, but should not be taken out of context. For most changes, the company will not have results that indicate the success or failure of the entire change effort until after the last chunk is implemented. You should recognize measurements made during the implementation phase for what they are: tentative and intermediate.

Accommodating Change

A change initiative rests on its underlying assumptions. In their analysis of an initiative, change initiators look at benefits, costs, and risks. They project them as far into the future as they reasonably can. The projected benefits, costs, and risks provide the basic assumptions on which the change initiators make their investment decisions.

> A change initiative rests on its underlying assumptions

As they proceed with development and implementation, the change initiators may find that the assumptions made when they started the initiative are no longer valid. When this happens, they should test the effects on the initiative. The most severe challenges come when the requirement for the initiative disappears— why do it if it is not needed anymore? Or, when the costs rise appreciably, are there enough benefits to justify the added costs? The company may find that a new technology or process has become available that can be incorporated into the initiative. Some of the planned risks may not materialize, so the reserve established for risk reduction can be decreased.

Modifications to the project plan, of course, carry risks. They need to be evaluated before being decided upon. It helps if work groups are conditioned to change, and if they view carefully considered changes as routine. It also helps if modifications are designed using lean practices that will minimize the effort of incorporating them into the existing design of the initiative.

Sometimes, the best thing to do when assumptions—especially about the market, about costs, or about the time of completion— change dramatically is to end the effort. After a reasonable attempt to get a failing initiative back onto a timely and productive course, it may be impossible to achieve projected benefits. That is the time when a lean company will cut its losses and seek a better way to meet the need.

Project Completion

When can you declare a change initiative to be complete? Is it when the company has switched from the old to the new way? Is it when the budget no longer carries an item for the change; that is, when the investment for change is completed? Alternatively, since the company is becoming lean, and will make improvements continuously, will the change initiative never be complete?

Completion is defined arbitrarily by the authors as that point in time when the change initiative is accepted as part of your company's routine operations and is subject to continuous improvement efforts. That is, completion is achieved after the development of new processes, systems, and procedures. It is after cutover and after the learning curve is asymptotically complete. Only then, will you know whether the change has been effective—only then will the measurements provide quantitative indicators of success (or failure).

Assessment Phase

The temptation, especially in small companies, is to make a change, see that it seems to be working, and go on to the next pressing problem. There is always another pressing problem. However, every company should analyze and evaluate results after a change is made to:

- Validate the initiative to ascertain whether the projected benefits have been achieved and have justified the investment decision.
- Learn what is good about the change and determine what is bad. This approach will identify opportunities for continuous improvement, improve judgment, and help the company avoid repeating errors.
- Package the lessons—pro and con for application elsewhere in the company or for use in other projects. A lean company reuses its learning wherever it can, minimizing the waste of re-inventing wheels.
- Understand the unpredictable consequences of change. The most costly aspect of a change initiative can be correcting a situation caused inadvertently by the change. You cannot always think of everything during the planning phase, so you need a mechanism to quickly identify and correct the unexpected.

Comparison of Results
with Targets and Baseline Measurements

The comparison of actual results with targets and baseline measurements should be straightforward. If the results come close to your targets, everyone can go away feeling good. Usually the results are mixed: you meet some targets, you fall short on others, and you may even overachieve. The comparisons flag important questions.

When a company does not meet its targets, is it because the change initiators were naïve? Was there a failure in project planning or execution? Did the company miss the window of opportunity? Was there an unexpected change in the external environment that blind-sided it? When targets are exceeded, the questions are subtler. Was it luck? Were the change initiators too conservative in their targets? What new opportunities did overachievement make available? What lessons apply to other change efforts?

The On-line Distribution Channel at Whiz-Bang

Suppose Whiz-Bang obtained the measurements shown in Table 11-2.

Assume the progress measurements were made after the front-end chunk for on-line interaction with customers had been implemented, but before the back-end linkage to inventory control had been made operational. The operational measurements are those made after the entire system has entered routine operations.

In this made-up case, Whiz-Bang achieved a significant reduction in the unit sales cost, contributing $15/unit to the gross profit. However, the reduction did not reach the target. This should raise an immediate flag—why not? Was it because of unrealistic expectations? Or, was it because of poor implementation? Or, did some of the risk factors lead to increased costs? Or, was there an unpredicted side effect that degraded the results? If Whiz-Bang understands the reasons why it did not achieve the target, then the company has a truthful basis for looking at opportunities to improve.

On the other hand, Whiz-Bang achieved the target for reduction in the product fulfillment time. Whiz-Bang should look now

Table 11-2. Results from the on-line distribution channel initiative

Strategic Perspective	Change Metrics	Baseline Measurements	Progress Measurements	Operational Measurements	Target Measurements
Financial	Per unit sales cost	$150/unit	$145/unit	$135/unit	$125/unit
Customer	Elapsed time for order fulfillment	12 days	9 days	8 days	8 days
Internal operations	Elapsed time to update inventory	24 hours	N/A	10 minutes	30 seconds
Globalization	Revenue from offshore sales	$1,000/week	$7,000/week	$17,500/week	$10,000/week
Innovation	Percent increase in earnings due to new system	—	50%	150%	250%
Learning & growth	Number of employees trained in on-line systems	0	10 developers 10 operations	15 developers 30 operations	10 developers 20 operations

at customer satisfaction and retention measurements to see if the project is having the desired contribution to corporate strategic goals.

Whiz-Bang did not meet the target for updating the inventory control system either, but the reduction of the time from a day to ten minutes is significant. The question now is whether updating on a ten-minute cycle is close enough to real time for the purposes of inventory control. Can Whiz-Bang use it to implement kanban?

The increase in global sales is gratifying and should encourage Whiz-Bang to analyze the data further in preparation for segmenting the market and targeting specific products to particular countries or regions.

The increase in earnings attributable to the new system should encourage further innovation, especially if the change initiators who proposed and carried out the change are rewarded visibly for their efforts.

Unexpected Results and Side Effects

One of the old saws of change management is that the solution of one problem inevitably introduces new problems. Some cynics even claim that the growth in new problems is exponential. While careful change selection and change project management can minimize new or unexpected problems, the analysis of a completed change should identify new problems and side effects.

In the Whiz-Bang example, perhaps the average sales cost/unit in the existing distribution channel rose because of distributor resistance to the new channel—balancing to some extent the gains made by implementing the on-line channel. This was a risk factor, of course, but an important side effect, too.

> The solution of one problem inevitably introduces new problems

A more pleasant side effect is that Whiz-Bang overachieved its goal in training people. This raises questions. Given that Whiz-Bang has a cadre of skilled people, how best can these workers now be employed? How can they be utilized in other internal on-line system developments? And are they competent enough that other companies might want to hire them to develop systems?

Effects on Strategic Goals

Finally, any significant, well-designed initiative that is aligned with the strategic goals at least should show up as a blip in the measurements of the corporate metrics. If there are no observable effects, the company should look deeper. Are there no observable results because other factors mask them? On the other hand, were the assumptions the company made about the effects of the change effort wrong?

The balance sheet in the Whiz-Bang example should be measurably affected. There should also be an indication of the success of the initiative on customer satisfaction and retention. In addition, increased global sales should help energize other globalization initiatives.

The Completion Phase

Completion of a change project that has been accepted as part of the company's routine operations does not mean that the change is cast in concrete. Lean companies will have some sort of continuous improvement program as part of their corporate strategy. Change becomes operational when it is just one more target for continuous improvement, either to reduce costs or to enhance function, but always to make the company more competitive.

The completion phase is, of course, also a starting point for the next change effort. While a company should celebrate a successful change, it should maintain vigilance, looking for changing conditions that will render the new, recently implemented initiative outmoded. There is an old saying, "Once you have drawn a line on paper your design is outmoded."

EXERCISE

1. Outline the project plan, including the plan for the implementation phase, for the change initiative you chose to analyze in the exercises of Chapters 9 and 10.
2. For the same initiative, describe what you would look for in the assessment phase.

Chapter Twelve

Making the Decision

Should Whiz-Bang Consumer Electronics invest in the on-line distribution channel initiative? Whiz-Bang cannot answer that question in isolation.

If you have empowered the work force to challenge the company's existing processes continually, you will receive proposals from many groups for change initiatives that seem equally compelling. However, some of the proposals will prove to be better than other proposals. Some will move the company closer to its strategic goals at less cost and with fewer risks.

Most successful companies are unlikely to adopt all proposals their people make. The costs, even though they all promise long-term financial gains, may exceed what the company can divert from cash flow or reasonably borrow. Even if the company has adequate cash on hand, the toll on its people of too much change, too quickly, may be more than it can absorb. Inevitably, these proposals must compete for the company's investment of time, effort, and money. Sometimes, corporate leaders and investors face difficult decisions about whether to invest, or not invest, in these initiatives. Each initiative carries with it a unique combination of benefits, costs, and risks. Quite often, the decision-makers must use their intuition based on a qualitative comparison and prior experience, because there can be no clear objective comparison among competing investment opportunities.

> Proposals compete for the company's investment of time, effort, and money

THE DECISION INPUTS:
THE ON-LINE DISTRIBUTION CHANNEL

Whiz-Bang's proposed on-line distribution channel initiative is an example of the types of inputs provided by its employees. The system consists of two chunks: a web-based order entry and tracking system for direct distribution to customers, and an interface for automatically updating the inventory control system as on-line orders are entered. The proposal includes four sources of inputs to the decision-making processes: benefits, costs, risks, and alignment with lean principles and practices.

Benefits, Costs, and Risks

As discussed in Chapter 9, Whiz-Bang could summarize benefits of proposed change by looking at the alignment of the change goals and targets with corporate strategic goals (refer to Table 9-6). The major projected benefit of this initiative is the reduction of cost of sales and the resultant addition of $8.75 million in earnings—assuming sales forecasts are met and prices are not reduced. Whiz-Bang gains additional financial benefits if targets for the other goals are also achieved, in particular reduction in the time to update inventory. Of course, Whiz-Bang positions itself as a stronger competitor.

In Chapter 10, the authors looked at costs and risks of the on-line initiative (refer to Tables 10-1 and 10-2).

Alignment with Lean Principles and Practices

The fourth input is the initiative's alignment with lean principles and practices, which was presented in Tables 9-7 and 9-8.

Summary of the Initiative

Having summarized the benefits, costs, risks, and alignment with lean principles and practices in tables like Tables 9-6, 9-7, 9-8, 10-1, and 10-2, it may be useful to reduce the summary to a graphical form, such as the one that was shown in Figure 10-3. This unified graphical representation of the project in itself may provide adequate information for comparison with other initiatives, or may invite further examination of specific questions.

COMPARING PROJECTS

The decision-making process is one of:

- Weighing benefits against costs and risks;
- Prioritizing initiatives in which potential benefits clearly justify their costs and risks with a minimum disruption of the operation.

To demonstrate the comparison, two additional initiatives might be proposed for Whiz-Bang. These initiatives provide different combinations of benefits, costs, and risks.

Initiative #2: Modular Assembly Cell

The second proposed initiative is intended to enable mass customization of assemble-to-order products. The motivations are to:

- increase Whiz-Bang's current assembly capabilities by 100,000 units/year to 450,000 units;
- broaden the family of products a customer can order by providing the opportunity to include any functionality from Whiz-Bang's three product lines in any item shipped;
- assemble only items that customers have ordered. That is, shift from a push system to a pull system, from batch assembly into inventory-to-assembly upon receipt of order, followed by immediate shipment.

The new assembly method represents a major change in the production paradigm for Whiz-Bang since its current capacity is the sum of the three fixed lines of the three operating divisions. These are lines that operate on a mass-production model with limited capacity to vary product functionality.

Benefits

Table 12-1 summarizes benefits of the modular assembly cell initiative. Here basic benefits are the revenue increase resulting

Table 12-1. Benefits of modular assembly cell initiative

Strategic Perspective	Change Goals	Change Metrics	Baseline Measurements	Target Measurements	Benefits
Financial	Control per unit production costs	Per unit production costs	$120/unit	$120/unit	Capabilities to add $50 million in revenue at no added cost per unit
Customer	Increase match with customer wants	Number of possible product configurations	1,000 configurations	21 million configurations*	Increased ways to satisfy customer demand
Internal operations	Reduce finished units inventory	Number of unsold units/week	2,000 units	0	Savings from inventory reduction
Globalization	Target products to specific markets	Number of configurations tailored for offshore markets	0	20 million	Expanded capability to market offshore
Innovation	Add capabilities for innovative new modules	Number of ways to add new functionality	5	1 million	Expanded flexibility for adding product innovations
Learning and growth	Train a cadre of modular assemblers	Number of employees trained	0	400	Work force suited to more flexible workloads and product mixes

* In principle, customers can order any of 1 million combinations of functionality in any of 20 language variations.

from an increase of 50% in Whiz-Bang's production capacity, coupled with greatly increased flexibility for meeting rapidly changing customer demand.

Customers will be able to order any model mix that Whiz-Bang offers in its three product lines: consumer electronics, personal computing, and home automation. The new production facility will be highly flexible. It will add enough capacity to generate $50 million in additional revenue, even more if the added value of assemble-to-order products with added functionality justifies higher prices. Since the more flexible capital equipment is capable of producing a larger quantity of higher-value products, Whiz-Bang's ROI should increase. The expanded capacity will cause a new risk: if demand for additional production does not materialize, Whiz-Bang might have to sell off the new facility or take an existing production facility out of service, perhaps with a substantial write-down.

Costs

Projected costs for the modular assembly cell initiative are described in Table 12-2. The bulk of these costs are for development and hardware for modular assembly cells and for educating and training those that operate the cells.

As noted in the previous section, the analysis assumes that existing production facilities continue to generate revenue. If projected increase in demand does not materialize, the revenue stream

Table 12-2. Costs for modular assembly cell initiative

Cost Category	Metrics	Budgeted Targets
Time	Time to routine operations	9 months
Development	Development budget	+$1.5 million
Operations	Operations budget/cell	+$840K/yr
Education and training	Education and training budget/cell	+$200K
Capital	Capital budget/cell	$600K

from the new channel will displace existing revenue streams. If that occurs, Whiz-Bang would have to discount benefits because of insufficient demand for utilization of production capacity of combined existing and new assembly facilities.

Risks

Table 12-3 summarizes the risks for the modular assembly cell initiative.

The Modular Cell Assembly Initiative carries a higher risk, the risk that Whiz-Bang ends up with excess capacity. There may be a need for an aggressive marketing campaign to make customers aware of added flexibility in Whiz-Bang's products.

The initiative means that Whiz-Bang's employees have to learn to operate a very different assembly system from the one they use now. The work force will have more responsibility for changing the cell to accommodate various products they are asked to assemble. There could be organizational disruption if the employees do not receive education and training needed to make them comfortable in their new roles.

Alignment with Lean Principles and Practices

Tables 12-4 and 12-5 show the modular assembly cell initiative's alignment with lean principles and practices.

The initiative will make a strong contribution to Whiz-Bang's ability to respond to change by reducing its dependence on the mass-production paradigm and creating the ability to offer customers assembly-on-demand.

Summary of the Initiative

Figure 12-1 summarizes the decision factors for the modular asssembly cell initiative. This summary should be compared with Figure 10-3.

Initiative #3: Hub Distribution System

The third proposed initiative would replace Whiz-Bang's physical distribution system. It assumes that Whiz-Bang has a traditional

Table 12-3. Risks for modular assembly cell initiative

Risk Category	Metrics	Degree of Risk	Risk Reduction Activities
Product acceptance	Product revenue	High	Aggressive marketing programs and targeted promotions of custom-delivered functions
Customer satisfaction	Customer satisfaction index	Medium	Project management, maintenance of quality standards
Partner satisfaction	Partner satisfaction index	Low	Education programs
Development	Time/cost to completion	Medium	Project management, phased implementation
Operations	Operations costs	Medium	Cost containment, continuous improvement
Organizational disruption	Employee satisfaction index	Low	Education and training

Table 12-4. Alignment of modular assembly cell initiative with lean principles

Lean Principle	Degree of Support	Alignment with the Initiative
Minimize waste	High	Reduces unsold units to a minimum.
Respond to change	High	Inherently more flexible assembly technique allows Whiz-Bang to respond much more easily to market change.
Right thing, right place, right time, right quantity	Medium	Provides customers with units that are assembled to their order.
Effective relationships within the value stream	Sustaining	Eliminates one step in value chain (warehousing of finished units).
Continuous improvement	Medium	Modular assembly facilitates combining three assembly lines and accommodating improved modules. Proper design and implementation of the assembly facility helps to accommodate modular improvements.
Optimal first-delivered unit quantity	Sustaining	The assemble-to-order facility allows delivery of product meeting specific customer need on demand.

regional warehousing and distribution system. The initiative would replace that system with a hub distribution system.

Whiz-Bang's products are amenable to distribution using commercial package delivery services such as those offered by UPS and FedEx. With these commercial services, distribution cost is not strongly dependent on distance from the shipping dock. This means Whiz-Bang can use a centralized distribution point as a

Table 12-5. Alignment of modular assembly cell initiative with lean practices

Lean Practice	Degree of Support	Alignment with the Initiative
Focus on customer . . . continuously	High	Supplies customers with functionality they want rather than with some preconceived understanding of their wants.
Implement IPPD	Sustaining	Opportunity to introduce IPPD for internal product and process development.
Identify and optimize enterprise flow	Sustaining	Reduces material handling and processing through warehouse operations.
Assure seamless information flow	Negligible	Seamless information flow from customer to assembly facility is required for this initiative to succeed.
Ensure process capability, maturity, and yield	Sustaining	Provides greater consistency in rate production and quality level.
Challenge existing processes for continuous improvement	High	The initiative represents a significant departure from Whiz-Bang's existing assembly processes, enhancing increased profitability.
Promote lean leadership at all levels	Medium	Places more responsibility on operators who have to be leaders in their cells.
Make decisions at lowest level possible	Sustaining	More decisions made at cell level.
Optimize capabilities and use of human resources	Medium	The system uses people to exercise the flexibility of assembly cells to meet customer wants.
Develop relationships based on trust and commitment	Sustaining	IPTs promote improved relationships across entire company.
Nurture a learning environment	Medium	A major departure from prior method of operation that requires significant learning—an example for a learning environment.
Maximize stability in a changing environment	Medium	Capability of assembling a variety of products using the same cell design and basic procedures, thus improving ROI of capital investment.

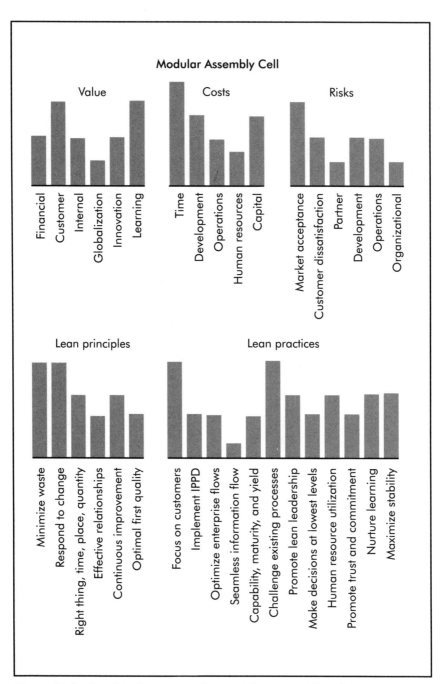

Figure 12-1. Graphical summary for modular assembly cell initiative.

hub. Such a distribution point can be located at or near the production line so that finished products can flow directly from line to customer. In contrast, a regional warehousing system requires trans-shipment from assembly point to warehouse, storing and handling at the warehouse, and then packing and shipping to the customer. The company can eliminate many steps that are subject to error if shipping is done directly from the assembly point, or from a nearby commercial shipping hub. The result is:

- reduced distribution time from plant to customer;
- reduced handling between plant and customer;
- simpler distribution system with fewer opportunities for errors or damage;
- reduced inventories in the pipeline from plant to customer;
- and elimination of costs related to regional warehouses and any company-owned transportation facilities.

Benefits

Benefits are summarized in Table 12-6. The hub distribution initiative reduces elapsed time between the time the customer enters the order and the time the product is delivered and paid for. Although reduced float is large enough to be significant on Whiz-Bang's balance sheet, the assumption is that the primary benefit is greater customer satisfaction and loyalty. The result should be higher retention of the customer for all of Whiz-Bang's products. The initiative also provides opportunity to redirect shipments while in transit if customer needs should suddenly shift.

Costs

Table 12-7 describes costs of the hub distribution initiative, which are lower than the costs of the previous two. Elimination of regional warehouses will save the costs of personnel, supervision, and transportation between factory and warehouses, as well as the costs of warehouses. The expectation is that these savings will exceed operating costs of the hub system. Although cost of package delivery services may be somewhat higher, those costs will be more than offset by the elimination of regional warehouses.

Table 12-6. Benefits from hub distribution initiative

Strategic Perspective	Change Goals	Change Metrics	Baseline Measurements	Target Measurements	Benefits
Financial	Decrease order to payment time	Average time elapsed from order to payment	14 days	10 days	Reduce float by four days (= $1.9 million assuming $175 million annual revenues)
Customer	Reduce time for delivery	Average elapsed time for order fulfillment	12 days	8 days	More immediate satisfaction of customer demands
Internal operations	Reduce distribution inventory cost	Value of units in distribution inventory	$2 million	$500K	Reduced need for working capital
Reduced inventory losses and errors
Globalization	Establish global distribution system	Number of countries to which products are delivered	10	200	Expanded capability to market offshore
Innovation	—	—	—	—	—
Learning and growth	Provide new skills	Number of people trained	0	40	Adequate labor force to support expansion

Table 12-7. Costs for hub distribution initiative

Cost Category	Metrics	Budgeted Targets
Time	Time to routine operations	4 months
Development	Development budget	+$400K
Operations	Operations budget	+$250K/mo.
Education and training	Education and training budget	+$125K
Capital	Net capital budget after sale of warehouses	–$500K

Risks

Table 12-8 summarizes risks for the hub distribution initiative. The highest risk lies in the termination of relationships with suppliers at regional warehouses. Whiz-Bang must be particularly sensitive to the effects on small businesses. They may require some help in recovering from loss of Whiz-Bang's business. The next highest risk lies with customer satisfaction. If customers perceive the new system to be less responsive in delivering the right product at the right time when compared to the warehousing system, they will be dissatisfied.

Alignment with Lean Principles and Practices

The alignment with lean principles and practices is shown in Tables 12-9 and 12-10.

The hub distribution initiative will move Whiz-Bang toward being a lean company. It is one piece in the puzzle. Its benefits may not be visible in the bottom line, but its implementation can fit with, for example, other initiatives proposed to make Whiz-Bang more responsive to the customer. If Whiz-Bang implements this initiative and on-line order entry, the initiatives can reduce significantly the time from order entry to delivery. Combining an improved order entry system with the new package delivery system will cut elapsed time by nearly a week. Overall, this would make the company much more responsive to customers, while accruing important financial benefits.

Table 12-8. Risks for hub distribution initiative

Risk Category	Metrics	Degree of Risk	Risk Reduction Activities
Product acceptance	Product revenue	Low	Demonstrate more reliable delivery
Customer satisfaction	Customer satisfaction index	Medium	Employee, supplier, and customer education Quality assurance
Partner satisfaction	Partner satisfaction index	High	Education of affected distributors Termination compensation
Development	Time/cost to completion	Medium	Project management Early pilot implementations
Operations	Operations costs	Low	Cost containment Continuous improvement
Organizational disruption	Employee satisfaction index	Medium	Reassignment and retraining

Table 12-9. Alignment of hub distribution initiative with lean principles

Lean Principle	Degree of Support	Alignment with the Initiative
Minimize waste	Medium	Reduces time and effort devoted to distribution, simplifying operations and reducing losses and time spent on corrective actions.
Respond to change	Sustaining	Permits more flexible delivery channels that are controlled from assembly point.
Right thing, right place, right time, right quantity	Medium	Reduces possibility that customer orders are lost or that wrong products are delivered.
Effective relationships within the value stream	Sustaining	Eliminates one step in value chain (regional warehousing of finished units).
Continuous improvement	Negligible	Provides opportunities for minor improvements.
Optimal first delivered unit quantity	Sustaining	Better ensures that delivered product meets customer needs in a timely manner.

Table 12-10. Alignment of hub distribution initiative with lean practices

Lean Practice	Degree of Support	Alignment with Initiative
Focus on customer . . . continuously	High	Supplies customers more quickly with the products they want.
Implement IPPD	Negligible	Simple, self-contained project. IPPD provides more discipline to planning process.
Identify and optimize enterprise flow	Medium	Initiative gradually eliminates regional warehousing entirely.
Assure seamless information flow	Sustaining	Package delivery services' tracking systems improve information flow and provide an automated system for real-time information on location of order.
Ensure process capability, maturity, and yield	Sustaining	Simpler process should reach maturity quickly and sustain process yield.
Challenge existing processes for continuous improvement	Medium	Initiative is a significant departure from Whiz-Bang's existing distribution processes, but provides more reliable and timelier delivery service.
Promote lean leadership at all levels	Negligible	Creates an atmosphere promoting continuous improvement.
Make decisions at the lowest level possible	Negligible	Creates an environment that encourages employees to suggest ideas for operational improvement.
Optimize capabilities and use of human resources	Medium	Reduces number of employees devoted to distribution and makes better use of the few who are assigned to it.
Develop relationships based on trust and commitment	Medium	Improves employee morale and encourages an improved work ethic.
Nurture a learning environment	Sustaining	Provides a learning experience for those who must operate the new system.
Maximize stability in a changing environment	Medium	Makes distribution operations more visible, reduces variations in regional operations.

Summary of the Initiative

Decision factors for the hub distribution initiative are summarized in Figure 12-2 in the same way as those for the two previous initiatives. The three figures—Figures 10-3, 12-1, and 12-2—provide a standard way to compare initiatives.

THE DECISION

In which initiatives should a company invest? Sometimes the decision is an easy one. Sometimes proposals have clear benefits and the company has sufficient funds available to fund them. Occasionally there is one proposal that is so obviously the most important one, the company is willing to pour investment funds into it.

More likely, however, the decision is not that simple. More likely, all proposed projects have worthwhile benefits. They further the company's efforts to become leaner. Nevertheless, they have substantial costs. Moreover, they have risks that are too large to ignore.

The three examples in this chapter are typical of realistic projects. They are not merely incremental changes. Each represents a significant change in the way Whiz-Bang does business. But neither are they make-or-break changes, so dramatic as to compel immediate advancement. They are good, sound ideas for a conservatively run company seeking to become leaner. Should Whiz-Bang make the investments in these changes? In which should Whiz-Bang invest first?

There is no silver bullet

There is no silver bullet—no simple and sure formula for deciding in which of these projects to invest. Although the authors have provided tables, checklists, and graphical descriptions for comparing projects, these tools cannot hide the subjective nature of the decision. Because of the complex combination of benefits, costs, and risks that each project presents, they are not directly comparable. They cannot be put on a single scale and weighed.

Approach to Benefits

The financial benefits of an initiative are always important. There is no reason to invest in an initiative unless it either provides a

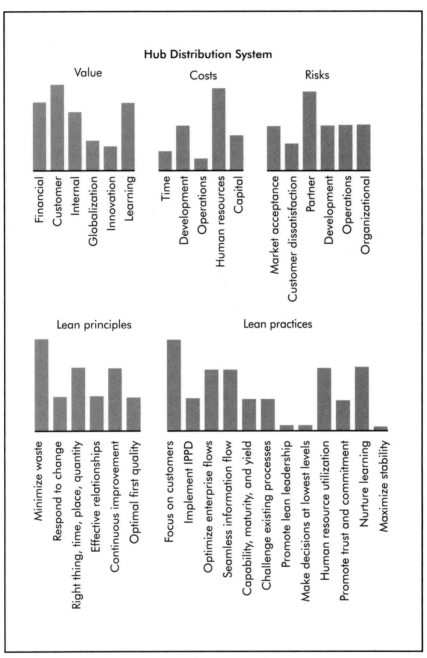

Figure 12-2. Graphical summary for hub distribution system.

direct financial benefit or enables other initiatives that provide obvious financial benefits.

Some companies' decision-making processes focus almost exclusively on financial benefits. In many instances, these companies aim for short-term results or improvements on a quarterly basis. They may believe such improvements are necessary to satisfy the financial community. Others take an approach—the one the authors espouse—that examines the initiative's contributions toward achieving a balanced set of strategic goals. When this is done, some goals loom more importantly than other goals in any planning period. That may be because of some pressing external event, or because the company perceives a weakness in one of the perspectives that requires special attention.

For example, if a competitor has started offering modular multifunction products, Whiz-Bang may conclude that capability of meeting customer demand for customized variations of its products is essential for its survival. In this case, it will invest in the modular assembly cell initiative. If it is clear, however, that Whiz-Bang is losing customers because it is not responding to orders fast enough, it will invest in one or both of the initiatives that cut delivery time. If Whiz-Bang thinks its most important nonfinancial strategic goal is globalization, then the extended reach provided by order entry and fulfillment initiatives may be more attractive.

Approach to Cost

Obviously, the company must be comfortable with the cost of initiatives in which it invests. Just as with family accounts, the company has its own definition of comfort. It can probably be defined in cold financial terms—level of reserves the business needs to run, percentage of cash flow, rating for debt, or the price-to-earnings ratio that satisfies shareholders.

Company leaders must be satisfied that there are no other ways to achieve equivalent benefits at significantly lower costs. More fundamentally, they must be comfortable that they can pay for the initiatives. Prudent financial planning sets aside funds for some change initiatives as an investment strategy for renewal and growth. Most companies divide funds for investment into two parts. One is built into the operating budget and covers expense items. The other is the capital budget for acquisition of facilities and equipment, the value of which appears on the asset ledger and costs of which are amortized over several years.

As noted before, the amount in the budget for lean change initiatives will probably be less than the cost of all the worthy proposals the company receives. Is it willing to take funds from other reserves? Is it willing to borrow, or even sell equity, to fund change initiatives?

Approach to Risk

The company and its executive leadership have a culture that defines their approach to the benefit-cost-risk equation. As noted, some companies seem to thrive by taking risks; others fail when risk overtakes them. Some companies thrive by making only considered decisions—decisions that look almost like a chess master's moves—in which risks are minimized. Other companies fail because they habitually are too conservative.

The authors do not argue for one approach to risk over another. The most important factors are honest appraisals of decision inputs, including risks. Whatever the approach, company leaders should make investment decisions using the most objective assessments possible. Although the decision ultimately may be made with the decision-maker's intuitive assessment of risk, that risk should be based on realistic scenarios, not on unnamed fears and inapplicable myths.

A Lean Decision Process

The authors do argue for a lean decision-making process because it provides timely, high-quality decisions. As with every other process in the lean company, the decision-making process should minimize waste and be responsive to change.

A lean decision-making process is one that accepts time constraints and seeks to make accurate decisions within those constraints. In a dynamic global competition, a company cannot afford to waste time in the decision-making process. The old adage, "Time is money!" is a mantra for 21st Century business. There is a time for all things—even for change initiatives.

A company cannot afford to waste time in the decision-making process

Time wasted in making a decision may be the difference between being first to market, or being just a secondary player in the market. Time wasted may mean that company leaders are stuck and cannot focus on the next decisions they must make. Worse, it may mean that those who would be affected by the decision are placed in a state of suspended animation. Do they continue to work toward the initiative, or do they return to their other work? If they return to their other work, are they available and prepared to return to the proposed initiative if it is finally launched? A crisp, timely decision eliminates uncertainty that can sap work force morale. It provides workers with the stability of knowing what they are or are not going to do next.

If someone deep in the organization can make as good or even a better decision than the change leaders would make, that person should make it and get visible support for his or her decision. That way, change leaders will be free to use their time on decisions that are their core competencies—the things only they can decide. They will demonstrate lean leadership by doing this.

Sometimes, time constraints require leaders to make decisions without as much information as they prefer to have. The decision-making process and change initiative design should recognize this and be flexible enough to accommodate additional information as it becomes available.

There are other costs in decision-making. Leaders need clear, concise, and complete information. But how much information do they really need? Line management in traditional American industry got into a habit of "staffing" nearly every decision. This meant that a staff person or group reviewed each proposal. The staff might, or might not, include experts as participants in the decision. Reaching a decision meant that the proposal team first had to convince the staff, usually buttressing its arguments with voluminous data to support the initiative and serve as advocates. In the worst of circumstances, decision-makers were shielded from raw information that might support or reject acceptance of an initiative. This technique wasted the efforts of the proposal team and often consumed more time than the actual initiative took to complete. It wasted talents of the staff, which could better be employed directly in activities that added value to the company.

Electronic communications has reduced the need for staff investigations. Raw information is more readily available, and executives can direct inquiries more precisely to experts within the company. The decision-makers in lean companies should be more active participants in the decision-making process, even going as far as examining raw data.

Other Prioritization Considerations

In Chapter 8, the authors wrote of the roadmap for transforming a company. The chances are that if you have used the checklist implied by the Lean Enterprise Model, or some other model of leanness, your initiatives will lie someplace on the roadmap. No matter how tempting the initiative, if it is not consistent with the roadmap, it is time to ask questions: is the initiative a good idea that simply does not fit with the directions you want to take your company? Or, have conditions changed such that you need to update your roadmap to accommodate your new ideas? If you do include the initiative in the roadmap, what else needs to change?

Some initiatives have prerequisites. If a company does not have plans to complete an initiative on which a second one depends, it makes little sense to invest in the second. For example, Whiz-Bang needs to have in place an electronic network that links its sales function to its production facilities before it completes the on-line distribution and inventory control system. Otherwise, its investment in on-line systems is diminished if not negated. The roadmap for lean transformation should provide a basis for precedence evaluations.

Some initiatives must be done now—they are "hole in the dike" initiatives required to fix an immediate problem. Toxic waste is found leaking from tanks on the plant site. This must be fixed now. Competitors have websites that are grabbing customers' attention. You may not have a clear view of how you can gain revenue from the website, but you may need to implement a presence immediately just to maintain your hold on customer mindshare. Or, in the case of our third example, the company may accelerate implementation of the hub distribution system if it has lost its leases on regional warehouses.

DECISION-MAKING

Decision-making in business is a multi-attribute process. In Chapters 9 and 10, the authors cataloged many attributes that decision-makers should consider before deciding to invest in a lean change initiative. The complexity of most decisions precludes an unambiguous mathematical description. Therefore, intuition or subjective judgment enters into most investment decisions.

For most, decision-making is a pattern-recognition process. Decision-makers consider the pattern of benefits, costs, risks, and lean alignment and, based on experience, evaluate the pattern.

Decision-making is a process that can be engineered. The first step in any process engineering effort is to make the steps of the process visible. The better leaders understand how they make decisions—even ones that demand intuition—the more systematic and consistent their decisions will be. The better they understand decision-making as a process, the more they can improve their decision-making—by improving the process.

In a lean, knowledge-based, company, where decision-making is expected at every level, the whole organization should have visibility into the decision-making process. Not only should the decision-maker understand the process he or she uses, but the process should be well enough understood so it can be explained in a rational way to anyone whose activities are affected by the decision.

The form the actual decision-making process takes is dependent on many factors:

- An experienced decision-maker may have a deep understanding of customer and business issues, and be able to read the pattern accurately enough to make decisions without a formal process. Clearly, this is a model that is most effective for companies with slowly changing markets, business processes, and technologies. In this situation, previous experience is almost mandatory.

273

- Decision-makers facing complicated decisions, or inexperienced decision-makers, may prefer a more formal process. If the market and competitive environment are dynamic, and prior experience does not provide reliable precedents, then a systematic consideration of decision factors presented in this book is warranted.
- The size of the commitment makes a difference, too. The "you bet your company" decision warrants a formal evaluation. The process for a decision that carries low costs and will affect only a small part of the company may be less formal.

Leaders can think of decision making as they would of any process used to manufacture a product. Here the product of the process is the decision. Some of the ideas of Integrated Product and Process Development (IPPD) help describe a lean decision-making process—including use of Integrated Product Teams (IPTs) and Rapid Improvement Teams (RITs).

Whether or not the ultimate decision-maker is a single individual, the decision-making process should be team-based, involving people from all affected areas of the company. This is not in contradiction to the argument against the process of staffing decisions. Here the issue is to have people directly affected by a decision represented by their leaders. There are several reasons to involve a team of this sort in decision-making. Few people in organizations of some complexity have all the information, understand all the nuances, and see all the benefits, or pitfalls, of a decision. The people most likely to see important factors are those charged with making a reality out of the decision. In the end, the decision will cost the company less if this group gets a chance to veto it first.

Since this is the team responsible for carrying out the decision, its member's involvement in the decision means that they can better communicate it to the work force. Communication will be quicker and more accurate, making it less likely that execution of the decision will be wasteful.

The more the company's leadership gains experience with lean decision-making, the better able each person will be to make decisions for which he or she is responsible.

As difficult as it is to buck human nature, the decision-maker and decision-making team should leave their egos at the door. The issue, of course, is the ultimate good of the company and its stake-holders, as defined by its strategic goals and leavened by its culture. Ideally, everyone on the team comes away convinced that the best choices were made for the good of the enterprise—even if a favorite initiative was left unfunded or given a low priority. That is why it is so important to provide objective information for the decision and to make the process as visible and understandable as possible—to reduce contention based on emotion. Even if a change leader disagrees with it, he or she should come away with an understanding of rationale for the decision based on the benefit, cost, risk, and leanness criteria adopted in the company.

The simple approach to investment choices posed in this chapter is a qualitative comparison of graphical summaries of the proposed initiatives. Figures 12-1, 12-2, and 12-3 provide examples of graphical summaries. This is a starting point, an alignment of the decision with the company's real or perceived priorities. As initiatives are sorted by precedence, alignment, affordability, and risk, the comparisons will be supported by reference to the tabular summaries.

EXERCISES

1. Prepare a presentation that gives your recommendations for prioritization of Whiz-Bang's three proposed initiatives.
2. Consider the three initiatives you developed in Chapter 9. Develop decision factors for them (you will already have done so for one of them). Prepare a presentation that presents your recommendation for investment (or non-investment) in the three.

Appendix A

Survey of Perceptions of a Company's Leanness

In Chapter 4, the authors suggest one way to assess a company's leanness, using 36 questions framed for specific stakeholder groups. Each pair of questions probes the group's perception of the company's current adherence and trend toward one of two lean meta principles, four enterprise principles, and 12 overarching practices. The questions in Tables A-1 to A-5 provide a sample of such a survey. In this survey, the authors provide variations for customers, executives, employees, suppliers, and investors.

The 36 questions are intended as a guide. A company may want to probe for perceptions of other aspects of the Lean Enterprise Model than those touched upon by these questions. The company also may want to probe perceptions of other stakeholder groups with questions tailored specifically for them, such as government or community leaders.

The questions can be answered with quick, scale-of-one-to-five answers. Answers can be quickly tabulated and summarized. Respondents should be given an opportunity to elaborate on these numerical values if a question strikes a passionate chord.

Odd-numbered questions probe the company's current state of leanness. Questions are designed so that answers for lean companies should average between 3.0 and 5.0 for all stakeholder groups. The closer to 5.0 the average is, the leaner the company.

Even-numbered questions probe perceived trends—is the company becoming more or less lean? Answers averaging above 3.0 indicate that the company is perceived as getting leaner. If the company is perceived as already being very lean (with averages for odd-numbered questions approaching 5.0), the rate of change may not be great and the average of even-numbered questions might be as low as 3.0. On the other hand, if the company has a so-so average on the odd-numbered questions, but averages 4.0 or above on even-numbered ones, it is making progress toward leanness.

Table A-1. Customer survey

Lean Principle or Practice	Question	Choose One Answer by Number				
		1	2	3	4	5
1. Respond to change	What is the company's response when you come to it with a new requirement?	Very poor	Poor	OK	Good	Very good
2.	Is the company better or worse at meeting your needs now than it was 12 months ago?	Much worse	Worse	Same	Better	Much better
3. Minimize waste	How efficiently does the company handle its transactions with you?	Very inefficiently	Inefficiently	OK	Efficiently	Very efficiently
4.	How much more or less efficient is the company now than it was 12 months ago?	Much less	Less	Same	More	Much more

Table A-1. Customer survey (continued)

Lean Principle or Practice	Question	Choose One Answer by Number				
		1	2	3	4	5
5. The right thing at the right place, the right time, and in the right quantity	Does the company deliver what you order, correct in all details, when you need it?	Never	Seldom	Some-times	Usually	Always
6.	Is the company fulfilling your orders better or worse than it was 12 months ago?	Much worse	Worse	Same	Better	Much better
7. Effective relation-ships within the value stream	Does the company blame its suppliers if problems arise in its products or services?	Always blames	Usually blames	Some-times blames	Seldom blames	Never blames
8.	Is there more or less evidence of poor working relationships between the company and its suppliers now than there was 12 months ago?	Much more evidence	More evidence	Same evidence	Less evidence	Much less evidence

Table A-1. Customer survey (continued)

Lean Principle or Practice	Question	Choose One Answer by Number				
		1	2	3	4	5
9. Continuous improvement	Does the company continually and aggressively find ways to better serve you?	Never	Seldom	Some-times	Usually	Always
10.	Is the company more or less aggressive with its improvements than it was 12 months ago?	Much less	Less	Same	More	Much more
11. Optimal first-delivered unit quality	Does quality of the first delivery of the company's products meet your standards?	Never	Seldom	Some-times	Usually	Always
12.	Are there more or fewer instances of the first delivery of a product meeting your standards now than there were 12 months ago?	Many fewer	Fewer	Same	More	Many more

Table A-1. Customer survey (continued)

Lean Principle or Practice	Question	Choose One Answer by Number				
		1	2	3	4	5
13. Focus on the customer . . . continuously	Do you trust the company to pay adequate attention to your needs and interests?	Never	Seldom	Some-times	Usually	Always
14.	Is the company paying more or less attention to your needs and interests than it was 12 months ago?	Much less	Less	Same	More	Much more
15. Implement Integrated Product and Process Development	Does the company include you, or customers whose interests are similar to yours, on its Integrated Product Teams?	Never	Seldom	Some-times	Usually	Always
16.	Does the company formally consult you more or less about your needs and interests than it did 12 months ago?	Much less	Less	Same	More	Much more

Table A-1. Customer survey (continued)

Lean Principle or Practice	Question	Choose One Answer by Number				
		1	2	3	4	5
17. Identify and optimize enterprise flow	How often do you perceive bottlenecks within the company that reduce its ability to provide you the goods and services you want?	Always bottle-necks	Usually bottle-necks	Some-times bottle-necks	Seldom bottle-necks	Never bottle-necks
18.	Are there more or fewer such bottlenecks within the company that reduce its ability to provide you the goods and services you want than there were 12 months ago?	Many more bottle-necks	More bottle-necks	Same amount of bottle-necks	Fewer bottle-necks	Many fewer bottle-necks
19. Assure seamless information flow	Does the company provide you with accurate information in a form you can use when you want it?	Never	Seldom	Some-times	Usually	Always
20.	Is the company providing you with information that is more or less usable than the information it provided 12 months ago?	Much less	Less	Same	More	Much more

Table A-1. Customer survey (continued)

Lean Principle or Practice	Question	Choose One Answer by Number				
		1	2	3	4	5
21. Ensure process capability, maturity, and yield	How often does the company delay shipment of products because of process bottlenecks?	Always	Usually	Some-times	Seldom	Never
22.	Are there more or fewer delays than there were 12 months ago?	Many more delays	More delays	Same amount of delays	Fewer delays	Much fewer delays
23. Challenge existing processes to achieve continuous improvement	Does the company work with you to develop better processes to meet your needs and interests?	Never	Seldom	Some-times	Usually	Always
24.	Is the company working with you on better processes more or less than it did 12 months ago?	Much less	Less	Same	More	Much more

Table A-1. Customer survey (continued)

Lean Principle or Practice	Question	Choose One Answer by Number				
		1	2	3	4	5
25. Promote lean leadership at all levels	Do the company's people respond quickly to your changing needs with no wasted effort?	Never	Seldom	Some-times	Usually	Always
26.	Are the company's people responding to your needs better or worse than they did 12 months ago?	Much worse	Worse	Same	Better	Much better
27. Make decisions at the lowest level possible	How often do the company's people with whom you work defer to others in the company for decisions that relate to you?	Never	Seldom	Some-times	Usually	Always
28.	Are the company's people making more or fewer decisions without referring them elsewhere in the company than they did 12 months ago?	Much fewer	Fewer	Same	More	Many more

Table A-1. Customer survey (continued)

Lean Principle or Practice	Question	Choose One Answer by Number				
		1	2	3	4	5
29. Optimize capabilities and utilization of human resources	Are the capabilities of the company's people with whom you come in contact utilized well?	Very poorly	Poorly	OK	Well	Very well
30.	Is the company using the capabilities of its people better or worse than it did 12 months ago?	Much worse	Worse	Same	Better	Much better
31. Develop relationships based on mutual trust and commitment	Do you trust the company and its people with whom you are in contact?	Never	Seldom	Some-times	Usually	Always
32.	Do you trust the company and its people more or less than you did 12 months ago?	Much less	Less	Same	More	Much more

Table A-1. Customer survey (continued)

Lean Principle or Practice	Question	Choose One Answer by Number				
		1	2	3	4	5
33. Nurture a learning environment	Are the company's people eager to learn and share what they learn with you?	Never	Seldom	Some-times	Usually	Always
34.	Are the company's people more or less eager to learn than they were 12 months ago?	Much less	Less	Same	More	Much more
35. Maximize stability in a changing environment	When circumstances demand a change, does the company change in a measured, dependable way?	Never	Seldom	Some-times	Usually	Always
36.	Does the company handle change better or worse than it did 12 months ago?	Much worse	Worse	Same	Better	Much better

Table A-2. Executive survey

Lean Principle or Practice	Question	Choose One Answer by Number				
		1	2	3	4	5
1. Respond to change	What is your company's response to changes in customer needs?	Very poor	Poor	OK	Good	Very good
2.	Is your company better or worse at meeting customers' needs now than 12 months ago?	Much worse	Worse	Same	Better	Much better
3. Minimize waste	How many areas in the company have activities where there is obvious waste?	Most areas	Many areas	Some areas	Few areas	Almost no areas
4.	How much more or less waste is there in your company compared to 12 months ago?	Much more waste	More waste	Same amount of waste	Less waste	Much less waste

Table A-2. Executive survey (continued)

Lean Principle or Practice	Question	Choose One Answer by Number				
		1	2	3	4	5
5. The right thing at the right place, the right time, and in the right quantity	Does your executive team make crisp, complete, and timely decisions?	Never	Seldom	Some-times	Usually	Always
6.	Are your executive team's decision-making processes better or worse than 12 months ago?	Much worse	Worse	Same	Better	Much better
7. Effective relation-ships within the value stream	How often do your operating groups escalate issues to you that you think should be resolved at lower levels of your company?	Always escalate issues	Usually escalate issues	Some-times escalate issues	Seldom escalate issues	Never escalate issues
8.	Are your operating groups escalating more or fewer such issues to you now than they did 12 months ago?	Many more issues	More issues	Same amount of issues	Fewer issues	Much fewer issues

Table A-2. Executive survey (continued)

Lean Principle or Practice	Question	Choose One Answer by Number				
		1	2	3	4	5
9. Continuous improvement	Is there continuous improvement in the measurements used to gage progress your company is making toward achieving its strategic goals?	Never	Seldom	Some-times	Usually	Always
10.	Is the rate of improvement greater or less than it was 12 months ago?	Much less	Less	Same	Greater	Much greater
11. Optimal first-delivered unit quality	How often do you receive complaints about the quality of work done by any of your operating groups?	Many more com-plaints	More com-plaints	Some com-plaints	Few com-plaints	No com-plaints
12.	Are you receiving more or fewer such complaints than you did 12 months ago?	Many more com-plaints	More com-plaints	Same amount of com-plaints	Fewer com-plaints	Much fewer com-plaints

Table A-2. Executive survey (continued)

Lean Principle or Practice	Question	Choose One Answer by Number				
		1	2	3	4	5
13. Focus on the customer . . . continuously	Do you make regular reviews of your company's relationships with its customers?	Never	Seldom	Some-times	Usually	Always
14.	Are your reviews of customer relationships more or less comprehensive than they were 12 months ago?	Much less	Less	Same	More	Much more
15. Implement Integrated Product and Process Development	Do you structure Integrated Product Teams to include customers, suppliers, and all relevant functional areas involved with the product throughout its life cycle?	Never	Seldom	Some-times	Usually	Always
16.	Are your Integrated Product Teams more or less comprehensive than they were 12 months ago?	Much less	Less	Same	More	Much more

Table A-2. Executive survey (continued)

Lean Principle or Practice	Question	Choose One Answer by Number				
		1	2	3	4	5
17. Identify and optimize enterprise flow	How often do you have to resolve contentious situations that arise because of a breakdown in flow of products, materials, or knowledge across the company's extended enterprise?	Always	Usually	Some-times	Seldom	Never
18.	Are there more or fewer contentious situations because of a breakdown in the flow of products, materials, or knowledge in the company than there were 12 months ago?	Many more situations	More situations	Same amount of situations	Fewer situations	Much fewer situations
19. Assure seamless information flow	How often do you receive accurate information to do your job in a form that is usable when you need it?	Never	Seldom	Some-times	Usually	Always
20.	Is the information you receive more or less usable than the information you received 12 months ago?	Much less	Less	Same	More	Much more

Table A-2. Executive survey (continued)

Lean Principle or Practice	Question	Choose One Answer by Number				
		1	2	3	4	5
21. Ensure process capability, maturity, and yield	How often does the company delay shipment of products because of process bottlenecks?	Always delays	Usually delays	Some-times delays	Seldom delays	Never delays
22.	Are there more or fewer delays than there were 12 months ago?	Many more delays	More delays	Same amount of delays	Fewer delays	Much fewer delays
23. Challenge existing processes to achieve continu-ous improvement	How often do you see proposals to revamp your company's processes?	Never	Seldom	Some-times	Usually	Always
24.	Are you seeing more or fewer proposals for improved processes than you did 12 months ago?	Much fewer	Fewer	Same amount	More	Many more

Table A-2. Executive survey (continued)

Lean Principle or Practice	Question	Choose One Answer by Number				
		1	2	3	4	5
25. Promote lean leadership at all levels	Does the company's leadership respond quickly and effectively to change, with no wasted effort?	Never	Seldom	Some-times	Usually	Always
26.	Does the company's leadership respond to change better or worse than it did 12 months ago?	Much worse	Worse	Same	Better	Much better
27. Make decisions at the lowest level possible	How often do you make decisions that affect only internal operations within one line organization reporting to you?	Never	Seldom	Some-times	Usually	Always
28.	Are you making more or fewer decisions that affect only internal operations within one of the line organizations reporting to you than you were 12 months ago?	Many more decisions	More decisions	Same amount of de-cisions	Fewer decisions	Much fewer decisions

Table A-2. Executive survey (continued)

Lean Principle or Practice	Question	Choose One Answer by Number				
		1	2	3	4	5
29. Optimize cap-abilities and human resources	Does the company utilize the capabilities of its people well?	Very poorly	Poorly	OK	Well	Very well
30.	Is the company using the capabilities of its people more or less than it did 12 months ago?	Much less	Less	Same	More	Much more
31. Develop relationships based on mutual trust and commitment	Do you trust your peers and the people who report to you?	Never	Seldom	Some-times	Usually	Always
32.	Do you trust your peers and the people who report to you more or less than you did 12 months ago?	Much less	Less	Same	More	Much more

Table A-2. Executive survey (continued)

Lean Principle or Practice	Question	Choose One Answer by Number				
		1	2	3	4	5
33. Nurture a learning environment	Are the company and its people eager to learn and share what they learn with suppliers and customers?	Never	Seldom	Some-times	Usually	Always
34.	Are the company and its people more or less eager to learn than they were 12 months ago?	Much less	Less	Same	More	Much more
35. Maximize stability in a changing environment	When circumstances demand a change, does the company change in a measured, dependable way?	Never	Seldom	Some-times	Usually	Always
36.	Does the company handle change better or worse than it did 12 months ago?	Much worse	Worse	Same	Better	Much better

Table A-3. Employee survey

| Lean Principle or Practice | Question | Choose One Answer by Number | | | | |
		1	2	3	4	5
1. Respond to change	Is your work more or less difficult when the company responds to changing customer needs?	Much more difficult	More difficult	No significant difficulty	No more difficult	Easier
2.	Is the company changing too fast or too often, or is it changing too slow?	Much too fast	Too fast	OK	Too slow	Much too slow
3. Minimize waste	How wasteful is the company in the activities you see in your daily work?	Always wasteful	Usually wasteful	Sometimes wasteful	Seldom wasteful	Never wasteful
4.	How much more or less waste is there today than there was 12 months ago?	Much more waste	More waste	Same amount of waste	Less waste	Much less waste

Table A-3. Employee survey (continued)

Lean Principle or Practice	Question	Choose One Answer by Number				
		1	2	3	4	5
5. The right thing at the right place, and in the right time, and in the right quantity	Do you have all the tools and inputs you need, when you need them to complete your job on time?	Never	Seldom	Some-times	Usually	Always
6.	Is the availability of tools and other inputs for your work better or worse than it was 12 months ago?	Much worse	Worse	Same	Better	Much better
7. Effective relation-ships within the value stream	How often does miscommunication by others interfere with accomplishing your work?	Always interferes	Usually interferes	Sometimes interferes	Seldom interferes	Never interferes
8.	Is there more or less miscommunication than there was 12 months ago?	Much more	More	Same	Less	Much less

Table A-3. Employee survey (continued)

Lean Principle or Practice	Question	Choose One Answer by Number				
		1	2	3	4	5
9. Continuous improvement	How often do you make changes in the way you accomplish your work in order to improve it?	Never	Seldom	Some-times	Usually	Always
10.	Are you making more or fewer changes than you were 12 months ago?	Much fewer	Fewer	Same	More	Many more
11. Optimal first-delivered unit quality	How often do you receive inputs of poor quality from other groups?	Always inputs	Usually inputs	Some-times inputs	Seldom inputs	Never inputs
12.	Are you receiving more or fewer poor quality inputs than you were 12 months ago?	Many more poor quality inputs	More poor quality inputs	Same	Fewer quality inputs	Much fewer poor quality inputs

Table A-3. Employee survey (continued)

Lean Principle or Practice	Question	Choose One Answer by Number				
		1	2	3	4	5
13. Focus on the customer . . . continuously	How often do you know who the internal "customers" are at work, and who the ultimate paying customers are?	Never	Seldom	Some-times	Usually	Always
14.	Are you communicating more or less with your internal "customers" and with the ultimate paying customer than you did 12 months ago?	Much less	Less	Same	More	Much more
15. Implement Integrated Product and Process Development	How often do you or your work group participate in cross-functional or Integrated Product Teams?	Never	Seldom	Some-times	Usually	Always
16.	Is there more or less participation than there was 12 months ago?	Much less	Less	Same	More	Much more

Table A-3. Employee survey (continued)

Lean Principle or Practice	Question	Choose One Answer by Number				
		1	2	3	4	5
17. Identify and optimize enterprise flow	How often do you have trouble receiving the inputs of material, parts, other supplies, and information and knowledge you need for your work?	Always trouble	Usually trouble	Some-times trouble	Seldom trouble	Never trouble
18.	Are you having more or less trouble receiving the inputs you need than you did 12 months ago?	Much more trouble	More trouble	Same	Less trouble	Much less trouble
19. Assure seamless information flow	How often do you receive accurate information in a usable form when you need it?	Never	Seldom	Some-times	Usually	Always
20.	Is the information you receive more or less usable than the information you received 12 months ago?	Much less usable	Less usable	Same	More usable	Much more usable

Table A-3. Employee survey (continued)

Lean Principle or Practice	Question	Choose One Answer by Number				
		1	2	3	4	5
21. Ensure process capability, maturity, and yield	How often do problems due to upstream capacity, maturity, or yield affect your work?	Always affects work	Usually affects work	Some-times affects work	Seldom affects work	Never affects work
22.	Are there more or fewer problems than there were 12 months ago?	Many more problems	More problems	Same amount of problems	Fewer problems	Much fewer problems
23. Challenge existing processes to achieve continuous improvement	How often do you suggest elimination of, substitutions for, or changes to the processes you work on?	Never	Seldom	Some-times	Usually	Always
24.	Are you making more or fewer suggestions than you did 12 months ago?	Much fewer	Fewer	Same	More	Many more

Table A-3. Employee survey (continued)

Lean Principle or Practice	Question	Choose One Answer by Number				
		1	2	3	4	5
25. Promote lean leadership at all levels	Do you and your work group respond quickly and effectively to change with no wasted effort?	Never	Seldom	Some-times	Usually	Always
26.	Do your and your work group respond to change better or worse than you did 12 months ago?	Much worse	Worse	Same	Better	Much better
27. Make decisions at the lowest level possible	How often do you make decisions that affect operations of your work group and its relationships with others?	Never	Seldom	Some-times	Usually	Always
28.	Are you making more or fewer such decisions than you were 12 months ago?	Much fewer	Fewer	Same	More	Many more

Table A-3. Employee survey (continued)

Lean Principle or Practice	Question	Choose One Answer by Number				
		1	2	3	4	5
29. Optimize capabilities and utilization of human resources	Is the company utilizing your capabilities well?	Very poorly	Poorly	OK	Well	Very well
30.	Is the company using your capabilities better or worse than it did 12 months ago?	Much worse	Worse	Same	Better	Much better
31. Develop relationships based on mutual trust and commitment	Do you trust your peers and your supervisor or manager?	Never	Seldom	Some-times	Usually	Always
32.	Do you trust your peers and your supervisor or manager more or less than you did 12 months ago?	Much less	Less	Same	More	Much more

Table A-3. Employee survey (continued)

Lean Principle or Practice	Question	Choose One Answer by Number				
		1	2	3	4	5
33. Nurture a learning environment	Are you eager to learn and share what you learn with others in the company, with suppliers, and with customers?	Never	Seldom	Some-times	Usually	Always
34.	Are you more or less eager to learn than you were 12 months ago?	Much less	Less	Same	More	Much more
35. Maximize stability in a changing environment	When circumstances demand a change, does the company change in a measured, dependable way?	Never	Seldom	Some-times	Usually	Always
36.	Does the company handle change better or worse than it did 12 months ago?	Much worse	Worse	Same	Better	Much better

Table A-4. Supplier survey

Lean Principle or Practice	Question	Choose One Answer by Number				
		1	2	3	4	5
1. Respond to change	How easy or hard is the company to work with when it has to change its orders from you?	Very hard	Hard	OK	Easy	Very easy
2.	Is the company handling the change process better or worse than it did 12 months ago?	Much worse	Worse	Same	Better	Much better
3. Minimize waste	How much wasted effort is there when you work with the company?	Extreme amount of wasted effort	Great deal of wasted effort	Some wasted effort	Small amount of wasted effort	Almost no wasted effort
4.	How much more or less wasted effort is there working with the company now than there was 12 months ago?	Much more wasted effort	More wasted effort	Same	Less wasted effort	Much less wasted effort

Table A-4. Supplier survey (continued)

Lean Principle or Practice	Question	Choose One Answer by Number				
		1	2	3	4	5
5. The right thing at the right place, the right time, and in the right quantity	Does the company provide a complete task description or specification for the work it asks of you?	Never	Seldom	Some-times	Usually	Always
6.	Are the task descriptions the company gives you more or less complete than they were 12 months ago?	Much less complete	Less complete	Equally complete	More complete	Much more complete
7. Effective relationships within the value stream	How often do your managers have to meet with the company's managers to resolve misunderstandings?	Always	Usually	Some-times	Seldom	Never
8.	Are there more or fewer mis-understandings than there were 12 months ago?	Many more misunder-standings	More misunder-standings	Same	Fewer misunder-standings	Much fewer misunder-standings

Table A-4. Supplier survey (continued)

Lean Principle or Practice	Question	Choose One Answer by Number				
		1	2	3	4	5
9. Continuous improvement	How often does the company make improvements in the ways it works with you?	Never	Seldom	Some-times	Usually	Always
10.	Is the company making more or fewer improvements than it did 12 months ago?	Much fewer	Fewer	Same	More	Many more
11. Optimal first-delivered unit quality	How often does the company give you adequate information and resources to ensure the supplies you provide are of high quality?	Never	Seldom	Some-times	Usually	Always
12.	Are the information and resources the company provides more or less adequate than 12 months ago?	Much less	Less	Same	More	Much more

Table A-4. Supplier survey (continued)

Lean Principle or Practice	Question	Choose One Answer by Number				
		1	2	3	4	5
13. Focus on the customer . . . continuously	Do you know the customers who will take delivery of the products containing the inputs you supply?	Never	Seldom	Some-times	Usually	Always
14.	Do you have more or less knowledge of the company's customers than you had 12 months ago?	Much less	Less	Same	More	Much more
15. Implement Integrated Product and Process Development	Are you, or suppliers similar to you, included in the company's Integrated Product Teams in order to contribute to the intellectual content of its products?	Never	Seldom	Some-times	Usually	Always
16.	Are you, or suppliers similar to you, more or less involved in the company's Integrated Product Teams than you were 12 months ago?	Much less	Less	Same	More	Much more

309

Table A-4. Supplier survey (continued)

Lean Principle or Practice	Question	Choose One Answer by Number				
		1	2	3	4	5
17. Identify and optimize enterprise flow	How often do you receive the inputs of material, parts, other supplies, information and knowledge that you need without difficulties?	Never	Seldom	Some-times	Usually	Always
18.	Are you having more or less trouble receiving the inputs you need than you were 12 months ago?	Much more trouble	More trouble	Same amount	Less trouble	Much less trouble
19. Assure seamless information flow	How often does the company provide you with accurate information when you want it, in a usable form?	Never	Seldom	Some-times	Usually	Always
20.	Is the company providing you with information that is more or less usable than 12 months ago?	Much less usable	Less usable	Equally usable	More usable	Much more usable

Table A-4. Supplier survey (continued)

Lean Principle or Practice	Question	Choose One Answer by Number				
		1	2	3	4	5
21. Ensure process capability, maturity, and yield	Are the company's manufacturing processes that interface with your processes unstable or arbitrarily changing because of the company's problems with capacity, maturity, or yield?	Always unstable	Usually unstable	Some-times unstable	Seldom unstable	Never unstable
22.	Are there more or fewer problems with the company's manufacturing processes than there were 12 months ago?	Many more problems	More problems	Same amount of problems	Fewer problems	Much fewer problems
23. Challenge existing processes to achieve continuous improvement	How often does the company accept suggestions to improve the processes you are involved in?	Never	Seldom	Some-times	Usually	Always
24.	Is the company more or less receptive to your suggestions than it was 12 months ago?	Much less	Less	Same	More	Much more

Table A-4. Supplier survey (continued)

Lean Principle or Practice	Question	Choose One Answer by Number				
		1	2	3	4	5
25. Promote lean leadership at all levels	How often do the company's people respond quickly to changing conditions with no wasted effort?	Never	Seldom	Some-times	Usually	Alwcys
26.	Are the company's people responding to changing conditions better or worse than they did 12 months ago?	Much worse	Worse	Same	Better	Much better
27. Make decisions at the lowest level possible	How often does the company make arbitrary decisions about the processes you use to provide it with the supplies it wants?	Always makes arbitrary supply decisions	Usually makes arbitrary supply decisions	Some-times makes arbitrary supply decisions	Seldom makes arbitrary supply decisions	Never makes arbitrary supply decisions
28.	Is the company making more or fewer such decisions than it was 12 months ago?	Many more arbitrary decisions	More arbitrary decisions	Same amount of arbitrary decisions	Fewer arbitrary decisions	Much fewer arbitrary decisions

Table A-4. Supplier survey (continued)

Lean Principle or Practice	Question	Choose One Answer by Number				
		1	2	3	4	5
29. Optimize capabilities and utilization of human resources	Are the capabilities of the company's people with whom you come in contact utilized well?	Very poorly utilized	Poorly utilized	OK	Well utilized	Very well utilized
30.	Is the company using the capabilities of its people better or worse than it did 12 months ago?	Much worse	Worse	Same	Better	Much better
31. Develop relationships based on mutual trust and commitment	Do you trust the company and its people with whom you are in contact?	Never	Seldom	Some-times	Usually	Always
32.	Do you trust the company and its people more or less than you did 12 months ago?	Much less	Less	Same	More	Much more

Table A-4. Supplier survey (continued)

Lean Principle or Practice	Question	Choose One Answer by Number				
		1	2	3	4	5
33. Nurture a learning environment	Are the company's people eager to learn and share what they have learned with you?	Never	Seldom	Some-times	Usually	Always
34.	Are the company's people more or less eager to learn than they were 12 months ago?	Much less	Less	Same	More	Much more
35. Maximize stability in a changing environment	When circumstances demand a change, does the company change in a measured, dependable way?	Never	Seldom	Some-times	Usually	Always
36.	Does the company handle change better or worse than it did 12 months ago?	Much worse	Worse	Same	Better	Much better

Table A-5. Investor survey

Lean Principle or Practice	Question	Choose One Answer by Number				
		1	2	3	4	5
1. Respond to change	How well does the company respond to the market or to external conditions?	Very poorly	Poorly	OK	Well	Very well
2.	How much better or worse is the company responding to unexpected news than it did 12 months ago?	Much worse	Worse	Same	Better	Much better
3. Minimize waste	How well does the company communicate investor and financial information?	Very poorly	Poorly	OK	Well	Very well
4.	How much more effective are the company's communications than they were 12 months ago?	Much less	Less	Same	More	Much more

Table A-5. Investor survey (continued)

Lean Principle or Practice	Question	Choose One Answer by Number				
		1	2	3	4	5
5. The right thing at the right place, the right time, and in the right quantity	Is the information the company provides you clear, accurate, and sufficient for good investment decisions?	Never	Seldom	Some-times	Usually	Always
6.	Is the information from the company better or worse than it was 12 months ago?	Much worse	Worse	Same	Better	Much better
7. Effective relation-ships within the value stream	Does the company maintain a positive relationship with its investors?	Never	Seldom	Some-times	Usually	Always
8.	Is the relationship better or worse than it was 12 months ago?	Much worse	Worse	Same	Better	Much better

Table A-5. Investor survey (continued)

Lean Principle or Practice	Question	Choose One Answer by Number				
		1	2	3	4	5
9. Continuous improvement	How often does the company make improvements in the ways it works with you?	Never	Seldom	Some-times	Usually	Always
10.	Is the company making more or fewer improvements than it did 12 months ago?	Much fewer	Fewer	Same	More	Many more
11. Optimal first-delivered unit quality	How often does the company have to correct the information it provides or the transactions it makes with you?	Always corrects	Usually corrects	Sometimes corrects	Seldom corrects	Never corrects
12.	Are the information and resources the company provides more or less adequate than 12 months ago?	Much less	Less	Same	More	Much more

Table A-5. Investor survey (continued)

Lean Principle or Practice	Question	Choose One Answer by Number				
		1	2	3	4	5
13. Focus on the customer . . . continuously	Does the company actively seek better ways to understand and communicate with customers?	Never	Seldom	Some-times	Usually	Always
14.	Are the understanding and communications better or worse than 12 months ago?	Much worse	Worse	Same	Better	Much better
15. Implement Integrated Product and Process Development	How often does the company, together with its customers and suppliers, appear to function as a team?	Never	Seldom	Some-times	Usually	Always
16.	Does the company, together with its customers and suppliers, appear to function as a team more or less than 12 months ago?	Much less	Less	Same	More	Much more

Table A-5. Investor survey (continued)

Lean Principle or Practice	Question	Choose One Answer by Number				
		1	2	3	4	5
17. Identify and optimize enterprise flow	Do you receive timely and accurate inputs of information and knowledge from the company to make investment decisions about the company?	Never	Seldom	Some-times	Usually	Always
18.	Are you having more or less trouble receiving the inputs you need than 12 months ago?	Much less	Less	Same	More	Much more
19. Assure seamless information flow	Does the company provide you with accurate information in a usable form, when you want it?	Never	Seldom	Some-times	Usually	Always
20.	Is the company providing you with information that is more or less usable than the information it provided 12 months ago?	Much less	Less	Same	More	Much more

Table A-5. Investor survey (continued)

Lean Principle or Practice	Question	Choose One Answer by Number				
		1	2	3	4	5
21. Ensure process capability, maturity, and yield	Does the company miss its financial targets and strategic goals because of problems with capacity, maturity, or yield of its processes?	Always misses	Usually misses	Some-times misses	Seldom misses	Never misses
22.	Is the company having more or less trouble making its financial targets and strategic goals than it did 12 months ago?	Much more trouble	More trouble	Same amount of trouble	Less trouble	Much less trouble
23. Challenge existing processes to achieve continuous improvement	Is the company bold enough in actively seeking better processes?	Never	Seldom	Some-times	Usually	Always
24.	Is the company more or less aggressive in seeking better pro-cesses than 12 months ago?	Much less	Less	Same	More	Much more

Table A-5. Investor survey (continued)

| Lean Principle or Practice | Question | Choose One Answer by Number | | | | |
		1	2	3	4	5
25. Promote lean leadership at all levels	How often do the company's people respond to your needs without wasted effort?	Never	Seldom	Some-times	Usually	Always
26.	Are the company's people responding to your needs better or worse than they did 12 months ago?	Much worse	Worse	Same	Better	Much better
27. Make decisions at the lowest level possible	Does the company have crisp and timely processes for making decisions?	Never	Seldom	Some-times	Usually	Always
28.	Are the company's decision-making processes better or worse than they were 12 months ago?	Much worse	Worse	Same	Better	Much better

Table A-5. Investor survey (continued)

Lean Principle or Practice	Question	Choose One Answer by Number				
		1	2	3	4	5
29. Optimize capabilities and utilization of human resources	Are the capabilities of the company's people with whom you come in contact utilized well?	Very poorly	Poorly	OK	Well	Very well
30.	Is the company using the capabilities of its people better or worse than 12 months ago?	Much worse	Worse	Same	Better	Much better
31. Develop relationships based on mutual trust and commitment	Do you trust the company and its people with whom you are in contact?	Never	Seldom	Some-times	Usually	Always
32.	Do you trust the company and its people more or less than you did 12 months ago?	Much less	Less	Same	More	Much more

Table A-5. Investor survey (continued)

Lean Principle or Practice	Question	Choose One Answer by Number				
		1	2	3	4	5
33. Nurture a learning environment	Are the company's people eager to learn and share what they learn with you?	Never	Seldom	Some-times	Usually	Always
34.	Are the company's people more or less eager to learn than they were 12 months ago?	Much less	Less	Same	More	Much more
35. Maximize stability in a changing environment	When circumstances demand a change, does the company change in a measured, dependable way?	Never	Seldom	Some-times	Usually	Always
36.	Does the company handle change better or worse than it did 12 months ago?	Much worse	Worse	Same	Better	Much better

Appendix B

Strategic Metrics

In Chapter 5, the authors described the modified Kaplan/Norton Balanced Scorecard[SM] as a way of helping companies set strategic goals from six different perspectives. Table 5-1 contained suggestions for metrics that companies could use in association with the six perspectives. This appendix describes these metrics in more detail.

1. FINANCIAL PERSPECTIVE METRICS

The most familiar goals and metrics come from the financial perspective. Most have been developed over many years by the accounting community and have standards that assume the force of government regulation or law. Suggested goals and metrics for the lean enterprise are covered in the following sections.

Return on Investment

From the view of the investor, the most important financial measure is return on investment (ROI). ROI is the amount of money earned by a business over a predetermined period divided by the amount of capital invested in the business.

Earnings-Change-per-Invested-Dollar

Earnings-change-per-invested-dollar is a measure for assessing a company's competitiveness. Every incremental investment should result in a growth of earnings. The higher the growth rate, the more effective the corporate business strategy. A reduced or negative growth rate introduces questions about strategy and could be indicative of a number of factors, such as ineffective management, rising operating costs, waste, price erosion, or shrinking market share.

Turnover Rate

Turnover rate is a measure of the efficiency with which a company or the extended enterprise uses its available capital. The turnover rate is the number of times that capital invested in a business is utilized during a 12-month period.

Margin

Margin is defined as the percentage of sales revenues retained as profit. Margin is important as a company-wide metric, as a metric of the extended enterprise, and as a metric of product line and market segment. Assuming revenues remain constant or increase, an increased margin shows up immediately in the company's bottom line.

Percentage of Revenues from New Products and Markets

Increasingly, lean enterprises gain revenue by customizing existing product platforms so that they can sell small batches of discrete, differentiated products. By differentiating products, the company is in a better position to enter new markets and to introduce new product platforms. The percentage of revenues derived from products introduced within the most recent 12 months and the percentage from markets developed within the same time measure competitiveness of the company.

Supplemental Financial Metrics

Additional important financial metrics include:

- average time between start of an investment and the time when it begins to contribute to earnings;

- revenue per full-time equivalent employee,
- and costs versus competitors' costs.

2. CUSTOMER PERSPECTIVE METRICS

The customer perspective is a two-way one. The first is the company's understanding of its customers. The company must understand them well enough so its present offerings will meet their demands. It must understand them well enough so it can introduce new offerings with confidence. The second view is the customers' perceptions of the company. Do customers have confidence that the company will deliver value? Suggested goals and metrics for the lean enterprise are outlined in the following sections.

Revenue Growth by Market Segments and Product Lines

The potential for revenue growth, over time produced by specific product lines and within specific market segments, is a key factor for making strategic marketing investments. Different market segments and different product lines are at different levels of maturity. It is important to track revenue growth to understand the dynamics of any given market segment or product line at any one time.

Net Profit by Customer or Segment

The lean enterprise views customers in many instances as individuals rather than as members of large groups. Mass customization means that deciding to offer, or not offer, products and services often is based on actual or potential demand and resulting profitability of sales to the individual customer or small market segment.

Customer Perceptions

Under the prevailing conditions of fierce competition, customers buy from the manufacturer whom they perceive provides the best total package of tangible and intangible value. This means customers' perceptions of the company and its products provide better insights than do internal measures relating to customers. Typical of this class of metrics is the degree of customer satisfaction, the extent to which the company's products match customers' product preferences, the company's preferred status with the customer, and retention of the customers over time. Another is brand loyalty, which measures the likelihood that a company's customers for one product will buy other products with the company's brand. These metrics are especially valuable if they also allow comparison with customers' perceptions of the competition.

Supplemental Customer Metrics

Additional important customer metrics include:

- total cost to the customer of product and service solutions (life-cycle cost);
- elapsed time to fulfill a customer need;
- percentage of products not delivered as and when promised;
- mean time products are out of service for repair.

3. OPERATIONS PERSPECTIVE METRICS

Over time, companies have used many different operations metrics. Here the authors present metrics that stress lean and agile operations. The goals are for every operation to drive costs and cycle times down while improving quality and reliability, and to be prepared for change with little additional overhead costs.

Break-even Time for Products and Processes

Products and processes that are leading-edge today will be obsolete tomorrow. Therefore, investment in a product or process should provide a profit before a fickle market rejects the product or before the process is replaced by improved technology. Break-even time is time required for the revenue stream from a product—or attributable to a process—to return original investment and start producing a profit. This assumes that products are priced on the total expected sales and average unit life-cycle costs, not on first cost.

Percentage of Six Sigma Designs

A Six Sigma design is one that is executed to minimize the rework at any point in the product or process life cycle, targeting a zero-reject rate. The objective is to drive rework and scrap during the manufacturing cycle to zero and offer the customer a highly reliable product. Any upgrade should be designed to the same standards as the original design and should clearly enhance functionality or reduce cost of product or process and cost of ownership to the customer.

Rate of Productivity Improvement

In the lean enterprise, continuous improvement means continuous gains in productivity. The metric is a measure of the rate at which improvements happen or whether they happen at all.

Accuracy and Completeness
of Information Provided to Work Units

The operations of a company, whose success is based on its optimal use of intellectual assets, must provide those assets accurately and where and when they are needed. The metric is the percentage of tasks that fail for lack of accuracy and completeness of information provided to a work unit.

Supplemental Operations Metrics

Additional important operations metrics include:

- time to obtain product;
- cost of scrap and rework as a percentage of sales or manufacturing cost.

4. LEARNING AND GROWTH PERSPECTIVE METRICS

The learning and growth perspective provides a sense of the company's readiness to accept and master change. The Kaplan/Norton perspective on learning and growth includes innovation.

Innovation is so important and so extensive a contributor to survival and growth that it warrants a separate perspective. Suggested goals and metrics follow.

Qualification Level and Percentage of Employees Qualified for Teaming

The NGM company will function and grow by teaming. Teaming is a learned skill and companies will want a work force highly skilled in teaming. The metric is the percentage of employees trained to established standards.

Cost of Training and Retraining to Meet Existing Job Standards

In an innovative company, training in new technologies and processes will be an ordinary, expected, and acceptable expense. A more important measure of work force readiness is the extra cost of the education and training needed to provide employees with an adequate knowledge and skill base for using available technologies and processes.

Perceptions of Trustworthiness

A lean enterprise will be one in which its stakeholders—customers, partners, suppliers, shareholders, and employees—can trust to meet or exceed its commitments and to act reliably and constructively as conditions change.

Supplemental Learning and Growth Metrics

Additional important learning and growth metrics include:

- percentage of critical decisions made by work units,
- information systems literacy rate.

5. GLOBALIZATION PERSPECTIVE METRICS

Globalization includes three important components: globalization of markets, products, and production. The company's globalization strategy probably involves these components. The first speaks to the company's ability to compete wherever it chooses. The second addresses design and production of products that can be sold globally with little added effort for regional customization. The third means the company must have production processes optimized for markets it chooses and for locations where it plans to produce the product. The following are suggested goals and metrics.

Market and Major Account Share by Geographic Region

Market share, the percentage of a given market that the company holds, provides an important basis for competitive position. Major accounts may be thought of as distinct markets. This metric is a measure of the universality and effectiveness of market strategy and product acceptance.

Market Penetration by Geographic Region

Since the markets in various geographic regions mature at different rates, market penetration provides a measure of remaining opportunity and guidance for regional or country strategies.

Percentage of Employees
Engaged in Transnational Activities

A responsive lean enterprise will focus the resources it needs from any of its globally distributed operations to meet a local market opportunity. This metric is a measure of the utilization of knowledge and skills of the total personnel resources of the company. Depending on the size of the business, the company may wish to break this metric down into geographic areas.

Supplemental Global Metrics

Additional important globalization metrics include:

- percentage of systems integrated, and
- information and knowledge systems' availability.

6. INNOVATION PERSPECTIVE METRICS

The 21st Century company lives by its brains. It thrives with timely and competitive use of the best available knowledge employed in new and creative ways. The innovation perspective recognizes this all-important quality explicitly.

Percentage of Revenue
Invested in R&D and Market Development

An important measure of the vitality of an NGM company is its investment in innovation. There are two elements to innovation:

- R&D of new technologies, products, and processes;
- creation of new markets.

The lean enterprise uses many different ways to stimulate innovation, including utilization of outside R&D facilities, such as university laboratories, industry groups, government laboratories, think tanks, and innovative start-ups.

The metric is the annual investment in innovation as a percentage of annual revenue. It is not enough to have a flow of innovations. They should make visible contributions to earnings commensurate with investments.

Percentage of Earnings Attributable
to Implemented Innovations

The metric is a measure of the success of the company's innovation strategies. It is the earnings attributable to innovations implemented over the past three years. This metric may be difficult to measure, depending on whether the company has identified innovation activities in its accounting systems.

Percentage of Compensation
Attributed to Innovation Contributions

Employee rewards should be aligned with their innovative contributions to the company. While new ideas should be rewarded, emphasis should be placed on their successful implementation. The compensation plan should include rewards based on earnings contributions attributable to innovations. In some industries, such as pharmaceuticals where there are many time-consuming steps to bring products to market, a reward structure should have intermediate gates as steps are completed.

Supplemental Innovation Metrics

Additional important innovation metrics include:

- average product and process lead (or lag) times relative to competition;
- average time to develop and implement the next product or process;
- number of implemented innovations attributable to outside R&D collaborations.

Index